MANAGING GLOBAL CUSTOMERS

# Managing Global Customers

## An Integrated Approach

**George S. Yip**
**Audrey J. M. Bink**

OXFORD
UNIVERSITY PRESS

## OXFORD
UNIVERSITY PRESS

Great Clarendon Street, Oxford OX2 6DP

Oxford University Press is a department of the University of Oxford.
It furthers the University's objective of excellence in research, scholarship,
and education by publishing worldwide in

Oxford  New York

Auckland  Cape Town  Dar es Salaam  Hong Kong  Karachi
Kuala Lumpur  Madrid  Melbourne  Mexico City  Nairobi
New Delhi  Shanghai  Taipei  Toronto

With offices in

Argentina  Austria  Brazil  Chile  Czech Republic  France  Greece
Guatemala  Hungary  Italy  Japan  Poland  Portugal  Singapore
South Korea  Switzerland  Thailand  Turkey  Ukraine  Vietnam

Oxford is a registered trade mark of Oxford University Press
in the UK and in certain other countries

Published in the United States
by Oxford University Press Inc., New York

© George S. Yip and Audrey J. M. Bink 2007

British Library Cataloguing in Publication Data

Data available

Library of Congress Cataloging in Publication Data

Yip, George S.
Managing global customers: an integrated approach / George S. Yip, Audrey J. M. Bink.
   p. cm.
Includes bibliographical references and index.
ISBN 978–0–19–922983–3 (alk. paper)
1. Customer relations–Management. 2. International business enterprises–Management.
I. Bink, Audrey J. M. II. Title.
HF5415.5.Y57 2007
658.8′4–dc22                                              2007020335

Typeset by SPI Publisher Services, Pondicherry, India
Printed in Great Britain
on acid-free paper by
Biddles Ltd., King's Lynn, Norfolk

ISBN  978–0–19–922983–3

1 3 5 7 9 10 8 6 4 2

To Jan and Jeanne Bink
and
Moira, Andrew, and Sarah Yip

We thank The Leverhulme Trust for its primary support for this project.

# Contents

# List of Figures

# Table

# Preface

Multinational companies need to manage their relationships with multinational customers with a globally integrated approach. This book provides a systematic framework for developing and implementing such global customer management programmes.

## Who Should Read This Book

We have written this book for several types of managers (and aspiring managers) as well as for those who teach and study international business, marketing, and sales management.

### Global and Regional Account Directors and Managers

This book is addressed first to those who have responsibility for directing and managing global or regional accounts and customers. You are pioneers in a demanding and challenging role. We intend this book to help you to be more successful in your jobs.

### Global and Regional Purchasing Directors and Managers

You are the executives who are on the receiving end of global and regional account management. This book will help you to get the best out of global and regional supplier relationships.

### National Sales and Purchasing Executives in Multinational Companies

If your job is confined to a national market, whether in sales or purchasing, but you work in a multinational company, then you need to understand how your national customer–supplier relationships fit within the broader context of multinational relationships. Increasingly, you will be expected to participate in global or regional programmes.

## Suppliers to Multinational Companies

Multinational suppliers to multinational companies need to learn how to deal with the new breed of 'global customers'. And purely local suppliers need to understand the new global strategy also. A local supplier to a local subsidiary of a multinational company can find that its business dries up quickly when the customer's parent company switches to a global sourcing strategy.

## Business Unit Managers

Selling to multinational customers is one of the prime activities of most business units. So the heads of business units need a good understanding of global customer management, this being critical to enhancing the competitive position and performance of their businesses.

## Top Corporate Executives

The most effective global account or customer management programmes will involve the top corporate executives, from the CEO downwards, in the relationships with their most important customers. This book will help you in that customer-facing role.

## Educators of Future Managers

*Managing Global Customers* can be assigned as a supplementary text in courses on international management, international marketing, or sales management.

# Acknowledgements

Many people have helped us with this project. We first started working on the topic of global account management with Tammy Madsen, David Montgomery and Belen Villalonga. Alan Nonnenberg, the creator of Hewlett-Packard's global account management programme gave us the access we needed to write our first case study in this topic, and has maintained support and interest over the last ten years. Claire Stravato and Angela Andal-Ancion worked on the Star Alliance case and Angela has also contributed editing work. Tomas Hult collaborated with us in the study that provided the primary supporting research for this book. Alina Kudina helped with literature searches. Omar Toulan and Matthew Myers have provided valuable input to our thinking. George Coundouriotis has provided some of the examples in this book. David Butter of Young and Rubicam Brands helped us to set up the Global Account Management Forum that has provided critical learning and evidence. Christoph Senn of the Account Management Center and the University of St. Gallen has given us the opportunity to test out our ideas in executive programmes and conferences over the last three years. George's secretary, Samantha Cantle, provided cheerful and efficient support for our work.

Audrey Bink's time and most of the expenses for this study were provided by a grant from The Leverhulme Trust. George Yip's time and additional expenses were supported by his Fellowship with the Advanced Institute of Management Research, which has been funded by the UK's Economic and Social Research Council and Engineering and Physical Sciences Research Council.

Lastly, we thank all the executives who have participated in forums, been interviewed, and completed surveys over the years. You have provided the essential material for this book.

# About the Authors

*George Yip* is Vice President and Director of Research & Innovation at Capgemini Consulting, based in London, Professor of Strategic and International Management at London Business School and Lead Senior Fellow of the UK's Advanced Institute of Management Research. He held the Chair of Marketing and Strategy at Cambridge University, and has also held faculty positions at Harvard Business School and UCLA, and visiting positions at China–Europe International Business School, Georgetown, Oxford, and Stanford. His book, *Total Global Strategy: Managing for Worldwide Competitive Advantage* (Prentice Hall, 1992) was selected as one of the 30 best business books of 1992, has been published in ten languages, and has been updated as *Total Global Strategy II* (2003). (He can be contacted at: george.yip@capgemini.com or gyip@london.edu).

*Audrey Bink* is Head of Marketing Communications at Uxbridge College in West London. She previously held a research position at London Business School, with her work focusing on Global Customer–Supplier Management.

As a product manager and market development manager, Audrey has also been active in global industrial marketing at DMV International, the ingredients division of dairy cooperative Campina. She holds an MSc in Industrial Engineering and Management Science from Eindhoven University of Technology (The Netherlands). (She can be contacted at: abink@uxbridgecollege.ac.uk).

# Part I

## Foundation

# 1    Managing Globally

> 'I am sorry but we are dropping your company as a supplier to us because you are unable to serve us on a globally integrated basis.'
>
> 'I am pleased to tell you that we have designated your company as a worldwide supplier because you have demonstrated your ability to serve us on a globally integrated basis.'

Multinational suppliers are increasingly hearing one or the other of the above two messages from their multinational customers. What is happening is a sea change in the way in which multinational customers and multinational suppliers work with each other. The old operating mode was that the national subsidiaries of multinational companies (MNCs) were free to make their own decisions about suppliers. This often meant that different national subsidiaries of one MNC customer might be buying from the national subsidiaries of an MNC supplier, but the relationships would be between national subsidiaries and not at the (multinational) company level. Figure 1.1 illustrates this mode of relationship, which we term 'multilocal buying'. Of course, there can be other variations, such as a customer in Country A buying from the same or different suppliers in several countries. But the central aspect of this mode is that subsidiaries make their own choices.

## The Globalization Context for Managing Global Customers

The need to manage customers on a global basis arises in the context of the ongoing globalization of countries, industries, and companies. In terms of countries, every major economy, and most minor ones, participate in the larger global economy, albeit with varying degrees of openness. Many countries have joined trading and other economic blocs, such as those of the European Union, ASEAN, or NAFTA, in which trade, investment, and other business cross-border barriers have been drastically reduced. The net effect is that most companies now have very wide geographic choices in terms of both where they sell and where they source. For example, Wal-Mart alone accounts for more than 10 percent of all of the United States' annual imports from China. Also, as

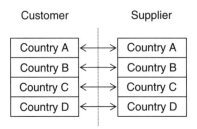

**Fig. 1.1** Multilocal buying

multinational companies expand the geographic scope of their activities, they expect their suppliers to follow them. In turn this spread raises the bar in terms of the scope in managing customer relationships on a global basis.

In terms of industries, competition increasingly occurs across as well as within national borders, although the extent of globalization varies by industry, depending largely on industry globalization drivers. These drivers include national culture, economies of scale, and regulation.[1] The industries with the strongest globalization drivers require competitors in them to respond with globally integrated strategies.[2]

In terms of companies, these globally integrated strategies involve strategies such as global market participation. C. Michael Armstrong, CEO of AT&T, was referring to this aspect of global strategy when he said, 'In the future there will be two kinds of corporations; those that go global and those that go bankrupt'.[3] Other strategies include producing global products and services, setting up a global location and coordination of activities, pursuing global marketing, making global competitive moves, and setting up global organization and management structures.

# The Globalization of Buying and Selling

So in response to globalization, both multinational customers and suppliers are adopting various aspects of global strategy. Customers who use global purchasing can be viewed as pursuing the strategy of global coordination of activities. Suppliers who manage customers globally can be viewed as pursuing the strategy of global marketing.

## Changes in Multinational Buyer Behaviour

In the global era, multinational customers increasingly seek to deal on a globally coordinated basis with their suppliers, demanding such services as global contracts, global pricing, product standardization, and a global account relationship. For example, in their drive to reduce costs, the major automobile manufacturers, such as General Motors and Ford, increasingly seek global contracts from their suppliers, such as Bosch and Goodyear. Nestlé and its competitors increasingly apply pressure on their suppliers, such as International Paper, to provide global prices and other terms. Even retailers, such as Wal-Mart and Carrefour, who have long taken national approaches, are seeking global or regional supply contracts, as they expand globally.

Historically, most multinational companies have allowed their national subsidiaries extensive independence in their purchasing behaviour, but the problems found with this approach (e.g., incompatibility of equipment and standards, and diseconomies in purchasing) have increasingly led them to buy on a more centralized or coordinated basis. Also, as multinational companies themselves develop more globally integrated strategies, they expect the same from their suppliers.

The electronics giant and Dutch MNC, Philips, illustrates this change in global purchasing behaviour. Until 2003, each Philips business unit was responsible for the procurement of its own supplies.[4] As purchases equate to approximately two-thirds of Philips' revenue, the company launched a new supply management strategy that should make procurement cheaper and more efficient. Whereas some companies decide to centralize all procurement in one central function in order to cut costs, Philips decided to combine economies of scale with rapid decision-making that is tied closely to the needs of the different businesses. In the new model, each of the five business groups has a central purchasing officer with responsibility for group-wide procurement of specific commodities. For example, the lighting division is responsible for procuring all the group's packaging while the consumer electronics division buys all its plastics. To keep the link with the other businesses, each central purchasing officer has a team that is dispersed around the different businesses.

Since 2003 Philips has cut the total number of its suppliers from 50,000 to 33,000. The percentage of combined (i.e., multi-unit) purchases, either for specific businesses or for the group as a whole, has risen from 6 percent to 55 percent. In 2005 the target for procurement savings was 16 percent, and Philips was well on its way to reaching that target. Another part of the new procurement programme is forging closer relationships with a number of key suppliers, whom Philips describes as 'partners for growth'. These key suppliers are increasingly involved at an early stage in innovation. In 2005 they provided 26 percent of the group's purchases. Barbara Kux, Philips' first chief procurement officer said: 'It is a two-way process. We ask each other: what can we do better together? There are always great ideas from our suppliers'. One example is the Philishave Coolskin shaver, for which Philips worked with Beiersdorf to make a soothing skin balm, under the Nivea brand name.

**Foundation**

Even supermarkets, one of the least globalizable of industries because of its strong local nature, is moving toward regional and global buying. A 1999 study by a leading consulting firm found that MNC suppliers to supermarkets faced increasing pressures as retailing giants such as Carrefour, Tesco, and Wal-Mart expanded into more and more countries and also accelerated the extent of their regional or global buying.[5] As a global customer of Philips', Wal-Mart's annual purchases of over $1 billion are larger than many of Philips' own businesses, such as that for shaving products.

As far back as 1997, a survey of 191 senior executives in 165 major multi-national companies found that their multinational customers were increasingly demanding global consistency in service quality and performance, global contracts, uniform terms of trade, global pricing, and the like. In turn, these multinational suppliers were responding with increased use of global customer management programmes.[6]

## Changes in Multinational Seller Behaviour

Most multinational suppliers find it very difficult to respond to the demand for global service. Their own organization structures and management processes have long been geared toward providing national, rather than global, customer management. But the savvier suppliers, such as AT&T, Bank of America, British Telecom, Citigroup, IBM, Hewlett-Packard, and Xerox are learning to play the new game of global customer management and are consequently reaping the corresponding rewards. This book is, first, about how suppliers can play this game more successfully and, second, about how customers can play their part. Managing customers and suppliers on a globally integrated basis can be viewed as a form of global customer–supplier relationship. As illustrated in Figure 1.2., such relationships typically involve coordination by global units

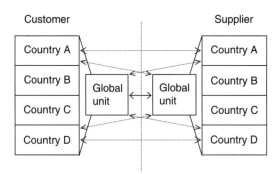

**Fig. 1.2** Global customer–supplier relationship

on both customer and supplier sides. On the customer side such a global unit may be their global purchasing function. On the supplier side, such a global unit may be their global account management function. This book concerns how to manage these global customer–supplier relationships, especially from the viewpoint of the supplier.

Advertising agencies provide a strong example of an industry effect. Many advertising agencies have seen a real trend of supplier rationalization among their largest customers. Instead of working with up to a hundred different agencies worldwide, clients increasingly want to work as much as possible with as few as possible suppliers. They do so for two reasons: to achieve greater global consistency in their communications messages and to achieve greater global coordination of their purchasing.

Particularly in the 1980s, many major advertising agencies faced some globalization drivers that spurred them on to adopt global account management.[7] First, some of their major clients, such as Procter & Gamble and Unilever, were themselves embracing a globally integrated strategy and starting to act as global customers. This change in behaviour included the increasing use of globally standardized advertising,[8] for example, Coca-Cola's sports hero/little boy campaign of the 1970s, British Airways' repositioning as a global and 'the world's favourite' airline in the early 1980s, and Toyota's global campaign introducing its new Camry model in the early 1990s (all partly legitimized by Theodore Levitt's 1983 proclamation of the globalization of markets).[9] Second, one agency, Saatchi & Saatchi, in its prime aggressively positioned itself as *the* global agency, spurring its rivals to respond.

Even a stellar creative reputation cannot save an advertising agency from the demands of global account management. In late 1993, Chiat Day, a US-based creative superstar among advertising agencies with the Apple Macintosh '1984' commercial and other gems to its credit but with little in the way of an international network, was dropped by Reebok International, the manufacturer of athletic shoes. Reebok consolidated its $140 million worldwide advertising account at Leo Burnett, a top ten international network. A key reason cited by Reebok's VP-marketing services worldwide was that Chiat Day did not have the global resources that the company needed. Reebok had 'wired together a global network using Chiat as the lead agency and Burnett and Euro RSCG (Paris-based) overseas, but there was no partnership between the three.'[10] Soon after the loss of this account, Chiat Day agreed in early 1995 to be acquired by Omnicom Group, and to be folded into the latter's TBWA network.

The trend in the advertising business toward global account management has perhaps been the major factor behind the top ten international agency networks steadily increasing their share of global advertising spending.[11] Most dramatic of all, in 1994 IBM's new CEO, Louis V. Gerstner, Jr., initiated the firing of over 40 different agencies around the world, and consolidated the company's entire

$400 to $500 million account at one top ten global agency, Ogilvy & Mather Worldwide (part of WPP, one of the largest advertising agency groups).

Many MNCs are using the need to serve customers globally as the basis for reorienting themselves from product- and geography-led organizations to becoming customer-led. For example, Reuters, the business information company, initiated in the early 2000s just such a move in order to better serve its top 22 global customers. In 2001 Reuters listed these top global customers:

- Europe: ABN Amro, Allianz, BNP Paribas, Commerzbank, Credit Suisse, Deutsche Bank, HSBC, Ing, Société Générale and UBS;
- USA: Bank of America, Citigroup, Fidelity, Goldman Sachs, Instinet, JP Morgan Chase, Lehman Brothers, Merrill Lynch, and Morgan Stanley Dean Witter; and
- Japan: Mitsubishi Tokyo Financial, Mizuho Holdings, and Putnam.

In the early 2000s, both IBM and Hewlett-Packard went so far as to break out from the rest of the organization their top 100 or so global accounts as separate businesses with their own profit and loss statements. Indeed, one of the few positives during HP's troubles of the early 2000s came from the success of its global accounts programme.

# Global Account Management

We now examine the key response by suppliers to the globalization of buying and selling—global account management.[12]

## From National Account Management to Global Account Management

In response to customers' demands for global coordination, MNC suppliers are increasingly adopting *global account management (GAM)*. Companies around the world have long used *national* account management to handle their most important accounts. Such national account management approaches include having one executive or team take overall responsibility for all aspects of a customer's business, whether directly or by coordinating the activities of others.[13] Typical applications include the use of national account managers for retail chains, and for business equipment and service customers. National account management approaches have also been used interchangeably with relationship marketing and management.[14] The global account management concept extends national account management across countries, not necessarily to all countries, but to the most important ones for the most important customers, and for the most important activities. Global account management can also be viewed as the new frontier in 'relationship marketing.'[15]

Different companies use different terms to refer to global customer management, such as 'global account management', 'parent account management', 'international account management', or 'worldwide account management'. Although we will use the first term in this book, this being the most common one, all these terms involve *an organizational form and process in multinational companies by which the worldwide activities serving one or more multinational customers are coordinated centrally by one person or team within the supplier company.* Global account management can be expensive to implement and carries its own risks (such as standardizing global prices at a low common level). So managers need to be able to diagnose the extent to which their customers will want such services, what sort of services to provide, and how to implement the programmes.

Correspondingly, multinational suppliers are creating global account management programmes, with such features as global account managers, double counting of revenues to incentivize both global and national sales people, and global measurement of customer revenues and profits.[16] Common objectives for these global programmes are increased account revenues, joint innovation and customer lock-in.

## Should a Company Adopt Global Account Management?

Taking a GAM approach sounds promising, and for some companies it seems that doing so is inevitable to keep up with the competition, but it is a costly exercise and therefore it is necessary that implementing a GAM programme will in fact bring some visible extra revenue to the company. GAM has the potential to be a very valuable asset to the company, if it is handled in the right way. The benefits of GAM also depend greatly on the product or service involved. The comments of a purchasing manager at the engineering giant, Asea Brown Boveri (ABB), illustrate this:

It is a combination of volume, how big is the spend, how big is the potential leverage and the globalization of the supplier. For example, electrical energy is high in volume but a domestic service. It is not a global commodity, whereas credit cards, for example, are a globally available product. So we will implement credit cards globally and energy locally. It is the product that decides if it makes sense to have a global process for procurement.

In Chapter 2, we will discuss how to analyse the industry globalization drivers that determine which products and services sold by a supplier offer the most potential for GAM.

GAM programmes are not cheap. They involve adding personnel, processes, and direct expenses, such as for travel and information collection. They also carry risks. The dominant fear is that a globally coordinated approach to a multi-national customer merely allows that customer to extract greater concessions.[17] Such concessions may swamp the various possible benefits. Often, companies are reluctant to implement a GAM programme because of the risks involved, especially those of a possible unbalanced relationship and the seemingly inevitable subsequent price squeeze.

On the other hand, there is plenty of evidence that GAM programmes work. One study found that GAM programmes were estimated to have a 20 percent improvement on overall customer satisfaction, about 15 percent improvement on revenues, and about 15 percent improvement on profits.[18] These benefits in GAM programmes have also been reported by a number of companies such as Asea Brown Boveri,[19] Adidas-Salomon,[20] Hewlett-Packard,[21] and the advertising agency Young and Rubicam.[22]

GAM programmes are also very demanding on the implementing company's capabilities for global integration and coordination. A company has to be truly global before a programme for global relations has any chance of success. This may sound trivial, but often companies have an exaggerated perception of their own global capabilities. A global account manager from Unisys, the US computer company, remarked: 'if a company says global account selling is easy, they probably haven't actually been doing it'. Therefore, an assessment of the company's own global situation and capabilities is a good place to start. In Chapter 3 we will discuss how to conduct such an assessment.

## Global Account Management as an Organizational Response

GAM can be seen as an organizational response to a changed business environment. A study in 2006 even identified GAM as one of the 100 most significant management innovations in business history, and one of the 11 most interesting recent (from 1987 to 2000) innovations.[23] The study cited Hewlett-Packard as being the first company to develop a formal GAM programme, implemented by Alan Nonnenberg HP's first director of global accounts. (However, Citibank did have a form of GAM programme as early as 1975.)[24]

From the perspective of organizational innovation, GAM can be seen as particularly affecting two capabilities: information processing and bargaining power.[25] First, GAM requires an increase in the information processing capacity of the organization, in response to increased information processing demands.[26]

Throughout this book, we will discuss how GAM programmes need to use information effectively. Second, GAM programmes affect the relative bargaining power of supplier and customers, and the way in which they depend on each other.[27] As a supplier moves from country–country relationships with a customer, the dependence of each partner on the other will change. On the one hand, the supplier becomes more dependent on the customer, as all or most of its sales now go through one point of customer contact. This greater dependence is the biggest fear of suppliers who are considering the adoption of GAM. On the other hand, the customer typically cuts down the number of suppliers it uses, which in turn increases its dependence on the supplier.[28] So the implementation of GAM creates a shift in bargaining power between supplier and customer; in whose favour this shift moves depends on the situation and, to a great extent, on who is better coordinated globally.

The mutual reduction in the number of bargaining and contracting points between supplier and customer (as shown earlier in the shift from Figure 1 to Figure 2) also greatly reduces transaction costs for both parties.[29] We will discuss, at various points later in this book, how suppliers and customers can realize these reduced costs.

## What Sort of GAM Programme?

The most effective form of GAM programme differs from company to company, and even from customer to customer within the same company. Many aspects need to be taken into account before designing and implementing such a programme. Key questions include: how should it be organized, how should it be implemented, and for which customers should it be implemented? Even if it were possible to isolate the top thirty or so customers, it would then still be an enormous task to have a separate customized GAM programme for each customer. How do you find a balance between customizing GAM programmes and minimizing the resources required to implement these plans. A typical error is starting a GAM programme just because the customer asks for it and doing the absolute minimum that is required by the customer. At the other end of the spectrum is the difficulty in implementing a comprehensive GAM programme without gaining any potential added value in the existing customer situation. It is important to find the right balance in GAM implementation for the situation the company is in.

One way to think about implementation is that effective GAM programmes need to provide the right balance between local autonomy and global integration. Achieving both is difficult but necessary in global management.[30] The balance between the two depends particularly on the industry of the supplier (as will be discussed in Chapter 2). For example, a computer supplier probably has

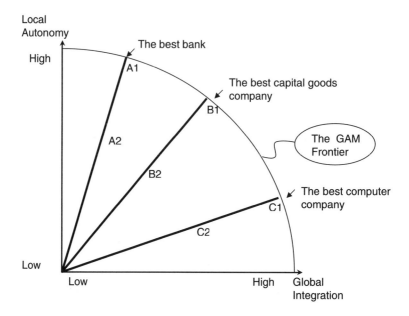

**Fig. 1.3** The frontier of GAM performance

a greater need for global integration than for local autonomy, while a supplier of banking services probably needs the balance the other way, and a capital goods supplier may be somewhere in between. These differences are illustrated in Figure 1.3. The best performing bank (A1) in terms of GAM is at one position on the 'GAM Performance Frontier', while the best performing capital goods company (B1) and the best performing computer company (C1) are at respectively different positions. Figure 1.3 also illustrates that other companies can be beneath the GAM performance frontier, that is, they under-perform in terms of both local autonomy and global integration in their GAM programmes. Such companies are exemplified in Figure 1.3 by A2 bank, B2 capital goods company, and C2 computer company.

## From Global Account Management to Global Customer Management

When pursuing a global relationship with a customer, potentially even a partnership, it is important to regard this customer as a whole company, not just as a purchasing department that happens to buy your products. Therefore, we introduce the concept of global customer management (GCM). GCM is not the same as GAM, nor is it something a company should do instead of GAM.

GAM, the formal global account management programme, is focused on coordinating the global business with the account. This is mainly a sales oriented programme, and the most important thing to focus on is good coordination of the different sales contacts throughout the world. When, however, a supplier wants to change the global relationship with a customer into a relationship that is more than just a global sales contract, it is crucial to involve other areas of both companies in the global relationship. Furthermore, it is important that the GAM programme is not an operation that is treated as being separate from the rest of the company's operations; rather it should be an integral part of the corporate organization's operations. This is where GCM comes in. GCM is the informal foundation for a total, integrated approach to GAM. This means that the GAM programme will be fused with the company strategy and organization.

---

**Siemens' Global Customer Management Approach**

German electronics company Siemens' Corporate Accounts programme works with the idea that the partnership, not the product, provides the differentiation. The president of its Information & Communications Corporate Accounts said: 'Customers do not want a single point of contact, but rather a collaborative multifunctional team aligned to their organization'. For this collaborative, cross-functional team, customer focus means having a deep understanding of the customer and its industry sector, focusing on the customer's business processes, having knowledge of and selling all of Siemens' assets. Next to the cross-functional team, sector boards provide a total portfolio to meet the customer's needs. These boards provide the best technology and innovation in their class, integrated systems and services; and sector focused business solutions from all groups. With this structure it is the whole corporation, not just the global account manager, that interacts with the global customer.

---

With GCM, the entire corporation accommodates the GAM programme, which in turn interacts with the rest of the organization, not being a separate organization entity (see Figure 1.4). GAM needs to be a part of the total organization that is aligned with all other company departments. Therefore, GCM will affect the whole company, and will incorporate the management processes that are needed to keep this integration effective. Within the GAM programme there needs to be a representative for every global customer in the programme, usually a global account manager (gam). The gam is responsible for the total global relationship with the account. He or she is organizationally situated within the GAM programme, but in the integrated approach, needs to have a network of contacts throughout the whole company. By having the gam work beyond the GAM programme, into the rest of the company, it is possible to lift the programme beyond a transactional strategy to true global relationship management. One of the best methods to give the gam outreach to the rest of

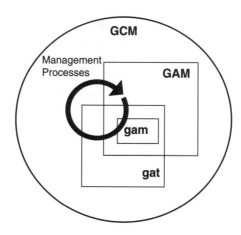

**Fig. 1.4** Components of global customer management (GCM)

*Note*: GCM = global customer management; GAM = global account management programme; gam = global account manager; gat = global account team. GCM covers the entire company. GAM is the formal part of GCM. The gam runs the GAM programme, and leads the gat, some of whose members are outside the formal GAM programme. Management processes, represented by the circling arrow, affect all components.

the company is the establishment of a multidisciplinary global account team (gat). This team will be a combination of both people who are working in the GAM programme and employees outside the global sales organization. The gat needs to have members from different departments (such as R&D, logistics and finance) to ensure a broader relationship network with the customer and within the company itself. Therefore, the gat should not consist solely of sales personnel. In most cases the gam will be part of the gat, either as a member or as a team leader. In the Dutch ingredients manufacturer DMV International, the composition of the gat is based on the customers' requirements. Next to the global key account manager, the core team will have members from particularly relevant departments for this customer, whereas the other departments are represented via a surround team that is less formalized. For example, if the customer is very active in new product introductions, the DMV R&D and marketing departments will be well represented in the core team, if the customer particularly values projects for cost reduction, focus will be on logistical and manufacturing representatives. As the core team members are encouraged to build relationships with their counterparts in the customer company, this will give more connections and opportunities for cooperation with the customer.

In summary, the focus for the implementation of a global relationship management programme should be on the integrated approach. When implementing a GAM programme it is important to embed it in the total organization of the company. It is vital to perceive GAM as an integrated part of the organization, and not as a separate programme. This way the GAM programme will get the respect and support within the organization that it needs to function to its full potential. The basic idea is that it is important to look beyond the 'sales–purchasing' relationship and perceive the relationship with the customer as being formed by a combination of contacts within all departments and geographies.

# The Integrated Approach

The two most important aspects of the integrated approach are that the GAM programme should be integrated within the organization and that the management of the global relationship should go beyond sales to having an integrated approach towards all aspects of the customer's organization. With this integrated approach, it will be easier to build a global relationship with the customer that will deliver the added value that is enclosed in the opportunities of global business. Admittedly, taking the integrated approach for global customer management will be a more complex change to the organization than just adding a global coordination department, but the rewards of truly global customer management will not be easy to reap without it. It is highly unlikely that a company with a very basic implementation of global account management will create a global partnership with its customers as there would be no methods in place for coordinating relationships outside the sales department, and even within the sales department it would be difficult to get the company behind certain global initiatives.

One of the important aspects of the integrated approach is the 'diamond' or 'web' structure in the relationships between the customer and the supplier. In a traditional 'sales–purchasing' situation, the relationship structure between the two companies resembles a bow tie with all the activities within one company leading to one person who has contact with the other company (account manager at the supplier end, and purchasing officer at the customer end). The integrated approach advocates a relationship structure that resembles a web or diamond in which employees from many different departments and functions have a direct relationship with each other and relevant people within the other company, as illustrated in Figure 1.5. This diamond structure changes the relationship with the customer from being purely sales-related towards being a partnership. The Dutch food ingredients company DMV International has actively worked on implementing such a diamond structure, encouraging employees from departments like marketing and R&D to create active relationships with their counterparts and other relevant people within the customer company. This has led to a better understanding of the customers by the cross-functional

## Foundation

**Fig. 1.5** From bow-tie to diamond relationships

*Note:* The figure on the right represents the multi-faceted, diamond-like aspect of a global customer–supplier relationship.

account teams (described earlier) and therefore to a more customized account management approach.

Our integrated approach results in a framework of four parts, which will also be used as the structure of this book: the foundation, the tools, the content and the process. Figure 1.6 shows the complete framework, and its components, which comprise the nine central chapters (2 to 10) of this book.

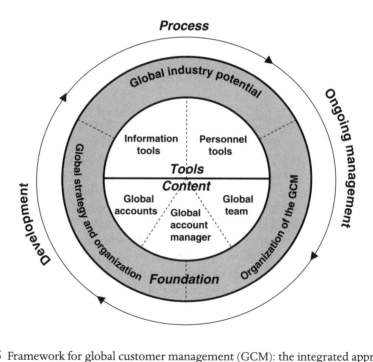

**Fig. 1.6** Framework for global customer management (GCM): the integrated approach

## Foundation

The foundation of the integrated approach is the research and preparation that needs to be done before implementing the complete programme. This starts with determining the potential for starting a GCM programme. There are many objectives for starting a GCM programme, many of which are discussed in Chapter 2. However, it is important that a company about to embark on GCM thoroughly determines the potential for its own situation. After the potential benefits and rewards have been determined, along with the necessary programme elements to tap into that potential, it is important to take care in exploring the company's strategy and organization with respect to the impending GCM programme.

The type of products or services that a supplier offers to its global customers will determine whether there is a need for global customer management. Typically, a supplier of commodities will have less need for complex coordination systems than a supplier of value added or complex products. This and other industry specifics will determine the elements that are needed within the GCM programme, and these need to be analysed before the organization is set up. Furthermore, the current strategy and organization must be analysed with respect to the alignment with a potential GCM programme. A company must have a global mindset for a GCM programme to work smoothly within the total organization. This means the global strategy of the company must be compatible with a potential GCM programme. The current organization structure is also an important item for analysis, as the company needs to have the capabilities to act as a global supplier before showcasing this with customers. Chapter 3 will discuss the analysis of the current company strategy and organization with respect to GCM.

After the current situation has been thoroughly analysed and, if necessary, changed, the organization of the GCM programme itself can be determined. There is not one best way of organizing the programme, but it is important that sufficient care is taken to choose the best possible structure for the company's situation, as the GCM organization is the bedrock of the total GCM programme. Chapter 4 will, therefore, not give a standard recipe for a GCM organization, but aims to give some ideas on different organization forms for GCM, and show some possible pitfalls.

## Key Choices

After the company situation has been thoroughly examined and a suitable GCM organization for the company's situation has been designed, it is important to take some care in providing the right content for the programme. A crucial part of the content that will largely determine the success of the programme is the selection of the right global accounts. Choosing the right accounts can be a daunting activity. Most customers will want to be part of the programme, but it is important that only those customers that can be of added value to the programme are included otherwise GCM will end up as a costly operation of price (and probably profit) reduction. Chapter 5 gives some pointers on selecting the right accounts for the programme and discusses what kind of relationship with the customer should be aimed at after the selection process.

The global account manager (gam) is another important feature of the GCM programme. As the GCM programme should lift GAM beyond a general sales approach, the role of the gam should be more than that of a salesperson. It takes specific skills and seniority to be a gam that can handle the complexity of the global situation while still being able to build on any extra potential. Therefore, selecting the right person for the position of gam can be the key aspect of lifting the programme beyond global account coordination towards global customer management. Chapter 6 discusses the role and the position the gam should have within his or her own company and toward the customer. Some general, preferred skills and specifications of a gam are also discussed. Next to the global account manager, the global account team (gat) can have some influence on the effectiveness with which the global customer is being managed. As the total relationship is a lot more complex than in a country-based relationship with a customer, the gam cannot handle the account completely on his or her own. Most companies have a formal or informal team that assists the gam in his or her activities. There are many different ways of setting up a global account team, but in the integrated approach, it is important to include members with different skills in the team. This will help the programme to be more aligned with the rest of the organization, and will give the programme greater recognition within the whole company. Chapter 7 discusses different forms of global account teams, such as virtual networks and cross-functional teams.

## Tools

Once the GCM programme is designed and running, its members will need to be provided with tools to help the programme to run smoothly within the rest of the organization, and to create the integrated approach. Customer information constitutes an important tool to reach a high level of integration. Especially in a globally complex situation it can be hard to keep track of every piece of information involving the account. The position of the gam can sometimes resemble that of an account specific 'information manager'. Many systems are available to help manage this information, but most companies agree it is hard to use this tool effectively and to its full potential to promote the integrated approach. Chapter 8 discusses the use of information management systems, the use of customer relationship management (CRM) systems and other knowledge management tools in GCM situations.

As employee perception can have a major effect on the programme, it is important to use tools that help motivate staff, and give them reason to work hard for the success of the GCM programme. Incentives and compensation can be an important tool in the development of the programme. Chapter 9 discusses the different levels of remuneration that are being used in global companies, and the problems that can arise from this. Many companies have to resort to some sort of 'double counting' to keep things fair for all involved parties. Chapter 9 also discusses the personnel perception of the GCM programme, and the way personnel tools can help to develop a positive perception.

## Process

Once the GCM programme has been implemented, the company will want it to run as smoothly as possible. Companies have to realize GCM is a process, not a project, and manage it accordingly. The programme needs to be developed over time, as improvements can be made and situations change. Chapter 10 discusses the processes that are needed to run the programme to its full potential, and to help develop the programme and make it fit in with the rest of the organization and the current times. The different supporting systems to help the programme develop are featured, as are the different approaches to improving relationship management. Furthermore some pointers on planning and potential pitfalls are given.

The book concludes with Chapter 11, which looks at critical success factors for managing global customers.

# Appendix

## Supporting Research

This book utilizes research on GCM by the lead author and various co-researchers over the last decade from 1996, and is also based on experience gained through interacting with executives in numerous executive programmes and conferences. In addition, this book builds on 20 years of research on the broader subjects of global strategy and organization.

## Foundation

TABLE 1.1 Global customer-supplier relationships researched

| Global suppliers researched | Their global customers researched | Global customers researched | Their global suppliers researched |
| --- | --- | --- | --- |
| Xerox (USA) | ABB (Switzerland) Siemens (Germany) Volkswagen (Germany) HSBC[1] (UK) | HSBC (UK) | IBM (USA) NCR (USA) British Airways (UK) Lowe[2] (UK) |
| DMV International[3] (Netherlands) | Three major European customers | BG Group[4] (UK) | Schlumberger (France) Bechtel (USA) |
| Unilever (UK/Neths.) | Wal-Mart (USA) Carrefour (France) Tesco[5] (UK) | Siemens (Germany) | Two major US suppliers |
| WPP[6] (UK) | Vodafone[7] (UK) Kellogg (USA) BP (UK) Royal Dutch/Shell (Neths./UK) | WPP (UK) | Vodafone (UK) |
| Royal Dutch Shell (Neths./UK) | Bosch (Germany) Daimler-Chrysler (Germany) Unilever (UK/Neths.) Wartsila[8] (Finland) | | |

Notes: [1] One of the world's largest banks. [2] One of the world's largest advertising agencies, and part of Interpublic. [3] Food ingredients, part of Dutch cooperation Campina. [4] Global energy, particularly gas. [5] The largest UK supermarket chain and one of the largest in the world. [6] One of the world's largest marketing communications services companies. [7] The world's largest mobile phone service provider. [8] Power generation and marine propulsion.


## Global Customer–Supplier Management Study

The primary supporting research for this book is a study of global customer–supplier management that we conducted in 2003 and 2004, along with Professor Tomas Hult of Michigan State University. This involved first hand research at 31 MNCs, both global suppliers and global customers, listed in Table 1.1. This research involved personal interviews with over 60 senior executives, as well as a detailed multi level survey completed by 27 executives. Information was obtained on the way global customer–supplier relationship programmes can be implemented, the barriers that can be encountered, and best practices that can lead to extra advantage. In this study we coined the term, 'Global Relationship Management (GRM)' to refer to either global customer management or global supplier management.[31]

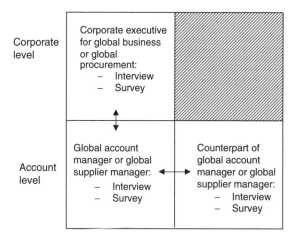

**Fig. 1.7** Levels in global customer–supplier management study

In the primary set up of the study eight global companies were selected as prime casestudy companies. For half of these companies, their global customer management programme was studied, and for the other half their global supplier management. For each company two to four global customers (for the global customer management companies) or global suppliers (for the global supplier management companies) were identified. The study per prime company was split into two levels and two sides, as shown in Figure 1.7. We interviewed executives at both the corporate/programme level and the account level. We did this in order to understand both the general, company-wide nature of the GRM programme, and the way in which the management of specific customers and suppliers might have been customized. At the corporate level we interviewed the executive responsible for the whole global programme. At the account level, we interviewed executives on both the managing side (e.g., a supplier) and the managed side (e.g., a customer) in order to understand both sides of the relationship pair. This also allowed us to get evaluations of the performance of the GRM programme from the viewpoint of both the managing and managed sides. This research design avoided the common research problem of potential bias from having the same respondent report on both the programme and its performance.

Large Sample Survey

The lead author and a co-author (Professor David B. Montgomery of Stanford Business School) developed a questionnaire about global account management, had it completed by 191 senior international executives from 165 multinational companies and conducted various statistical tests.[32]

## Foundation

Our sample came from four different sources: one postal survey and three convenience samples from senior-level executive education programmes conducted at Stanford and UCLA business schools during 1997. In all four samples, respondents were nearly all at the level of vice president or higher.

Statistical tests showed that the four samples provided very similar results and could be pooled into one sample for analysis. The respondent multinational companies came from a very wide mix of industries and from 33 different countries spread across all the regions of the world: North, South, and Central America; Western and Eastern Europe; East Asia; Africa; and Oceania. On average, the companies had operations in four of these regions. US companies made up 70 percent (133 out of 191) of the sample. Median company revenues were $1,956 million (just below the US *Fortune 500* cutoff of 1997).

### GAM Forum

Additional supporting research comes from six sessions of a global account management forum, based in London, that we conducted during 2001. During these sessions, senior executives from 13 multinational companies discussed issues about GAM. These companies included: BP Amoco, Castrol International, Herbert Smith (a leading law firm), IBM, Hill & Knowlton, Merrill Lynch, PricewaterhouseCoopers, Regus (a leading provider of office space around the world), Siebel Systems (a leading provider of CRM and other systems), Spirent (a leading telecommunications technology company), Standard Chartered Bank, Wunderman (a marketing services company in the WPP group), and Xerox.

### Case Studies

We wrote detailed case studies on Hewlett-Packard's global account management programme and about how the Young & Rubicam advertising agency managed the Star Alliance (of airlines) as a global customer.[33]

### Other Research

We conducted supplementary interviews with senior executives involved in global customer management at BT, Citigroup, Dun & Bradstreet, Ford Motor Company, and Reuters. The lead author advised in a research study conducted by McKinsey & Company on how multinational suppliers to retailers perceived the effects on their business of the internationalization of retailers.

### Executive Education Programmes and Conferences

The lead author benefited from interacting with participants in executive education programmes that he conducted on global customer management for

ABN Amro, Deutsche Bank, and Wallenius Wilhelmsen Lines. He also spoke at the St. Gallen GAMPRO programme in 2004, 2005, and 2006, at which participants included global account directors and managers from Areva T&D, Balzers, Brewer Science, Brita, Ciba Specialty Chemicals, Clariant International, Degussa, Deutsche Bank, Dow Chemical, Experian-Scorex, Frantschach Industrial Packaging, GN Netcom, Halcrow, Hubert+Suhner, IBM, MAN Turbo, Mondi Packaging, Narimpex, Nike, Oracle, Prionics, Rockwell, SAP, Scandinavian Airlines System, Siemens, SIG Combibloc, Sika, Sun Chemical, SWIFT, Swisscom Fixnet, Swiss International Airlines, Telekurs Financial Information, Vodafone, W.L. Gore, and Wacker Chemie.

In 2004, both authors participated in a special workshop in London on global customer management, organized by ITC Solutions, at which participants included executives from WPP, C&A, Unisys, Intel, IBM, BT, Delta, Royal Dutch Shell and Hewlett-Packard.

Lastly, in late 2006, the lead author presented and discussed the framework of this book at the St. Gallen University annual conference on global account management. Participants included executives from AMC Account Management Center, Bossard, Citigroup, Farnell InOne, Heidelberger, Holcim Group, Kone, Lufthansa Cargo, Marriott International, Philips International, PricewaterhouseCooper, Rogers Corporation, Schott, Shell Chemical, Sika Services, Suez Industrial Solutions, Tesco Stores, Vectia, Vitra International, Voith Paper Fabrics, and Zurich Insurance.

# Notes

1. For a full discussion of industry globalization drivers, see Chapter 2 in George S. Yip (2003) *Total Global Strategy II: Updated for the Internet and Service Era*. Upper Saddle River, NJ: Prentice Hall.
2. For a review of global strategy see George S. Yip (1989) 'Global Strategy...In a World of Nations?', *Sloan Management Review*, 31 (1): 29–41; and George S. Yip (2003) *Total Global Strategy II: Updated for the Internet and Service Era*. Upper Saddle River, NJ: Prentice Hall.
3. M. Gabel and H. Bruner (2003) *Global Inc*. New York: New Press.
4. See 'Smarter Links in the Modern Supply Chain', *Financial Times*, 8 November 2005, p. 13.
5. McKinsey & Company (1999) *Managing International Retailers*. London: McKinsey & Company.
6. David B. Montgomery and George S. Yip (2000) 'The Challenge of Global Customer Management', *Marketing Management*, 9(4): 22–9.
7. George S. Yip and Tammy L. Madsen (1996) 'Global Account Management: The New Frontier in Relationship Marketing', *International Marketing Review*, 13(3): 24–42.

8. Dean M. Peebles (1989) 'Don't Write Off Global Advertising: A Commentary', *International Marketing Review*, 6(1): 73–8.

9. Theodore Levitt (1983) 'The Globalization of Markets', *Harvard Business Review*, May–June, pp. 92–102.

10. Pat Sloan (1993) 'Why Reebok Fired Chiat, Once and For All', *Advertising Age*, 30, September, pp. 13–158.

11. From 23 percent to 48 percent over the ten-year period to 1993. See Laurel Wentz (1993) 'Shops Flourish in '90s: Decade of Alignment', *Advertising Age*, 30 September, pp. 11–110.

12. Global purchasing by customers is the other key response but is not the central subject of this book. See instead, Philip B. Schary and Tage Skjott-Larsen (2001) *Managing the Global Supply Chain*, 2nd edn. Copenhagen: Copenhagen Business School Press.

13. Benson P. Shapiro (1989) *Close Encounters of the Four Kinds: Managing Customers in a Rapidly Changing Environment*. Boston, MA: Harvard Business School, Note No. 9-589-015; and Benson P. Shapiro and Rowland T. Moriarty (1980) *National Account Management: Emerging Insights*, Report No. 80-104. Cambridge, MA: Marketing Science Institute.

14. Barbara B. Jackson (1985) *Winning and Keeping Industrial Customers*. New York: Lexington Books.

15. Yip and Madsen (1996). See also Atul Parvatiyar and Thomas Gruen (2001) 'Global Account Management Effectiveness: A Contingency Model', working paper. Goizueta School of Business, Emory University, Atlanta, GA, 25 May. GAM can also be viewed as an extension of relationship marketing. For a discussion of the latter concept see, for example, U. Manohar Kalwani and Narakesari Narayandas (1997) 'Long-Term Manufacturer–Supplier Relationships: Do They Pay Off for Supplier Firms?', *Journal of Marketing*, 59: 1–16; and Christian Grönroos (1997) 'Value-Driven Relational Marketing: From Products to Resources and Competencies', *Journal of Marketing Management*, 13(5): 407–20.

16. Researchers have been writing about global account management programmes for at least the last ten years. See Yip and Madsen (1996); Tony Millman (1996) 'Global Key Account Management and Systems Selling', *International Business Review*, 5(6): 631–45; Christian Belz and Christoph Senn (1999) 'Global Account Management', special issue of *Thexis* (University of St. Gallen), 4: 1–64; David B. Montgomery and George S. Yip (2000) 'The Challenge of Global Customer Management', *Marketing Management*, 9(4): 22–9; David Arnold, Julian Birkinshaw and Omar Toulan (2001) 'Can Selling Be Globalized? The Pitfalls of Global Account Management', *California Management Review*, 44(2): 8–20; Julian Birkinshaw, Omar Toulan and David Arnold (2001) 'Global Account Management in Multinational Corporations: Theory and Evidence', *Journal of International Business Studies*, 32(2): 231–48; Kevin Wilson, Nick Speare and Samuel J. Reese (2002) *Successful Global Account Management: Key Strategies and Tools for Managing Global Customers*. London: Miller Heiman; G. J. Verra (2003) *Global Account Management*. London: Routledge; H. David Hennessey

and Jean-Pierre Jeannet (2003) *Global Account Management: Creating Value*. New York: Wiley; and Nirmalya Kumar (2004) *Marketing as Strategy*. Boston: Harvard Business School Press, chapter 5.

17. Arnold et al. (2001) and Birkinshaw et al. (2001).

18. Montgomery and Yip (2000).

19. Anton Fritschi (1999) 'Global Key Account Management bei ABB: Erfolg Kennt Keine (Länder-) Grenzen', *Thexis*, 4: 26–9.

20. Faris Momani and Tobias Richter (1999) 'Standardisation versus Differentiation in European Key Account Management: The Case of the Adidas-Salomon AG', *Thexis*, 4: 44–7.

21. Yip and Madsen (1996).

22. Angela Andal-Ancion and George S. Yip (2004b) 'Star Alliance (B): A Global Customer', Cranfield, UK: European Case Clearing House, No. 504-128-1.

23. Julian Birkinshaw and Michael Mol (2006) 'How Management Innovation Happens', *MIT Sloan Management Review*, 47(4): 81–8.

24. Robert D. Buzzell (1984) 'Citibank: Marketing to Multinational Customers', Boston, MA: Harvard Business School, case No. 9-584-016 Harvard Case Services, revised 1/85.

25. See exposition of this argument by Julian Birkinshaw, Omar Toulan and David Arnold (2001) 'Global Account Management in Multinational Corporations: Theory and Evidence', *Journal of International Business Studies*, 32(2): 231–48.

26. For a review of information processing theory in relation to multinational companies, see William G. Egelhoff (1992) 'Information Processing Theory and the Multinational Enterprise', *Journal of International Business Studies*, 23(3): 341–68.

27. This dependence can be seen in the light of resource dependency theory. See R. M. Emerson (1962) 'Power Dependence Relations', *American Sociological Review*, 27: 31–40.

28. This more dependent global customer can be seen as an increase in resources of the supplier, according to the resource-based view of strategy. See Birger Wernerfelt (1989) 'From Critical Resources to Corporate Strategy', *Journal of General Management*, 14(3): 4–12; and Jay B. Barney (1991) 'Firm, Resources and Sustained Competitive Advantage', *Journal of Management*, 17(1): 99–120.

29. For an exposition of transaction cost theory, see Oliver E. Williamson (1945) *Markets and Hierarchies: Analysis and Antitrust Implications*. New York: The Free Press; and for relevance to international business, see Alain Verbeke (2003) 'The Evolutionary View of the MNE and the Future of Internalization Theory', *Journal of International Business Studies*, November, 34(6): 498–504.

30. See the discussion of local responsiveness and global integration for MNCs in Prahalad and Doz (1987) and Bartlett and Ghoshal (1989).

31. George S. Yip, G. Tomas M. Hult, and Audrey Bink (2005) 'Static Triangular Simulation as a Methodology for Strategic Management Research', in *Research Methodology in Strategy and Management*, Vol. 4, David J. Ketchen and Donald D. Bergh, (eds.), Oxford: Elsevier JAI, 2007.

32. This study is reported in David B. Montgomery and George S. Yip (2000) 'The Challenge of Global Customer Management', *Marketing Management*, Winter, 9(4): 22–9; and in David B. Montgomery, George S. Yip and Belen Villalonga (1999) *Demand For and Use of Global Account Management*. Cambridge, MA: Marketing Science Institute, report No. 99-115.

33. See Angela Andal-Ancion, under the direction of George S. Yip (2004b) 'Star Alliance (B): A Global Customer', European Case Clearing House, No. 504-128-1; and also G. S. Yip and T. L. Madsen (1997) 'Hewlett-Packard (A): The Global Sales Problem' and J. K. Johansson (1997) 'Hewlett-Packard (B): The Global Account Solution', *Global Marketing*. New York: Irwin, pp. 684–91; Jose de la Torre, Yves Doz and Tim Devinney (2001) 'Hewlett-Packard (A)', *Managing the Global Corporation: Cases in Strategy and Management*. Maidenhead: McGraw-Hill, pp. 364–74.

# 2    Exploiting Globalization Drivers and Potential

Global industries are not born.
They are created by global companies.
The rewards of globalization go to the first movers.

Should a company develop a global customer management (GCM) programme? How can it determine whether to do so? What are the potential benefits and costs? These are the questions that we address in this chapter. We do so by examining several drivers and benefits for the adoption of GCM.

## Drivers to Adopt GCM

There are four major categories of drivers for adopting GCM—customer, financial, market and technology:[1]

1. Customer drivers:
   - customers in multiple countries;
   - more globally coordinated customers;
   - global purchasing programmes;
   - demand for standardized products and services.
2. Financial drivers:
   - more revenue and return from customers;
   - lower selling costs.
3. Market drivers:
   - consolidation of industry;
   - commoditization of products, shift to marketing solutions;
   - competition.
4. Technology drivers:
   - fast-changing technology;
   - risk of imitation;
   - improvements in information and communications technology.

## Customer Drivers

Not surprisingly, as a customer focused programme, GCM is very much driven by changing customer behaviour. Several of these behaviours are critical for GCM.

### Customers in Multiple Countries

Most MNC customers are expanding their businesses geographically, thanks to increased globalization. Market deregulation and macro-economic factors have created these growth opportunities. Customers in saturated markets are seeking new markets where they can introduce their products and services. In 2004, the Shell global account manager for global electronics concern Bosch said: 'Initially, the focus for Bosch was on the big amount of German business. With the new global focus, we started identifying potential business over Europe and eventually over the whole world'. As Bosch was growing and getting more global, so too did Shell's business with this customer.

The 'how' of this expansion can vary. Customers may move to countries where the supplier is present only through an agent. For example, a global customer of office solutions provider, Xerox, expected service in Malta, a country where Xerox did not have a subsidiary but worked with an agent. This arrangement proved to be a real barrier for good global service, with the need for extensive extra coordination with this agent. Likewise, IBM says it can be difficult to take advantage of global opportunities for those of its customers who have developed in countries where IBM is mainly represented by agents. Another scenario is where customers enter new markets not yet served by their suppliers. When Siemens and Xerox set up their global relationship, it was unprecedented. A lot of customization was required, and the size and uniqueness of this account at times created difficulties, as not every local operation of Xerox had the knowledge and capability that Siemens demanded. Both Siemens and Xerox had to invest a lot of time to make their local staff understand the business model they were working with. This problem recurs whenever Siemens expands into a new country. Many day-to-day problems of language and culture are a result of the current growth. In particular, global customers have the same service expectations in different countries regardless of how long the supplier has operated there. When a supplier expands into a new country they face the difficulty that customers typically still demand the same products and services that they enjoy in countries where the supplier has established markets and an existing relationship with the supplier.

More Globally Coordinated Customers

As just described, multinational companies continue to become more international, spreading their sales and other activities over more of the globe. This greater international spread in itself generates greater demands on multinational suppliers to serve their multinational customers in the countries they have expanded into. But more important is the accompanying trend for multinational customers to become more globally, or regionally, coordinated in their purchasing. So more and more MNC customers are moving towards more centralized purchasing models and demanding to purchase products and services in global agreements. The continuing globalization of most industries drives this change. In some instances, the customer initiates the move toward global coordination, developing the knowledge and infrastructure required to extract global efficiencies ahead of its suppliers. For example, energy multinational Royal Dutch/Shell has implemented specific processes to manage all stages in its relationships with global suppliers. Shell has cast most activities in the pre-award stage into globally consistent processes used worldwide, such as those for selecting contractors, online bidding, gathering market intelligence and evaluation systems. As of 2004, Shell was working on a new step to develop consistent processes for the post-award stage of global contracts, such as relationship management with the suppliers.

Like Shell, most globally operating companies have started with some form of global purchasing. Many supplier companies, however, have also been quick to anticipate this trend, and have geared up their processes to fit this growing demand for global agreements. For example, an international sales and operations executive at IBM said in 2001:

We are reengineering our worldwide sales, services and support infrastructure, so that we can offer our customers wherever they are, the full power of our global resources ... The network of teams is, in effect, one global agile organization—unimpeded by traditional business unit boundaries, supported by our worldwide resources and those of our business partners—presenting a single face to our customers.

## Global Purchasing Programmes

As customers expand geographically and as they seek more global coordination of purchasing, a common response is to set up a formal programme for global purchasing.[2] The primary objective is to save on purchasing costs, but secondary objectives include greater global consistency in quality and specifications, and a more complete global overview.

## Foundation

To implement global purchasing, customers create centralized purchasing teams. For example, Volkswagen (VW) now works with a strict central decision structure—all sourcing decisions over € 250,000 a year are made at VW's headquarters in Wolfsburg, Germany, by a corporate sourcing committee that meets weekly. If a purchase is needed in Mexico, it is decided in Wolfsburg who the supplier will be. In this way, up to 98 percent of the sourcing for any one car is coordinated from Wolfsburg, allowing for an almost complete global overview.

Information systems have also encouraged the adoption of global purchasing programmes by exposing cross-country price differences for similar products and services. Suddenly, supplier companies can no longer apply different prices for different markets. Global customers demand the best price to be applied uniformly across all its operations. Once they have adopted global purchasing, customers also further develop their information and communication systems to support it.

A multinational supplier working with a customer that uses global purchasing needs to respond with GCM. IBM's initiation in 1995 of its GCM programme allowed it to cope effectively when one of its largest customers, a major British multinational bank, moved to global purchasing. This bank's customer initially made good progress in its global coordination, but did not move as fast as IBM. By the early 2000s, however, the bank began to evolve at a faster pace and to overtake IBM in terms of global coordination. For example, this bank started sharing pricing information, in particular, among its different procurement regions. It took IBM over two years to react effectively to this evolution, but now this customer is managed as a single business unit in IBM's integrated model of customer management.

### Demand for Standardized Products and Services

Globalization has brought greater use by both customers and suppliers of products and services with a high degree of global or regional standardization.[3] Standardization has many benefits on both the demand and supply sides.[4] On the demand side many customers, whether individuals or businesses prefer the global consistency, compatibility and quality guarantee that can come from standardization. On the supply side producing standardized products or services can allow a single production facility to fill the demand of multiple countries, and marketing initiatives can be applied across different markets. Standardization of specifications, as well as ingredients and components, also allows a global customer to simplify its supply chain management. Therefore, customers who choose to produce globally standardized products and services will demand the same from their global suppliers.

# Financial Drivers

Customers expect and usually achieve significant financial benefits from moving to global purchasing. But suppliers also face financial drivers to manage customers globally.

## More Revenue and Return from Customers

Customers use global agreements to boost their bargaining power in securing the best terms for their business. Hence suppliers dealing with global customers face a classic dilemma. On the one hand, global agreements almost always lead to more business for suppliers. On the other hand, these agreements also almost always lead to lower prices being set than otherwise existed. Hence suppliers have to achieve a greater total return from the combined higher volume but lower margins to make this change worthwhile. But GCM can lead to further favourable developments. First, it is usually easier to sell higher value-added products and services to a globally managed customer, partly because of the greater depth of trust that develops in the relationship. Second, the total cost of serving the customer should be lower, with less cross-country duplication of service activities and the greater stability of the business. The latter characteristic can mean lower cost, not having to gear up and down to serve the customer. Third, global agreements open doors for further geographic expansion, essentially conquering new markets using the customers' international network and business infrastructure.

## Lower Selling Costs

Over the long term, suppliers can enjoy lower selling costs from global agreements. They can spread their costs over a wider base of products, thereby exploiting economies of scale in their transactions. Instead of separate agreements for each country, there is now only one agreement to be made, possibly in the form of an umbrella contract with alterations in place for different countries. Once established, a global relationship should mean less selling effort is required to retain the customer, especially in terms of re-bidding.

Perhaps the biggest selling benefit from GCM comes from elevating the global supplier into a much more rarified level of competition. In most industries there are only a few suppliers capable of serving customers globally, while there are many who can do so nationally. The computer systems industry is a case in point. It has many local players, but only about four with global capabilities. Thus, a supplier with global capabilities has to compete with only two or three other companies to win a global contract, compared to a local supplier who has to compete with at least 20 other companies for a much smaller amount of business. So while the global supplier's selling cost is only a fraction of the size of a subsequent contract, the local supplier's selling cost may be significant, relative to the business for which it is competing. Furthermore, the chances of winning a global contest are one in four rather than one in 20 in a local contest. Hence, global capabilities for a supplier can lead to a competitive advantage that can then lead to lower selling costs.

## Market Drivers

GCM is a market-oriented strategy. So market drivers play a key role in deciding on its adoption.

### Consolidation of Industries

The ongoing global consolidation of many industries creates fewer but bigger customers. We recognize that industries actually go through cycles of consolidation and then fragmentation, rather than moving in one direction toward consolidation. But globalization means that each cycle usually ends up with fewer, larger players. For example, the personal computer industry is now in a consolidation phase, dominated by a small number of global players. Similarly the food consumer world has seen a high rate of consolidation in the last decade, leaving the industry with fewer, larger players such as Unilever and Kraft. As such major customers represent a significant chunk of the total market, it becomes imperative for large MNC suppliers to win their business. GCM and its attendant global capabilities has become a major source of competitive advantage for MNC suppliers seeking to gain the business of mega-customers. A virtuous circle ensues for the winners, as suppliers encourage their customers to rationalize their list of suppliers, and customers increase their total purchase volume.

### Commoditization of Products, Shift to Marketing Solutions

As many industries mature, many of their products are becoming increasingly commoditized. Product features become easily replicable, making differentiation a bigger challenge. So the battle for business gets fought at the service level. Customers and suppliers need to add value to their products by bundling them with services providing a marketing solution. An example would be the shift by Xerox from selling photocopiers to selling document management. To create the most value-added solutions, suppliers need an intimate understanding of their customers. Relationship building is key, especially on a global level where the scale of marketing solutions can be generalized or customized according to customers' needs. To customize its marketing solutions for Siemens' needs,

Xerox mapped Siemens's requirements and divided its geographical market area into two levels. Level 1 countries (Germany, China, USA, UK and France), have the highest level of focus. All Xerox personnel involved with Siemens in these countries are part of a larger, global community. The remaining countries are Level 2. Within these countries only a few key individuals with a coordination role are involved in GCM, and hold the Siemens 'linking pin' function. The resulting global account network consists of about 100 people, approximately half of them being at each level.

## Competition

The competitive landscape drives many suppliers to adopt GCM programmes. Competitors with the best global capabilities (in terms of the combination of local delivery and global coordination exploit their advantage to become early adopters. Such suppliers take the competition to a new, global level, as customers enjoy the benefits of GCM and begin to demand it as a standard. Any supplier wishing to keep its customers must now develop its own GCM programme to stay competitive. Competition between global suppliers then takes place at three levels: first, based on the actual products and services offered and their terms; second, based on the quality of the general GCM programme of the supplier; and third, based on the extent and effectiveness of the customization of the GCM programme to that particular customer. So the winner of global contracts may not offer the best in terms of products and services, but it may win on the basis of its GCM programme.

# Technology Drivers

Technology has both a general and a specific effect in driving the adoption of GCM. The general effect lies in the speeding up and accentuation of competition and hence the need to find more sources of competitive advantage. The specific effect arises in that technology is an enabler of the systems needed to run GCM programmes.

## Fast-Changing Technology

Short product life cycles, due to rapidly changing technologies, is a key driver for globalization and GCM. Suppliers now have less time to achieve a decent return on investment on their products. They can get a quicker return by selling for more or just selling more. When selling for more is not possible, suppliers can rely on their big customers to sell more. Having a global relationship with such customers makes this job easier.

Risk of Imitation

Another consequence of shorter product life cycles is the risk of imitation by competitors. First mover advantage is key in technology-intensive products, not only from a brand perspective but also for future sales. So suppliers seek to accelerate the speed of product introductions worldwide. One way to do this is to take advantage of global relationships to persuade major customers to become early buyers on a global basis. Thus, using global agreements with customers is an effective way to build a broad base for business in the introduction phase.

Improvements in Information and Communications Technology

The Internet and other related communications technologies have encouraged customers and suppliers to share information on a global scale. The ability to communicate anytime and anywhere without too much cost builds vital GCM relationships. Furthermore, developments in information systems, such as customer relationship management (CRM) and enterprise resource planning (ERP) systems enable the supplier to collect and analyse data faster and more accurately worldwide. Suppliers can use this more sophisticated analysis to improve their relationships with their global customers. (Chapter 8 will discuss how suppliers and customers can make better use of their available information and systems.)

# Realizing the Benefits of Global Customer Management

The various drivers for GCM discussed above offer many potential benefits to both suppliers and their customers. But managers must work to reap these benefits. We now discuss what managers need to do to attain the benefits from the four types of drivers.

## Attaining Customer Benefits

GCM gives the key stakeholders—the customer and the supplier—the potential to drive their relationship to mutual advantage. Key stages in this drive include building a stronger partnership, sharing information and gaining more inside knowledge, understanding customer strategy and goals, and influencing the customer's agenda.

Building a Stronger Partnership

GCM creates a virtuous 'trust and understanding' spiral, particularly if the supplier implements a more integrated global customer management programme and not just a narrow account-based programme. Both parties benefit from the trust and openness that develops.[5] When Schneider Electric, a French producer of electrical products, started its GCM programme the first customer with which it implemented this programme was an American company with which it had a long-standing relationship. As Schneider developed a deeper understanding of the customer's needs, it could tailor products to better suit its market. By working together in a global account relationship the two companies identified mutually beneficial initiatives in product development, reduction of project cycle time, improvement of productivity, minimization of down-times, savings in maintenance costs, and reduction of inventory and purchasing costs. Furthermore, their worldwide cooperation helped ensure global consistency in product and service quality. As a result of the success, Schneider became this customer's first and only globally certified electrical supplier.[6]

Sharing Information and Gaining More Inside Knowledge

GCM leads to information being more freely shared between customer and supplier. As explained in Chapter 1, having a diamond structure of contacts between customer and supplier plays an important part in any GCM relationship, as it creates a multidisciplinary network between the two companies.[7] The diamond structure ensures more contact between people from the two organizations, and hence more sharing of information on different levels and subjects. If this information is processed well, for example, by an effective customer information management system, then it can be a valuable resource for new developments, innovations and business between the two companies. It can also be an effective way to recognize potential problems before they escalate. Due to the global agreement between British energy company BG Group and its supplier, American engineering company Bechtel, these companies trust each other with more information in the start-up phase of new projects than they might have done without the agreement. By sharing more information in this early stage, the start-up phase can be better aligned to fit requirements and, therefore, it is shorter, which leads to a better time to market, and eventually an increased competitive advantage for BG Group.

Understanding Customer Strategy and Goals

GCM means business strategy and goals are aligned as customer and supplier work together to improve their processes to achieve better results. This teamwork builds over time, which further strengthens the partnership between the two parties. The supplier can use its in-depth knowledge of its customer to develop new products, services and processes that will directly benefit the customer. Gaining the customer's buy-in will be easier as the potential benefits and the existing supplier relationship come into play.

Aligned suppliers also have greater potential to widen the scope of business with their customers. For their part, customers prefer to work with suppliers with whom they have a long-standing relationship. GCM helps suppliers to achieve this better alignment and understanding of customer strategy and goals.

### Influencing the Customer's Agenda

The real test of the strength of relationship between customer and supplier is their level of influence on each other's agendas. This influence works both ways. The obvious example is where a supplier makes changes in its production facilities in response to a customer's request. A supplier will be reluctant to make such custom modifications if its relationship with the customer lacks a long-term business outlook and shared goals. The flipside also applies. For example, a supplier may want to influence a customer into changing its global logistical processes to better fit with the supplier's own, in order to derive greater efficiencies. Gaining the customer's buy-in and commitment will depend on the strength of their relationship.

In both cases, customers and suppliers can succeed in influencing each other's agendas if they can derive a win-win outcome. This also builds loyalty, which strengthens the relationship. Thus, a virtuous circle is created. In one example where a telecommunications company started a reciprocal partnership with its global advertising agency, the latter agreed to aim for early adoption of new products and services of the telecommunications company. Based on the knowledge that the telecoms global account manager had of the advertising agency he advised them to use Blackberry communication devices when these were first introduced. The Blackberries helped the advertising firm to save many man-hours, and at the same time gave the telecommunications company an ideal test site before rolling out this new technology to other accounts.

## Achieving Financial Benefits

As discussed earlier, the financial benefits of GCM stretch beyond volume sales and direct savings in sales costs. Suppliers can better gain the indirect benefits by using GCM to reduce total costs, gain business efficiencies and better utilize global resources.

Reducing Costs and Increasing Business Efficiencies

Global relationships can deliver significant cost reductions and more stream-lined business processes. In particular, such relationships enable the more effective deployment of shared productivity tools. For example, a common tool that customers and suppliers use is the automated order system (AOS), which is a web-based application that speeds up the order process, and ensures its accuracy and cost-effectiveness. In the early 2000s, Unilever started the E4US, a project to implement online ordering systems for its suppliers. Not all suppliers were pleased with this announcement, as they saw it as a costly exercise that would bring benefits mainly to Unilever. The suppliers that had an open mind toward E4US, however, got Unilever to help them streamline their order processes, which led, not just to logistical savings, but also to an increase in business, as Unilever preferred doing business with the companies that had implemented E4US. Furthermore, this shared system raised the threshold at which it might change suppliers, as Unilever would not like to abandon the investment it had made in these suppliers.

Fully Utilizing All Global Resources

Suppliers can fully utilize their global resources through better global coordination with their customers. In particular, suppliers can exploit economies of scale from combining similar customer requirements across the world, and spreading their delivery and operational costs across more customers. Even when only one customer is involved, a supplier can gain from better global utilization. As a global account of Xerox, Siemens wants the former to deliver a global interface, consistent systems, consistent products, consistent quality, a single level of global escalation and standardized logistics. Delivering this level of global consistency and standardization requires significant investment on the part of Xerox. But Xerox sees a return through achieving better economies of scale and from reducing duplication. So global consistency and standardization can be beneficial to both the customer *and* the supplier.

## Attaining Market Benefits

Suppliers can attain benefits from GCM by building on their global relationship with customers to strengthen their market positions.

Winning Market Share at the Global Customer Level

Suppliers can use GCM programmes to gain a greater market share through global agreements: the customer promises the supplier increased and sustained volume from the global agreement in return for favourable terms. While some may view global agreements as one-way—customers squeezing the supplier for every penny in return for its business—these global agreements provide an opportunity to achieve two-way benefits. The secret lies in establishing good global customer–supplier relationships. This way, the customer receives the economies of scale from the global agreement, while the supplier gains market share, volume and sometimes even cross-selling opportunities. The global purchasing leader at Shell commented, 'as part of the global supplier management, Shell has converted its relationships with many smaller advertising agencies to one strategic alignment with JWT'.

Gaining Competitive Leverage

For suppliers, global capabilities and good global relationships are real sources of competitive advantage that they can use as leverage. Customers all over the world are rationalizing their purchasing strategy, preferring to deal with only one or two suppliers instead of a myriad of companies.[8] Suppliers can view this rationalization trend as a threat or as an opportunity. Those suppliers who are threatened by rationalization should not be competing and can be discounted. This leaves only those suppliers who are prepared to compete for a place in customers' 'preferred list of suppliers'. At this point, suppliers can exploit their competitive advantage as customers seek companies that can help them meet their global challenges. In some instances, it may even be the suppliers' global capabilities and relationships that spur their customers to do business on a global scale. For example, the ability of personal computer component suppliers to deliver anywhere in the world has enabled final producers to globalize their own operations.

For a supplier on the preferred list, the opportunity to cultivate its global relationship with the customer is priceless. Trust and understanding will give rise to loyalty as both supplier and customer choose to accommodate each other's interests in every deal. In some instances, the relationship is even formalized, as illustrated in the case of Siemens. The company uses a 'lead communication manager' for global strategy with the supplier. This lead manager is in regular contact with the local buyers. In addition, local Siemens personnel are responsible for the day-to-day and operational communications with the supplier. But Siemens realizes there is the need to have more than just the basic purchasing relationship with the supplier. There is a quarterly cross-functional team meeting involving the main actors. Siemens' purchasing, logistics, quality and technology functions all rate the supplier in a very advanced supplier evaluation system. From this evaluation system, a supplier is awarded a 'factor' that is used as a guideline for improvement. One of the most direct ways in which this factor is important for the supplier is the fact that it is used when comparing quotes. The suppliers' factors are compared to the total average, and used to alter the price quote a supplier gives. For example, when a supplier is 5 percent better than the average supplier, its price will be regarded 5 percent lower than the original price quote. This way, even though a supplier may not have had the lowest price quote, it may still be chosen as the preferred supplier because of the good evaluation factor. With this system Siemens ensures that a supplier is rated by its complete performance, not just the sales price it offers.

### Increasing Credibility as a Long-Term Partner for Customers

To build and sustain the competitive advantage from GCM, a supplier needs to increase its credibility as a long-term partner for its customers. That applies in any selling relationship, but even more so given the extra challenges of a global one. So suppliers need to undertake GCM as a long-term strategy and realize that they will reap many of the potential benefits only years into the relationship with their global customers.

Therefore, suppliers need to treat GCM as an investment that may not yield an immediate return. Suppliers who are willing to invest financial and other resources into GCM send a strong signal to customers of their long-term commitment. In return, customers may initiate new and bigger projects for their suppliers. The more projects they work on together, the stronger their relationship becomes. Customers too must invest their time and money in GCM if they want to achieve their global objectives.

## Achieving Innovation and Technology Benefits

It is well established that closer supplier–customer relationships produce better innovations. GCM can do so even more, as it provides the supplier with multiple points of contact, geographic diversity in its interface with the customer, and an integrated view of the customer's needs. So the strength of the GCM relationship becomes a key ingredient in realizing innovation and technology potential.

### Fitting Innovations Better to the Customer

Suppliers can utilize their long-term relationships with their customers to develop new products, services and processes. Having inside knowledge will ensure that these new developments meet the actual needs of their customers, or assist them in realizing their business strategies. Royal Dutch/Shell works with customer value propositions that recognize the specific customer needs that Shell can help with. A Shell sector business manager said: 'We work with customized Customer Value Propositions (CVP). This way the global customer management organization deals with all the different elements that different customers seek from Shell'. The CVP strategy has often been shown to provide a real competitive advantage for Shell, as it gives customers a real sense of having a supplier who understands them and is looking out for their best interests.

Going one step further, the development could be through cooperation between the customer and the supplier, in which, for example, R&D employees of the two companies work together on the same project, or where the customer's facilities are used as a trial field for the developments. Schneider Electric does this in some of its most mature customer relationships. Schneider and the client form a product development team with members from both organizations to design new products together. This effort requires a high level of involvement from senior management in both organizations as well as a deep level of trust.[9]

Innovations from customer–supplier partnerships are often commercialized and offered to other customers or suppliers. A global partnership creates even more opportunities to do this. For example, Unilever wanted its suppliers around the world to become more efficient by following the Total Productive Maintenance (TPM) rules it had implemented in its own factories. Using its expertise Unilever helped some of its suppliers to install TPM in their factories, which led to benefits for both Unilever and the suppliers. The benefit for Unilever is that it knows that the goods it is buying have been manufactured under its TPM rules, which has generated an efficiency advantage and consequently a lower price. This efficiency, however, now applies to all products manufactured in each supplier factory, which therefore enables the supplier to offer lower prices or to enjoy higher margins with their other customers as well.

### Outsourcing of Technology from Customer

A customer–supplier relationship can become so tight that the customer begins to outsource its technology development (in part or in full) to its supplier. When this happens, the customer and supplier must strike the right balance of power in order to preserve their relationship. Too much dependence of the customer on the supplier is not sustainable, not only on the R&D level, but also on the human level. Negative feelings from the customer's staff can sabotage all the benefits that a strong global relationship might bring. In one example, an energy company outsourced its basic R&D activities to its global supplier of engineering services. But this move triggered a negative effect on the motivation of the energy company's staff when working with this supplier. Employees were very wary about providing the supplier with information as the employees were afraid the supplier was 'out to get their jobs'. It was not until the energy company managed to assure its employees that there were no plans to out-source any other work, that they became more open and trusting towards the supplier.

# Timing

GCM is a long-term strategy. It takes time to design and implement. Both IBM and Xerox took over ten years to fully develop their GCM programmes. Results do not come overnight. Adopters need to evolve through different phases toward achieving the full benefits of GCM. In particular, adopters need to start with a trial phase, where suppliers use GCM for a select number of customers before proceeding to the wider roll-out and integration phases, where GCM is integrated in the company's organization structure. Aligning the GCM function with the rest of the organization takes a particularly long time.

Successful GCM programmes need time to develop into strong relationships between customer and supplier. Trust and openness are not achieved overnight.

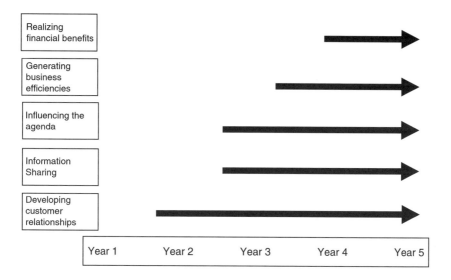

**Fig. 2.1** Benefits of global customer management over time

*Source*: Institute of Grocery Distribution, (IGD), based on a benchmark study of 25 leading suppliers in the grocery and food industry, 2004.

## Foundation

Both parties need to work at fostering the relationship before seeing tangible results. The different potential benefits tend to materialize over time, with financial benefits being among the last benefits to be realized (typically in the fourth or fifth years after adoption). As an illustration, Figure 2.1 shows a timeline of different benefits of implementing a GCM programme, based on a benchmarking study of 25 leading global companies in the grocery and food industry.

---

### Best Practices

The business world is getting more global. Suppliers are driven by many factors to adopt a more global approach to managing their customer accounts. Many multinational suppliers have responded to the demands of today's customers by setting up basic global account management (GAM) programmes. There are, however, a few more savvy suppliers who have taken the extra step of integrating the global coordination function throughout their organizations. Doing this delivers the benefits of a well implemented global customer management (GCM) programme.

The following points highlight the key drivers for global customer managing, as well as its benefits:

- for many industries, having global capabilities (local delivery and global coordination) is not a choice, but a necessity;
- when properly integrated in the total organization, a GCM programme delivers benefits on customer, financial, market and technology levels;
- the right GCM programme will lead to a positive spiral of trust and understanding;
- GCM is a long-term strategy, with its benefits being realized over time.

---

# Notes

1. This list of drivers for GCM is developed from the list of industry globalization drivers in George S. Yip (1992) *Total Global Strategy*. Upper Saddle River, NJ: Prentice-Hall.
2. Philip B. Schary and Tage Skjott-Larsen (2001) *Managing the Global Supply Chain*, 2nd edn. Copenhagen: Copenhagen Business School Press.
3. For a fuller discussion of global products and services, see chapter 4 in George S. Yip (2003) *Total Global Strategy II*. Upper Saddle River, NJ: Prentice-Hall.
4. As far back as the late 1980s, companies offering globally standardized products have been found to perform better than those offering local ones. See Masaaki Kotabe and Glenn S. Omura (1989) 'Sourcing Strategies of European and Japanese Multinationals: A Comparison', *Journal of International Business Studies*, Spring, 20 (1): 113–30.
5. See A. Cox, C. Lonsdale, J. Sanderson and G. Watson (2004) *Business Relationships for Competitive Advantage*. London: Palgrave.

6. A-V. Ohlsson and J. DiStefano (2000) 'Schneider Electric Global Account Management', case study IMD-3-0949, Lausanne, Switzerland.
7. P. Cheverton (2003) *Key Account Management—The Route to Profitable Key Supplier Status*. London: Kogan Page.
8. A. J. van Weele (1997) *Inkoop in strategisch perspectief*. Samson: Alphen aan de Rijn.
9. A-V. Ohlsson and J. DiStefano (2000) 'Schneider Electric Global Account Management', case study IMD-3-0949, Lausanne, Switzerland.

# 3    Integrating GCM with Global Strategy and Organization

You will all have to cooperate in an integrated European strategy, because if even one of you does not, the strategy will fail, and if you don't want to participate in the strategy you should leave the room now.

(Louis V. Gerstner, Jr., CEO of IBM)

The previous chapter examined how a supplier should decide whether to adopt a global customer management programme. In this chapter we discuss how to evaluate the GCM drivers in both the customer's and the supplier's industry, and how to integrate the GCM programme into the supplier's overall global strategy and global organization.

A GAM programme works better if it fits in with the company's overall global strategy and organization. But, when adopting a new business programme like global customer management, many general managers will be cautious about integrating it immediately into the company's strategy and structure. Therefore, the GAM organization often operates separately, alongside the existing company organization, so that it can first prove its success. However, it is in fact integrating the GAM programme into the rest of the company organization that can be key to making the programme a success. Having the programme integrated into all other company departments is one of the main capabilities needed to upgrade a GAM programme into a global customer management (GCM) programme. Furthermore, the company must have a global mindset for a programme as demanding as GCM to be effective. So before a company embarks on GCM, managers need to assess the company's current industry, strategy and organization to identify how a GCM programme can be best implemented.

## Global Potential of Industry for a GCM Programme

A GCM programme works better if the relevant industry is appropriate for its implementation. But many managers get confused as to which is the relevant industry. Most focus on the industry of the customer. But it is the industry of the supplier or the supplied product that matters much more. The nature of the customer's industry can also be important but usually much less so, as each customer buys hundreds or thousands of different products and services, some of which need global coordination and others of which do not. In this section we will discuss both the customer's and the supplier's industries, to show what issues are important indicators for the potential of a GCM programme.

## GCM Drivers in the Customer's Industry

Contrary to popular belief, it is not the customer's industry that leads in the need for GCM. An examination of the automobile industry as a customer illustrates the greater importance of the supplier's industry. The automobile industry has mostly globalized participants who act as global customers demanding global account management for many of their purchased inputs but not others. Why is that? First, they demand a GAM relationship for their more differentiated, less commodity-like, purchases that provide a competitive advantage in the market place, such as safety features (airbags, rollover protection and brake-by-wire systems). Second, they are more likely to demand a GAM relationship for more critical inputs, so that they can achieve joint design, for example of tyres. In contrast, automobile companies would be wasting their time to try to procure their stationery on a global basis. Third, automakers will act as global customers for items where cost savings can be achieved through global buying, even if these inputs are not differentiated or critical. But global suppliers may not exist for some of these inputs. In the case of automobile companies, some of their highest costs are for labour and healthcare. But to date those inputs can be procured only on a local basis, i.e., those industries have not become globalized. So from a customer perspective, even the most globally integrated companies have to adjust their demand for GAM to fit in with the industry of the purchased item.

Hence, there are perhaps no customer industry characteristics that drive the demand for GCM or GAM. There can, however, be an interaction between the customer industry and the supplier industry that makes the purchased product or service more strategically important and hence more likely to need GCM. For example, nearly every company buys computers. But in some industries, such as those that are transaction-based and information-based, such as financial services, office computers are critical to performance and competitive advantage. In other industries, such as food processing, office computers (although not process-control computers) are much less critical. So customers in the financial services industry are more likely than those in the food processing industry to behave as global customers for office computers. In summary, among the many thousands of products and services that a multinational customer buys, some will have much greater strategic importance than others. After all, a customer is more likely to aim for global supply of a key part of its end product, than for the window cleaning of its offices.

Lastly, an industry may have many companies acting as global customers because those companies operate with a high level of global integration and can hence operate global strategies such as global buying. But it is better to think of this effect as belonging to individual companies rather than as being a characteristic of the customer industry.

So although for many suppliers the increasing globalization of their customers is a major driver to start globalizing themselves, the fact that they have global customers in the first place says more about their own industry than about that of their customers'. The supplier's industry and product category play a major role in deciding on the benefits a global programme will have for the company.

Although the customer's industry does not directly lead the need for GCM, this does not mean that a company should not be interested in its customers' industries. Analysing the customer's industry is a good way to get thorough customer understanding. When doing this, it is important to also assess the customer's place in the whole industry: Who are the customer's competitors? Who are its customers? How can we help our customer to be a better player in its industry? Knowing what issues the customer has to deal with enables the supplier to act on these issues, and build a stronger relationship with the customer, which is the foundation for effective GCM.

Finally, there should also be some focus on the trends and issues in a customer specific industry. For example, in the automotive industry there is a trend of moving production facilities to Eastern Europe and China, for both cost and market reasons. In 2003 Volkswagen sold more cars in China than in its home market in Germany. This trend is important for suppliers of automotive parts or services, and something to take into account before planning a GCM programme.

So the customer's industry is not a strong driver for GCM. *But that does not mean that the customer itself is not a strong driver.* In fact, both the customer and the supplier, particularly their overall global orientation and global integration capabilities, drive the success or otherwise of a GCM relationship.

## GCM Drivers in the Supplier's Industry

The dominance of the supplier's industry becomes even clearer as we take the supplier's perspective. Most suppliers face a very diverse customer base in terms of the latter's industry. For example, computer manufacturers sell to customers in almost every industry. From the broad anecdotal and case evidence, and from our research, they are also perhaps the leaders in the adoption of GAM. A false interpretation would be that computer companies are simply responding to their customers' requirements. However, it is the inherent characteristics of the computer industry that causes its customers to demand GAM.

A few characteristics of the supplier's industry or product category affect the potential need for GCM:

### Need for Global Consistency or Compatibility

Products or services that vary little in consistency or standards have correspondingly little need for a global customer management programme to achieve global consistency and standardization. That is typically the case with commodities. In contrast, GCM is needed for complex products or value-added commodities. For example, Castrol, the specialized fuels division of BP, views selling fuel to airlines in the spot market as a commodity transaction that does not need GCM, while selling a global fuelling service or specialized lubricants may well need GCM. Similarly, most banks operate a weak form of GCM, mainly because the products they sell, financial instruments and services, are quasi-commodities that vary a lot less than products such as technical components. (Chapter 4 will elaborate on what we mean by weak versus strong forms of GCM.)

### Complexity of Product or Service

Product or service complexity can increase the need for GCM. For example, the Dutch food ingredients supplier, DMV-International, may not need extensive global coordination for the worldwide sales of its caseinate, a commodity milk protein. Global coordination of the customer relationship is very necessary, however, when DMV deals with its more exclusive, advanced nutritional ingredients, even though this might involve the same customers.

While most complex products and services may also qualify under the previous count for a need to offer global consistency or compatibility, the two effects can be independent. For example, management consulting firms supply a complex service that usually needs to be carefully tailored to whichever specific geographic unit of a multinational client that is buying the service. But the complexity of the consulting work means that it usually behooves the supplier to globally coordinate what it does for different units of a given client. The same need applies to other suppliers of complex business services, such as accounting and law firms.

### Need for Central Specification or Quality Control

When discussing the customer's industry, we mentioned the role of products and services that are strategic to the customer. While this can be related to the customer's industry, it is mostly an effect of the supplied product or service. Strategic purchases are those that have a potentially significant effect on the buyer's competitive position or business performance. Typical examples include advertising services for consumer product companies and process control equipment for many manufacturers. For instance, Honeywell finds that many of its multinational customers want to specify centrally what sorts of controls are installed in their factories around the world.

### High Margins Available

GCM programmes are costly. So the products and services to which they are applied need to have sufficient margins to support the additional expense. Of course, the previous three industry characteristics—the need for global consistency or compatibility, the complexity of products or services and the need for central specification or control—tend to go with higher margins. So there is usually no conflict over this additional requirement. Nevertheless, industry conditions can reduce margins to levels below which GCM programmes cannot be supported.

### Global Suppliers Exist

Even if all the other favourable industry characteristics apply, a customer cannot buy globally if global suppliers do not exist. As discussed above in the automobile industry example, there are many important purchase categories that customers might want to procure on a global basis but where global suppliers do not exist. Indeed, suppliers can see such industries as providing opportunities for globalization. Such latent demand from would-be global customers provides a strong business case to build a global operation through organic expansion or acquisition. This is what happened in both the accounting and advertising industries: global suppliers were created to serve global customers. Law firms too are now going down this route of global consolidation.

### Summary

In support of the above GCM industry drivers, our research has found the strongest applications of GCM by suppliers in capital goods industries, particularly technology-based ones. Such industries include computers, electrical equipment and process controls. Industries producing inputs for manufactured goods, such as automotive components, also tend to have high levels of GCM. Most service industries tend to be at the lower end, although technically based services, such as telecommunications tend to be at the upper end.

# What the Supplier Needs to Know about Its Own Industry

As it is the supplier's industry that leads the need for a GCM programme, it is vital for the supplier to have comprehensive knowledge of its own industry. This may seem trivial, but is not always the case. Having knowledge about an industry does not mean simply having knowledge about the products themselves and their use, but also about the more general elements of this industry and its players. As every manager knows, when asking himself or herself, 'What industry am I in?', a mobile phone manufacturer's answer should not just be, 'mobile phones', but also the more general and overlapping areas like, 'communications', 'electronic devices'. For example, Motorola has carefully defined one of its businesses as neither 'mobile phones' (too narrow) nor 'communications' (too broad), but as 'mobile communications'.

Managers need to know a number of other industry factors that may affect GCM. What are the qualifiers to being able to participate in an industry? What are the real key success factors (KSFs) that set players apart from others? An assessment of the total customer field and its characteristics is also essential, as the customer's industry and its respective customers can have an influence on the supplier's industry. Knowing about end-customers and the importance a supplier's products have for them provide another indicator of the need for a GCM programme.

Lastly, it is important to know the current and potential share of worldwide supplier industry purchases made by global (or regional) and other types of customers. As defined in Chapter 1, global (or regional) customers are those who buy on a globally (or regionally) coordinated basis. These are by definition also multinational customers. But many multinational customers are not also global customers, i.e., they buy in multiple countries but not in a coordinated way. Some subsidiaries of multinational companies (MNCs) may buy in their local country and some from other countries.

The various possible types of multinational customers are illustrated in Figure 3.1. The vertical axis shows the extent to which customers buy in domestic or foreign markets and from domestic or foreign suppliers. The horizontal axis shows the extent to which purchasing is globalized by headquarters (HQ) involvement. In the lower left cell is the *'Free' Local Customer*, who buys in its local market from local suppliers, without any involvement from its HQ. In the top left cell, is the *Foreign Customer*, who buys, without HQ involvement, in foreign markets from foreign suppliers, and then ships the purchases home, or uses a foreign sourced service. For example, an American subsidiary might, on its own, decide to buy parts from a Mexican supplier for use back in the US, or it might outsource some of its information technology work to India. In one of the middle cells is the *International Customer*, a subsidiary that buys in its domestic

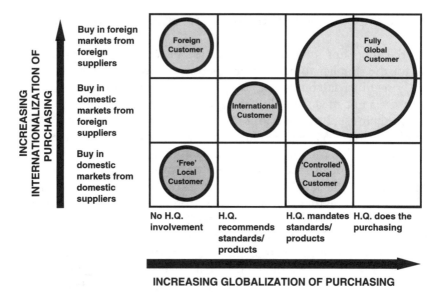

**Fig. 3.1** Types of multinational customers

market from foreign suppliers, with some guidance from its HQ in terms of standards or products. If the supplier has been designated a global one, and manages the customer as a global account, then this International Customer becomes part of a global customer relationship. On the lower right of the matrix is the *'Controlled' Local Customer*, who still buys in the local market, but follows HQ mandates about standards or products. In this case the mandate might require the customer subsidiary to buy from the local subsidiary of a designated global supplier. In that case this subsidiary also becomes part of a broader local customer relationship. Lastly, in the top right cells, is the *Fully Global Customer*, where the HQ either mandates standards or products or actually does the purchasing.

# Global Strategy

GCM is in itself an element of global strategy. To work effectively it needs to be part of, and fit with, a total global strategy. The latter includes the following key elements.[1]

- *Global market participation*: involves having the choice of country-markets in which to conduct business, and conducting that level of activity, particularly in terms of market share.

- *Global products and services*: are those that a worldwide business offers that are the same or different in different countries.

- *Global location of value-adding activities*: a company must choose where to locate each of the activities that comprise the entire value-added chain— from research to production to after sales service.[2]

- *Global marketing*: a worldwide business must decide to what extent they will use the same brand names, advertising and other marketing elements in different countries.

- *Global competitive moves*: a worldwide business must decide to what extent they will make competitive moves in individual countries as part of a global competitive strategy.

---

**How Xerox's Global Strategy Helped Win a Global Account**

Xerox's winning of Siemens, the huge German electronics company, as a global account illustrates the benefits of a GCM programme that fits into a broader global strategy. When Siemens started a project in 2000 to globally coordinate its purchasing, it chose document management as the targeted category. At that time, a lot of document management was done in-house, and all over the world. Siemens needed a supplier to which they could outsource some of this and was looking for a supplier that could combine local operations and global management. Siemens wanted one company dealing with document management, and one price for all services. Standardization and single point of contact were also very important. Siemens chose Xerox. In the words of a Siemens purchasing manager: 'Xerox's global strategy was one of the reasons to choose them as our global supplier. They are a worldwide player, and will fit in the Siemens global purchasing strategy once we have the buying efforts for this category fully combined'.

---

## Global Market Participation

When choosing markets in which to participate, companies will initially look for countries that have a high potential for revenue and profit. When the company is working with a global strategy, however, the reasons to participate in a certain country or region go beyond these considerations. The strategy may ask for participation in a country that is economically unattractive in its own right, but having a presence there represents an advantage for the company as a whole. Perhaps the most important difference between market participation for the sake of internationalization and that for the sake of global strategy is the role of *globally strategic countries*. Such countries are important beyond their intrinsic attractiveness. There are several ways in which a country can be globally strategic as a market-place: [3]

- offers a large source of revenues or profits;
- it is the home or other key market of global customers;
- it is the home market of global competitors;
- it is a significant market of global competitors;
- it plays a major role in of industry innovation.

As listed above, participating in the home or other key markets of global customers is a central part of global strategy. In selecting the country-markets in which to participate or operate, a supplier applying GCM should take into account the key markets of its key global customers. Such customers prefer to work with suppliers that cover their entire geographical area. Therefore, it could be worthwhile to have operations in a seemingly uninteresting market, in order to provide these key customers with a service that other global competitors might not offer, and thus win a greater market share in other countries.

### Service in Markets in which a Company Has No Customer Operations

Global customers often operate in more countries than do their suppliers. One of the world's largest banks complained to us that it operates in many more countries than any of its suppliers. Typically, the more geographically spread out multinational companies (MNCs) are the more likely they are to demand GCM services. A particularly tough requirement is for a supplier to serve a customer in a country or region where the supplier does already operate. A truly responsive supplier would set up operations in the new geographical area to avoid the risk of losing the existing global account by allowing a competitor to serve that customer in that location. The US advertising agency that used to have the Coca-Cola account (one of the largest in the world) was unable to serve Coca-Cola when it expanded to Brazil. So McCann-Erickson, another American but more global agency, took the account in Brazil. Then McCann used the Brazilian relationship to win the entire Coca-Cola account worldwide. To avoid a similar occurrence, many Japanese automotive parts suppliers have expanded globally with Toyota, Nissan, and Honda. Having established themselves, at significant cost, in these new countries, many of these suppliers subsequently have been able to find additional, non-Japanese customers.

---

#### Citigroup's Increase in Market Participation

Financial giant Citigroup has run one form or another of GCM from as early as 1974, initially by Citicorp (the banking company that became part of Citigroup). Its most recent form of GCM is primarily in its Global Relationship Bank (GRB), which was formed in 1995 to build upon its past successes in its 'World Corporation Group'. Since Citigroup started GRB, it has greatly increased its global market participation and local coverage. Key advantages for multinational clients of the GRB include a homogeneous quality of service globally and bank

---

clearing capabilities in most countries. Today, this business covers over 1,600 multinational clients who have significant global presence or activity.

GRB operates in every region of the world where a client meets global target market criteria or where it has an operating subsidiary with a banking wallet. For each global client, the total global responsibility is given to one person who is supported by other employees at the country level. Parent account managers (PAMs) are the global relationship managers, located in the country of the customer's headquarters, on the basis that a client's headoffice drives decisions. In support of the PAMs, subsidiary account managers (SAMs), who are local managers reporting to their country heads, also play a role, allocated according to the needs and the importance of a client's buying centres. The PAM has to make sure that all SAMs work with their country managers to get resources devoted to GRB customers. Having a GRB customer tends to increase the level of cross-border financing by Citigroup, which is inherently riskier. But, as the best clients are covered they offer a much better return on the capital employed to serve them, which offsets the higher risk. Citigroup calculates only one, global, profit-and-loss statement for each GRB customer.

## How GCM Helps Meet Customer Demands for Global Market Participation

The essence of global market participation is enhanced commitment to markets that may not be so attractive in themselves. Making such a commitment can be organizationally and politically difficult, especially when country managers are evaluated on the basis of performance in just the countries or regions for which they are responsible. A GCM programme can make a big difference in helping the organization to take a strategic decision to commit to markets of importance to global customers. A global relationship manager at a major multinational bank gave us an example. In each country, particularly in smaller, emerging economies, the bank can deploy only limited capital. In Malaysia, an important market for this bank, it faces more demand for loans from local, non-multinational customers than its allocated capital can support. Furthermore, loans to the local customers are made at higher interest rates than those to large multinationals. But the bank also faces demands for loans from the Malaysian subsidiaries of a number of its global customers. The bank's local manager would, if left alone, use all his capital in lending to local customers. The GCM programme intervenes, however, to ensure that some priority and capital is allocated for the local subsidiaries of global customers. The bank's Malaysian operation ends up with a lower profit margin than it would otherwise, but this loss is made up by the strengthening of the bank's wide relationship with each of its most important global customers.

## Global Products and Services

In a multilocal product strategy, the products and services offered in each country are tailored to meet local needs. In a global product strategy the ideal is a standardized core product that requires a minimum of local adaptation. Cost reduction is usually the most important benefit of product standardization. Some companies stress the need for a broad product portfolio, with many product varieties being offered in order to share technologies and distribution channels; or they stress the need for flexibility.[4] In practice, multinationals have already pursued global product standardization to a greater or lesser extent some of the time.[5]

More and more multinational customers are developing products and services with high degrees of global or regional standardization. Indeed, most MNCs have shifted from assuming that products and services will be local unless proven otherwise to assuming that they will be global, with as few adaptations as possible. Beiersdorf, the German consumer goods marketer of the Nivea and other brands, sums up this view with the philosophy, 'as global as possible, as local as necessary'. Standardization by customers means that they increasingly seek standardized products from their suppliers. Furthermore, when customers start to produce standardized products around the world, they demand that their suppliers also deliver standardized equipment or inputs in all the countries in which the customer operates. When Unilever develops a plan to introduce the same ice cream around the world, the company demands that its suppliers deliver the same ingredients around the world.

---

### Standardization at Ford

By pushing for standardization as part of the *Ford 2000* globalization initiative, Ford's global manager for global testing operations (GTO) managed to realize savings in the millions. This standardization required Europe and the United States to reconcile their approaches and specifications. Buying ten pieces of (standardized) equipment meant savings of about $2.5 million—a large percentage of the total purchase. One of Ford's suppliers, the Japanese company Horiba Instruments, recommended the new specifications, which would have elevated European standards and reduced US standards slightly. Of course, the US and European labs involved pushed for different standards. The European buyer for Ford said,

I presented the proposal to the global manager of GTO. He was very excited because, besides his purchasing objective, he also had a savings objective. Now we had aligned objectives. For North America, I was the strategist and placed the purchase order. For Europe, I was just the strategist. The Europeans still did the day-to-day buying and purchase orders, but I selected the suppliers, and worked on standardizing the specifications. My initial reaction was always to ask if the specifications could be standardized. What we [concluded] was that everything [could be] standardized. Customization could slow an order from six months to two-and-a-half years. So globalization also saved time.

How GCM Helps Meet Customer Demands for Global Products and Services

Developing global products and services is not easy. Doing so requires taking a proactive approach in diagnosing customer needs around the world and making the necessary compromises and adjustments to develop products and services that have the broadest global appeal, while avoiding the classic problem of appealing to the lowest common denominator.[6] Developers of global products also need to overcome the inherent organizational barriers to cross-border cooperation (which will be discussed later in this chapter). Developing global products or services that are customized to individual global customers' needs means overcoming barriers in two organizations. Having a GCM programme offers perhaps the only way that an MNC supplier can easily work with its MNC customers to develop globally standardized but client-customized solutions.

## Global Location of Value-Adding Activities

In a multilocal activity strategy, all or most of the value chain is reproduced in every country. In another type of international strategy—exporting—most of the value chain is kept in one country. In a global activity strategy, the value chain is broken up and each activity may be conducted in a different country, operating in a global network. The major benefits lie in cost reduction. One type of value chain strategy is partial concentration and partial duplication. The key feature of a global position on this strategy dimension is the systematic placement of the value chain around the globe.[7]

To provide its global customer support service, Hewlett-Packard maintains a global chain of activity—its more than 30 response centres around the world are integrated into a global network headed by four major centres: Bracknell (UK), Atlanta (Georgia, USA) and Mountain View (California, USA) and Melbourne (Australia). Each centre is staffed during extended daytime hours, seven days a week, by between 12 and 200 engineers. Problems that cannot be resolved in a smaller centre may be transferred to one of the major centres. Because of time-zone differentials, this arrangements means that at least one of the major centres is always in full operation at any time.

In serving global customers, a global supplier has to design allocation configuration that meets the key needs of its most important customers, as well as meeting the supplier's own internal needs and economics. For component suppliers, locating production activities close to key customer production sites is obvious. For example, as US producers of automotive parts, such as seats, move more production to China, their suppliers, such as those of seat cover materials, are doing the same. A less obvious requirement may be the need to locate supplier R&D near the customer's R&D centres in order to enhance their ability to cooperate.

How GCM Helps Meet Customer Demands for Global Location of Activities

A global strategy for the location of value-adding activities requires many complex judgments and tradeoffs in its design, and ongoing challenges in its operation. Adding the need to mesh with the global activity networks of multiple global customers greatly complicates both the design and operation of a supplier's own activity network. A GCM programme and the input of its global account managers, who represent the needs of different global customers, makes this challenging task much more feasible.

## Global Marketing

Global marketing constitutes the fourth lever that companies can use to globalize their strategy.[8] A worldwide business uses global marketing when it takes the same or similar approach or content, globally, for one or more elements of the marketing mix, i.e., using the same or similar brand names, advertising and other marketing elements in different countries. Multinational companies increasingly use global marketing by taking a uniform approach to some elements of their worldwide marketing, and have been highly successful— for example, Nestlé with its common brand name applied to many products in all countries; Citibank with its global advertising themes; and Xerox with its global leasing policies. But *global marketing is not about standardizing the marketing process*. Standardizing the way in which country subsidiaries analyse markets and develop marketing plans is merely good multinational practice—a way of transferring skills and setting high standards for the marketing function.[9]

Global marketing and selling means striving for the appropriate balance of global uniformity and local adaptation in all elements of the marketing mix, but with a probable bias in favour of uniformity unless a good case can be made for local exceptions. This means casting aside the previous conventional wisdom that companies should globally standardize the marketing process but not the marketing content. Global excellence in marketing now means looking for uniformity. Every element of the marketing mix—product design, product and brand positioning, brand name, packaging, pricing, advertising strategy, advertising execution, promotion and distribution—has potential for globalization. As with other global strategy levers, the use of global marketing can be flexible. A business can make some elements of the marketing mix more global and others less so. Within each element, some parts can be globally uniform and others not. For example, a 'global' pack design may have a common logo and illustration in all countries, but a different background colour in some countries. So both marketing as a whole and each individual marketing element can be global to a greater or lesser extent in its *content*.

Global marketing can also vary in its geographic *coverage*. Few global market-ing programmes can realistically apply to the whole of a worldwide market. A marketing element can be global without being 100 percent uniform in content or coverage.

GCM constitutes a particular type of global marketing strategy, probably the most challenging one. It affects all elements of the marketing mix, but generally has the greatest effect on the selling and pricing elements.

How GCM Changes Selling

In terms of selling, GCM changes the process from a focus on individual supplier–customer relationships in single countries to a focus on the global relationship, coordinated across countries. In practice, this usually means adding a global account manager (gam) in a global account management (GAM) pro-gramme. The gam has a different role from the national sales managers. We will discuss this role in depth in Chapter 6. For now, let's just say that the gam has three essential tasks. First, the gam has to manage the global relationship at a central locus of the customer organization. Second, the gam has to take an overall, long term, strategic view of the customer—in practice this usually means focusing more on the relationship and less on sales than would be the case for national sales managers. Third, the gam has to coordinate the activ-ities of the national sales managers who deal with the particular customer in individual geographical areas.

Multinational customers increasingly demand that they be sold to on a global rather than multicountry basis: they seek one point of contact. Global suppliers need to respond by changing the way in which they sell to such customers. Visteon, a US-based supplier of automotive systems went so far as to run advertisements proclaiming its ability to supply globally (Figure 3.2).

---

You don't want to talk to a big company.

You want to talk to one person who'll put a big company to work for you.

Global? Naturally. These days you have to be. But here's an even bigger challenge: making worldwide resources easily available to customers. So at Visteon, we dedicate one person to be your link to one of the industry's largest arrays of automotive system technologies. One person who understands your needs. One person with one purpose: to make you feel confident that you'll get whatever you need whenever you need it. Period…

---

**Fig. 3.2** Visteon's advertisement

## Foundation

How GCM Changes Pricing

In terms of pricing, most global customers want global pricing agreements. This does not necessarily mean the same prices in each country for the same items. But it does mean an integrated rationale for why prices are the way they are in different geographical areas. In particular, the supplier can no longer trade on the customer's ignorance of what it is paying in different countries for the same items. So the traditionally most flexible marketing mix element, price, becomes especially subject to customer demands for standardization. Due to differences in world markets and conditions it is often very difficult for a supplier to give a uniform price. Therefore, many companies work with purchasing price-plus methods, where a global base-price is negotiated, that will be subject to a surcharge that depends on the market of delivery.

IBM has a pricing policy to not have only one, global price. The company sets a series of measures and metrics for customers who may want a global price. To avoid the customer playing the different IBM regions against each other, the IBM global account team is penalized if it sells products that get diverted geographically. For example, if a country sells ten units in one country and gets these installed in another country, the team has 15 percent of the revenue taken away.

As part of its GCM operation, IBM has a centralized organization in charge of setting the price or so-called 'Global Customer Offering'. The overall objective is to maximize global bottom line profit, using an offsetting mechanism to manage profit adjustments between countries. Also when a customer asks for a discount, IBM works on relationships around the world to try to increase the volume in exchange for the discount.

Xerox works with a price rationale for each country, because discounts do not have the same effect in each country. Cost structures differ between countries. For example, discounts cost more in Spain than in Finland. Xerox sets global contracts with umbrella framework agreements that allow for unique country terms and conditions, and even last minute variations that may be required at the local level. Overall though, in order to reinforce customer loyalty, Xerox sells its global agreement programme on the basis of added value and not better prices. When Dutch packaging company Van Leer sells steel drums to French oil company Total, it also follows a global pricing policy. The best price in each location is based on the total volume in all locations. Prices are set for one year, and an annual rebate is given on global purchasing levels.

All the above examples show that even if a supplier does not want to give a single global price, it should have some form of global pricing policy in place to ensure that the customer understands the rationale for international price differences, and cannot play suppliers in different geographical areas against each other for the best price. The supplier that does its homework on geographical idiosyncrasies and competitive environments can suggest improvements to a customer's proffered global contract that will benefit both enterprises. In particular, the supplier should scrutinize customers' strategies in individual markets and quantify the variances in the service-level needs across country markets.

### How GCM Affects Other Aspects of Global Marketing

Having a GCM programme also makes it easier to formulate and implement other aspects of global marketing, including global branding, advertising, and promotion. The GCM role particularly helps when there is no other global marketing function, such as a global product or marketing manager.

### How GCM Helps Meet Customer Demands for Global Marketing

Global customers increasingly seek some elements of global marketing, especially global selling and global pricing. The latter can, in particular, pose severe risks for global suppliers. GCM programmes provide an effective way to meet these customer demands.

## Global Competitive Moves

In a global strategy, competitive moves need to be integrated across countries, as opposed to focused on competition within a specific country.[11] A multinational company, which faces competition from another multinational company in a specific market, traditionally will attack the competitor in that specific market. As multinational companies often work in an overlapping set of markets, however, the options for competitive moves have expanded extensively. In a global strategy, the world becomes a chessboard, where every market is available for action. For example, a company can make the same competitive move in multiple countries at the same time, to keep competitors from subsequently arming themselves for the move in other overlapping countries. Other global competitive moves are to attack a competitor in one country in order to drain its resources for another country, or counter an attack in one country with an attack in a different country. In one case, when a supplier saw a global competitor lower its prices in a strategic market, the company retaliated by also lowering its prices, not in the strategic market, but in the home market of the competitor, which the latter traditionally used as a 'cash cow'. This move drained the competitor's revenue, which eventually forced it to increase prices in the strategic market where the contest began.

When global customers are involved, the global chessboard becomes three-dimensional. Apart from having a score of markets to choose from when making competitive moves, there are also whole customers to target, who often represent more total business than some specific market places. Furthermore, differences in customer portfolios create differences as to which markets are strategic to which global suppliers.

How GCM Helps Suppliers to Make Global Competitive Moves

Globally coordinating competitive moves poses a tough challenge for most multinational companies, as most country-based managers usually focus on local competitors. A GCM programme brings a clear focus on global customers and what needs to be done to win their business around the world. Suppliers who can take a globally integrated view of the competitive moves they need to make gain a significant advantage over those who cannot.

# Global Organization

A GCM programme makes many new demands on an organization.[12] So the global organization of the company provides the foundation on which the organization of the programme itself must build.[13] What is a global organization?[14] Four sets of factors affect the ability of an organization to develop and implement global strategy: organization structure, management processes, people and culture. Each of these categories comprises several individual elements of organization:[15]

- *organization structure*: the reporting structure of a company;
- *management processes*: includes activities like budgeting, planning and information systems;
- *people*: represents the total human resources of a company in their worldwide operations;
- *culture*: comprises the values and rules that guide behaviour in a company.

The company's organization has to accommodate the GCM programme in its mission and strategy. Without the proper global organization to back it up, the GCM programme will be a standalone structure that lacks reach throughout the whole company and as a result will not be very effective. Proper alignment of a GCM effort with the global organization of the company means: enough organizational support, and a fitting culture and management processes, to provide the necessary resources and company commitment. In the first place, a global organization will be necessary to substantiate the global capabilities that a supplier promises a global customer in a global relationship. Secondly, a proper alignment and integration between the global organization of the company and of the GCM programme is necessary to capture all the potential benefits (described earlier in Chapter 2).

## Organization Structure

Nearly all GCM programmes involve adding the key organizational position of a global account manager (gam). The key role of the gam is to globally (or regionally) coordinate all of the supplier's selling activities with regards to a particular global customer. There are many ways in which this role can be performed. In Chapter 5 we will discuss this role in detail. Here we will address the broader issue of the positioning of the gam within the overall organization structure.

The introduction of the gam position asks for an organization structure that can handle a position with many cross-links. In the first place, a global organization structure needs integration of global authority, so that all units of the same business worldwide report to the same person globally. This is a good way to avoid geography-driven decisions within the business. However, many companies have grown traditionally, with a country-based organization where the main line of authority runs by country rather than by business. This can be a particular problem when adopting a GCM programme, as it gives the programme no room to escalate possible problems above a geographically enclosed level.

Also, the common split between domestic and international organizations presents a very common threat for good GCM. When there is a high level of autonomy for any separate part of the company, it can be hard to get all involved parties on the same wavelength. In general, this is easier when the company focuses more on the business dimension than the geographic dimension. As large, global companies often operate in several different businesses, they need to be managed across both a geographical and a business level. Many companies solve this by using some form of matrix organization structure in which employees report to both a geographically defined as well as a business-specific manager.

When a company adopts a GCM programme, it needs to determine to whom the key position holders in the GCM programme, most particularly the global account managers, will report. The reporting lines are directly linked with the perceived importance of the position, and the priority the company has for the GCM programme. For example, when a gam reports to a country manager it gives them a whole other image than when he or she reports directly to the head of a global business unit. Furthermore, the authority the gam has over local relationships with his or her customer needs to be determined. Many companies have a gam who can only coordinate global sales, but the GCM approach we advocate requires that the gam also should have a certain level of power on the local level.

Companies take many approaches to the structure and authority issue for gams. Integration of the GCM programme in the total organization is key to an effective and efficient system. Xerox works with an escalation scheme, where possible friction between global and local entities that cannot be resolved by talking, will be escalated to a more senior manager who is responsible for both areas. At one major advertising agency, the gams have a certain level of authority over the local people dealing with their customers. In contrast, many banks give only a coordinating power, rather than direct authority, to their gams. Regus, a worldwide operator of business centres, works with a three-tiered structure for global sales. Field sales executives run a cluster of centres with customers from many different sources. National account managers operate mainly within their geographic territories. But Regus gams deal with the truly global accounts. These gams have worldwide revenues credited to them and lead a virtual team, spread throughout the company's geographical area, to coordinate the global customer needs.

### How GCM Affects Organization Structure

A GCM programme changes the organization structure by creating a position—the global account manager (gam)—that has authority over others in the company. In particular, the gam now has a say over what national managers do with their customers. The extent of this authority can vary from direct control and veto to more that of coordination and advice. While national account managers typically control their accounts, the geographic scope of global account management makes such control much more difficult, and perhaps politically hazardous. Where there is organizational resistance, a gam can probably be more effective by merely coordinating the selling efforts of national sales forces. The gam also needs to act as the one interface with the customer at its headoffice. So in almost all cases the gam should be located in the home country of the global customer.

## Management Processes

The different management processes power the entire organization system and some of them are particularly important for global business. In particular, developments in *information systems* have made global management much more feasible. A globally managed company needs to have more information from its different geographical areas. This information needs to flow not just to the headquarters, but from there across the geographical company network. Another important process is *global strategic planning*, not to be confused with the corporate strategic planning process. A global strategic plan might integrate the plans of a specific business in different countries, or integrate strategies across worldwide businesses. When a company refrains from taking a global view of the strategic planning process, it is easy to lose the overview of the total potential that a global business can bring. Adopting a GCM programme will give a global company a good line of action for a strategic plan, i.e., a global customer strategic plan. It is still advisable, however, to keep a broad view of the total global opportunities, across countries, and possibly even customers.

Having global strategies and programmes implies having *global budgets* to implement them. Adding up the country budgets into a global total for each product line provides a first step in global resource allocation. Surprisingly few companies do this thoroughly. Many companies do not even know how much profit they make worldwide in a particular business. Typically, the profit contribution is spread across many national and regional accounts. Most alarming is that many managers believe that the global figures are readily available, only to find it is otherwise when asked to produce them. It is essential for GCM programmes to be able to add up on a global basis all the revenues, costs and profits for a given global customer. We have found many early adopters of GCM that are not able to do this. But we have also found that nearly all those with fairly developed programmes can do so.

Global budgeting also provides the critical ability to transfer funds and profits between countries—a frequent need in GCM, especially when global customers demand global prices. For example, one company had difficulty delivering the agreed price to a global customer in Malta because its total business was very small there. But the gam was able to use the global budget process to reallocate profits to subsidize the global price in Malta in order to ensure that the total business with the global customer was secure.

---

### How Xerox Spread the Cost

A contract between US Xerox and a global customer, a major British bank, stated a minimum print amount. The data in the tender, however, were erroneous and after implementation of the contract, only half of the prints were actually made. The global account manager discussed this with his opposite number in the global customer company and restructured the contract. This left the US Xerox organization with a high level of credit outstanding after the amended contract, which that organization could not afford. Therefore, the costs of this amendment were spread over all of Xerox's organizations in countries that had major dealings with this customer. It was a difficult thing to do, but it showed Xerox's commitment to the customer and it made clear that Xerox had the global capabilities to handle such situations.

---

In many ways, the most important global management process involves the *performance evaluation and reward system*. Getting this system to support global strategy can go a long way to offsetting deficiencies in the other systems. If the financial reporting system cannot be changed, managers can still be motivated to undertake loss-incurring strategic actions if they are evaluated and rewarded appropriately. So rewards, especially bonuses, need to be set in a way that reinforces the company's global objectives. This particularly applies to GCM, which needs the cooperation of country managers and national sales managers who are mostly evaluated and rewarded on national performance. Hewlett-Packard evaluates its gams on the worldwide performance of all their global accounts, while it evaluates country managers on the worldwide performance of global accounts headquartered in their country as well as on the account's performance in that country. For example, this means that HP rewards its country manager according to Germany not just according to what HP sells to global account Volkswagen in Germany, but on what it sells to Volkswagen worldwide. This approach provides incentives to HP country managers to coordinate and cooperate with the gams.

### How GCM Affects Management Processes

GCM is in itself a process and can also affect several other key management processes and systems. It improves the global strategy information system by providing a focal point responsible for collecting all strategic information about a multinational account. By definition, it provides cross-country coordination. The gam contributes to the global strategic planning process. GCM makes global budgeting more possible and more effective by providing an integrated viewpoint of customer related expenditures. Lastly, it can move a company toward global performance and compensation practices rather than solely country-based ones.

## People (Human Resource Policies)

A global organization, supporting a global strategy, needs to have a global human resource policy.[16] That means taking a global rather than a national view of how to select staff. The solution may not always differ, but it does mean searching globally for the best candidate for each significant open position. In practice, a global HR policy usually results in more cross-border postings. Such postings involve decisions by more than one geographic unit and may need support from the centre to make it happen. After all, managers seldom want to give up their best people, especially when it means sending them to another country. A global HR policy also requires plans to recruit, develop and retain the types of executives who will be needed in different geographical areas and functions in the future. Again, this will not happen without central intervention. In particular, the geographical areas that have the most future potential usually have a relatively small existing share of a company's employees and are seldom in a position to make long term investments in developing future pools of managers. For example, most Western companies today face a great shortage of managers able to function in the largest high-growth markets: the 'BRIC' countries (Brazil, Russia, India, and China).

A global HR policy means more than developing managers who can work in particular countries. It also needs to create a subset of managers who have the ability to work across many countries and cultures. A gam certainly needs to have such a global capability. (We will discuss in Chapter 6 the detailed requirements for a good gam.) In addition, the gam needs to enlist the cooperation of many other managers from around the world. The more there are of these other managers who also have had some international experience, the easier the gam's job will be.

How GCM Affects People (Human Resource Policies)

GCM requires a few managers to take on global responsibilities and requires many other managers to interact with these global managers. Companies can implement a global account management programme without immediately adding to the staff headcount. Initially, one manager may be able to wear two hats—as a national sales executive and as a global account manager. Such an approach can reduce turf battles and jealousy—national sales managers tend to resent interference with their local customers. If one manager becomes a global account manager he or she may get little cooperation from other national sales managers. But if several national sales managers are assigned global account responsibilities then they all have to cooperate with each other.

# Culture

Culture is the most subtle aspect of an organization, but it can play a formidable role in helping or hindering a global strategy. *Geographic identity* is the aspect of culture most relevant to global strategy, A company needs to find a good balance between the global and local identities of the company. Some level of a feel for national culture is important, as country cultures often differ, and not having knowledge of local customs can be a guarantee for creating embarrassing situations, or worse, losing customers. The different geographical locations in the organization, however, must also embrace the global identity of the company. Since 2000 or so UK-based HSBC, one of the world's largest banks, has been running a series of advertisements in which it positions itself, as 'the world's local bank'. This tagline states that HSBC is both a truly global company and has the knowledge of, and feel for, national markets.

Another important aspect of a global culture is that key managers should have a global mindset or a 'matrix in the mind'. [17] For GCM the company's culture can play a significant role in the success or failure of the programme. A global mindset is extremely important, as an 'us versus them' mindset will lead to unnecessary resistance to global initiatives. The more managers who have at least the beginnings of a global mindset, the easier it will be to implement GCM.

How GCM Affects Culture

Having a global culture steers managers toward global rather than local profit maximization. A GCM programme can significantly contribute to building the global culture of a company by getting national managers to think about the global implications of what they do for the national units of multinational customers.

---

**Best Practices**

A company that is planning to implement a GCM programme needs to implement a global strategy and global organization. Furthermore, it is good to remember that having a GCM programme is not the best solution for every company, as the need and potential of such a programme largely depends on the company's global industry potential. The following guidelines need to be taken into consideration when building the foundation for a GCM programme:

- Analyze the customer's industry.
- Analyze your own industry and your place in it.
- Assess the five global strategy levers: global market participation, global products and services, global location of value-adding activities, global marketing, and global competitive moves.
- Assess how a GCM programme will fit with the elements of your global organization: organization structure, management processes, people and culture.

---

# Notes

1. The elements of global strategy are drawn from George S. Yip (2003) *Total Global Strategy II.* Upper Saddle River, NJ: Prentice Hall.
2. For a full description of the value-chain concept see Michael E. Porter (1985) *Competitive Advantage.* New York: The Free Press.
3. See more detailed discussion of global market participation in chapter 3 of Yip (2003).
4. Gary Hamel and C. K. Prahalad (1985) 'Do You Really Have a Global Strategy?', *Harvard Business Review,* July–August, pp. 139–148; and Bruce Kogut (1985), 'Designing Global Strategies: Profiting from Operational Flexibility', *Sloan Management Review,* Fall, pp. 27–38.
5. Peter G. P. Walters (1986) 'International Marketing Policy: A Discussion of the Standardization Construct and its Relevance for Corporate Policy', *Journal of International Business Studies,* Summer, pp. 55–69.

6. See more detailed discussion of global products and services in chapter 4 of Yip (2003).

7. See more detailed discussion of global activity location in chapter 5 of Yip (2003).

8. See more detailed discussion of global marketing in chapter 6 of Yip (2003).

9. Some researchers have focused on a standardized marketing process as the key attribute of global marketing. See discussion by Pradeep A. Rau and John F. Preble (1987) 'Standardization of Marketing Strategy by Multinationals', *International Marketing Review*, Autumn, pp. 18–28.

10. Das Narayandas, John Quelch and Gordon Swartz (2000) 'Prepare Your Company for Global Pricing', *MIT Sloan Management Review*, Fall, 42(1): 61–70.

11. See more detailed discussion of global competitive moves in chapter 7 of Yip (2003).

12. GCM can be viewed as a new organizational form that responds to the increased interdependencies arising from globalization. See Janine Nahapiet (1994) 'Servicing the Global Client: Towards Global Account Management?', paper presented at the 14th Annual Conference of the Strategic Management Society, Groupe HEC, Jouy-en-Josas, France.

13. See also George S. Yip and Tammy L. Madsen (1996) 'Global Account Management: The New Frontier in Relationship Marketing', *International Marketing Review*, 13(3): 24–42.

14. See more detailed discussion of global organization in chapter 8 of Yip (2003). See also Christopher A. Bartlett and Sumantra Ghoshal (1989) *Managing Across Borders: The Transnational Solution*. Boston: Harvard Business School Press; and C. K. Prahalad and Yves L. Doz (1987) *The Multinational Mission: Balancing Local Demands and Global Vision*. New York: The Free Press.

15. Chapter 8 of Yip (2003).

16. For a general discussion of global human resource policies see, for example, J. Stewart Black, Hal B. Gregersen, Mark E. Mendenhall and Linda Stroh (1998) *Globalizing People Through International Assignments*. Reading, MA: Addison Wesley; and Morgan W. McCall, Jr. and George P. Hollenbeck (2002) *Developing Global Executives*. Boston: Harvard Business School Press.

17. Christopher A. Bartlett and Sumantra Ghoshal (1990) 'Matrix Management; Not a Structure, a Frame of Mind', *Harvard Business Review*, July-August, pp. 138–45; and Christopher A. Bartlett and Sumantra Ghoshal (1992) 'What is a Global Manager?', *Harvard Business Review*, September–October, pp. 124–32.

# 4 Structuring the Global Customer Management Programme

> Customers love global account management programmes. The key is to get your organization aligned behind them.
>
> (Bart Logghe, Senior Director of the International Retail Board,
> Royal Philips Electronics)

The previous chapter discussed how the global customer management (GCM) programme should fit into the company's overall global strategy and global organization. In this chapter we move onto the GCM programme itself. The organization of the programme forms the bedrock of the total GCM effort. But there is, of course, no single best way of organizing GCM, as the right structure depends on the company and its situation. The one commonality is that a global account management (GAM) programme nearly always sits at the core of the GCM organization (see Figure 1.4 in Chapter 1). The GAM programme constitutes the formal part of GCM, usually with a specific organization and reporting structure for the main players in GCM. As such the GAM programme will be the most visible part of the GCM organization, but needs to be integrated with the rest of the company. In that way, GCM becomes part of the company culture, so that the GAM programme does not have to work on its own, but can cooperate with the various other account structures and supporting departments, in order to successfully mange global customers. This chapter will describe the various elements that make up a GCM organization. We will also discuss the three major forms of GAM organization, along with their benefits and possible pitfalls.

## Citibank's Evolving GCM Approach

Citibank has been pioneering global account management for its corporate customers since the 1970s and has since rebranded and reorganized the programmes to better serve client needs. The World Corporation Group (WCG) started to exist in the late 1970s and after a shakey start has continued more or less in the same form ever since. The group originally worked with about 250 corporate clients. Those companies were all global players, mainly in the chemical, petroleum, shipping, aviation, automobile and retail industries, but there were no financial institutions among them. The WCG was expanded in 1995 and became the Global Relationship

Bank (GRB) business. The organization seeks to create and add more value by focusing on industries. The GRB covers about 1,600 multinational customers, made up by Fortune Global 500 and other companies with global presence and / or global activity (e.g., some global financial institutions, such as fund managers, do not have overseas branches but do trade extensively overseas).

# Elements of a GCM Organization

There seem to be as many organizational forms for GCM as there are companies, given the need for tailoring to fit the situation of each company. In particular, each company implements each element of GCM in a somewhat different way, producing unique configurations. These elements include the GAM programme, selection of accounts, global general manager, global steering committee, global account manager, global account team, information management, executive sponsorship, local account managers, global reporting structure, global remuneration system, and customer councils.

## GAM Programme

The GAM programme is the formal part of the GCM organization that prescribes the general way of working with global accounts. A GAM programme should outline the reporting structure and who defines the general global accounts strategy and the account specific strategies. The programme should identify who is responsible for the global account and what authority they have to enforce this responsibility. Global general managers need to ensure that the GAM structure is unambiguous and that the whole company knows and understands the objectives and structure of the programme. Despite many companies seeing the GAM programme as encompassing all global customer involvement, we propose that there is more to managing global customers. The GAM programme should be integrated into the total company organization structure and culture, so as to develop a true global customer management organization.

As defined in Chapter 1, GCM involves effort from the entire organization, both formal and informal, in managing global customers. So GCM includes the GAM programme, with all of the interactions with the rest of the company that the latter requires. *The GCM organization should be as big as the company itself.* By integrating the GAM programme into the total organization, more trust, support, and dedication towards the GAM programme will develop across the total company, so improving the programme's chances of success. Therefore, the programme elements we describe in this chapter apply both within the GAM programme and within the total GCM organization.

## Selection of Accounts

Which accounts should be selected for a GAM programme? As the success of the GAM programme is linked to the success of the separate accounts within the programme, a meticulous selection of these accounts is crucial. If possible it is sensible to have the GAM programme and its strategy outlined before selecting the accounts to participate in the programme, but in many cases these activities happen in parallel, and in some cases the company finds itself in need of a GAM programme after starting to work with accounts on a global basis. Although it sounds the wrong way round, this last situation is not so strange. Many companies are forced into global account management by customer demands, leaving them with little scope for making their own account selections. Not every customer is suitable to be in a GAM programme, and the customers themselves are mostly a bad judge of their suitability. Therefore, companies should keep a fierce grip on this selection process.

Royal Dutch Shell's initial set of accounts for its global key account management programme was mostly determined by the demand of the accounts at the time of the start of the programme. After a few years working with these accounts, however, some of them emerged as less suitable for GAM, and Shell decided to work with only those accounts that satisfied the selection criteria, and took some of the initial accounts out of the programme.

In order to select the right accounts, managers need to compile a set of selection criteria that suit the company after determining the strategy and organization of the total programme. The selection criteria need to reflect the objectives the company has for embarking on global account management, and the capabilities of the programme. These criteria will vary for different companies, but typical criteria include size, market potential, extent of global purchasing, growth rates, geographic spread, reputation and industry standing, openness for partnership and the mutual importance. Chapter 5 focuses on the global account, and will discuss the selection of accounts further.

## Global General Manager

A GAM programme needs a global general manager who is responsible for the programme and its strategy and operation. He or she needs to be a senior manager at the corporate or business unit level. Many companies, however, do not have such a position in place, and in some cases the responsibility is given to a manager who also has other duties. For some smaller global companies having a general manager who is solely responsible for the development of the global programme is a luxury they cannot justify. DMV International, a European supplier of ingredients for the food and pharmaceutical industries, has its global key account managers report into the (European) regional sales manager, who is also responsible for all other sales in that particular region. Even though the regional sales manager strongly supports the global account management, there is still the possibility of conflict of interest between local and global issues.

When there is no opportunity to have a global general manager who is dedicated to the programme, companies should at least use a reporting structure that minimizes conflict. This can be achieved by giving overall responsibility for GAM to a high level manager who has no direct links with any particular geographical area. Whether there is a dedicated general manager or a shared one, this person needs to have the authority and the desire to help develop the programme in the best way possible. Many company examples show that as soon as there is a person at the head of the programme who really believes that global relationships are the way forward, things change for the better. For example, when Unilever appointed a new senior vice president for global customer development, the existing situation, in which there were no systems, processes, or real support for the global account managers, started to evolve leading to a more empowered organization with more dedicated teams, and one that is more embedded in the total Unilever organization.

## Global Steering Committee

Many companies with successful GCM attribute part of this success to having a global steering committee. Such a committee typically comprises a group of senior executives who are committed to the global programme, but who have other general responsibilities. The global steering committee will meet on a regular basis to decide on the overall strategy and objectives for the programme and monitor its development. The collective power of the executives should outweigh that of any one country or regional manager to make sure that any conflicts on allocating resources or any other global–local friction can be easily resolved.

Having a global steering committee means that it is easier for the company to handle the tension that comes with the global–local disparity, and creates much visibility in the company's dedication to global relationships. Some companies even have separate global steering committees for specific relationships, where there is often a direct relationship between the members of the committee and senior managers at the customer or supplier company. Admittedly, a structure like this is very costly in terms of executive resources, and will realistically be created for only very special relationships.

Having global steering committees can be just as valuable for a global customer as for a global supplier. In the case of British energy company BG Group there are currently two relationships with suppliers that are deemed important enough to invest in a steering committee. For every global relationship, BG Group has established a committee consisting of senior managers from both BG Group and the supplier. These committees meet on a regular basis to focus on strategic issues that arise within the relationships. Both global steering committees are being chaired by a BG Group executive vice president, which demonstrates the high level of commitment BG Group has for the global relationships.

## Global Account Manager

A good global account manager (gam) is key to a successful global account relationship. The global account manager is responsible for the relationship with the account company and the resulting performance of the account. Ideally, the gam is dedicated to one global account, although in some smaller companies it is necessary to spread gams over multiple accounts. In many less advanced GAM programmes, the gam is a mid-level manager with a career background in sales. As managing global customers is about more than just the GAM programme, so it is also about more than just sales. More and more companies are starting to realize that the relationship with important global account companies should not just revolve around the transactional aspects, but be more integrated into other parts of the company in order to achieve a more rounded relationship that provides a good foundation for creating more opportunities between the companies in the long run. Therefore, it is important to realize that the skill set of a gam is not, as the head of one GAM programme put it, 'the same set of skills as a local account manager, plus having a passport'. In fact, it is not unheard of any more to have gams who do not have a background in sales. Xerox realizes the importance of knowing the customer's industry, and takes this into account when choosing the right gam for an account. The gam for global bank HSBC spent a large part of his prior career in finance, and the gam for the Volkswagen account used to be a Volkswagen employee.

Besides having knowledge of the customer's industry, other necessary gam skills include cultural awareness, team management, and sensitivity. In general, a gam takes responsibility for the strategic planning of the account, deciding on goals and determining and obtaining the right amount of resources. Furthermore, often the gam will lead the team of people that supports the global account—the global account team (gat). The gam needs to guide the gat members in their particular roles and help them develop their individual relationships with the account. Sourcing of information is also an essential task for the gam. He or she needs to be the ultimate expert on the account, and combine all the information that is available with the separate gat members or local account managers. The gam should, however, also have a thorough knowledge of the capabilities of his or her own company, and how these can help the customer. At Xerox many of the gams have a background in either Xerox itself or with the specific account they are managing. For example, the gam for Volkswagen has more than 25 years of experience in positions either with or relating to this customer. A complete outsider would have a much harder job getting to know all the ins and outs at both companies, and therefore would find it harder to identify mutually advantageous, or other, opportunities for the two companies.

In terms of organizational position, many companies have a structure in which the gam reports within the geographic area in which he or she is based. This occurs when no separate reporting structure exists for the GAM programme. But to avoid conflicts of interest between the global and local parts of the company, it is better to have the gam reporting to a senior manager at the corporate level.

Chapter 6 will discuss the role of the gam in more depth.

## Global Account Team

The composition and organization of the global account team (gat) provides a good indicator of the level of integration of GCM. When a gat is very informal, and consists only of the different local account managers, then the GAM programme probably focuses only on sales, and the gam does not have enough authority to be able to take full responsibility for the relationship with the account company. A company with an integrated approach to managing global customers will have formal global account teams that are both cross-function and cross-country. For example, DMV International works with global account teams that consist of both sales managers for the account from different geographical areas and representatives from different function areas that have contact with the customer (e.g., R&D).

The gat plays a crucial role in getting the relationship with the customer beyond the transactional phase into a partnership. The gat needs to implement the global strategy for the account while taking the existing organization of the company into consideration. Having a cross-functional team helps to get all relevant views on board, keeps the links with the different departments and ensures that the global account organization will not lead a life of its own separate from the existing organization. The gat is also key in building the diamond structure of relationships, described in Chapter 1, as a crucial part of the integrated approach. Building on existing relationships, the gat can engage the customer in new plans and opportunities.

The team members will also be an invaluable source for getting information from different parts of the customer's company, a good information system can support this. In the relationship between ABB and its supplier Xerox, the latter has arranged a broad range of contact points by mirroring the ABB organization. ABB has a group supply chain management function that is divided into direct and indirect activities and a national procurement organization in each of the top 22 countries. Xerox maintains a customer contact person in all of these countries, so ensuring a broad basis for relationship management and information gathering. Furthermore, the team members act as 'ambassadors' for GCM in their respective departments, ensuring support throughout the company.

Some companies have full-time team members, but it is not always optimal to have employees dedicated to one account. Best practice sharing and integration of the global programme with the rest of the company come as important benefits of having gat members with multiple roles. Which way to go will differ between companies and needs to be determined based on the company's situation.

Chapter 7 will focus more on the gat and will discuss necessary skills and some typical structures.

---

**Young and Rubicam's Global Account Team**

To develop a global account strategy, Young and Rubicam established a global management structure that oversees both the development and the execution of every global campaign. Global managing directors and their teams represent the core of Young and Rubicam's global management structure. Each global managing director provides a corporate global perspective for each campaign and is responsible for all communications with the client. Team members must be devoted to the client, have a global perspective and a broad understanding of not only their clients' markets, but also the key success factors of each region. Furthermore, because execution is always carried out locally, the firm must have access to and be able to coordinate a wide network of resources. Few clients begin by establishing a globally integrated campaign. Typically, campaigns are developed for one country and diffused to other countries once proven successful.

---

## Information Management

As managing global customers comes with a complex structure of relationships, measurements and information streams, a sound information management system is essential for the success of the programme.[1] The gam needs to be very knowledgeable about the customer and its industry, but he or she will not be able to gather this information without the help of the gat and a well functioning information system. Two types of information management systems are important here: firstly, the results measurement system and, secondly, the customer relationship management (CRM) system.

Many companies still have trouble getting both types of systems geared up for global relationships. Measurement systems need to track the sales of the global accounts and, therefore, the results of the GAM programme. A common problem is that most of the current systems identify every delivery address as a separate customer, and when a manager wants to see the results for a complete account, this has to be combined manually, which is complicated by differences across regions. Another common problem is that many gams do not have easy access to a good overview of the complete results of their account. Besides missing a good management tool, this can make things very complex when it comes to remuneration of the gam. Many companies traditionally link remuneration for national account managers to the account's revenues. This link should be less strong for global account management, as it should be based more on long term relationship development than short term sales. But not having information on global revenues for an account strongly undermines the ability to judge a gam's performance. This shows, once more, how important it is to have the GAM programme integrated into the whole company.

When choosing and implementing a new information system, managers need to think about the necessary capabilities of the system, including tracking global sales and profits. While the situation for sales measurement can be bad, it is often even worse for the internal information systems that support customer relationship management. Almost all big companies have some form of internal information system, such as Siebel, Lotus Notes, or Livelink. But when we asked if these systems were used to their full potential, the majority of global managers had to admit that they were not. Many companies implement these costly systems without thinking about the actual use of the systems. Training people on how to use these systems is necessary, but incorporating the actual use into their everyday tasks is at least as important. People will go looking for information at the moment they need it, but what incentive do they have to load information they already have into the system and how will they find out that there is vital information for them on the system if they don't know they should be looking for it? Often this situation ends up as a negative cycle of thinking: there is no useful information on the system therefore they never go on the system, and so they never upload information.

HSBC encourages its relevant employees to visit its Lotus Notes system at least once a day to deposit or access information. Other firms, like engineering company Schlumberger, have integrated the internal information system with measurement and logistics systems, to make using the information system a natural thing to do in everyday tasks.

Chapter 8 will discuss customer information in more depth.

## Executive Sponsorship

GCM will be successful only with a high level of executive sponsorship. The complex nature of managing global customers needs a high level executive with whom to raise conflicts between global and local business units. Even though the executive sponsor should not be involved in operational problems, having the position in place will give a visible signal to the organization that GCM is something to which top level management are dedicated, thus helping to gain support and commitment at lower levels. Having executive support also helps in getting essential people and other resources for the global account. So, in addition to a 'programme champion' in the form of the, ideally, board-level director who has overall responsibility for the GCM programme, many companies choose to have a system of executive sponsorship for the different accounts that involves more top level executives.

In an executive sponsorship system for GCM, every global account gets assigned a senior manager, typically at the CXO level such as chief financial officer or chief technical officer, who keeps in contact with a senior manager on the customer side. This shows the customer that it is important to the supplier, and helps to develop the relationship. The executive sponsor will often be able to help the gam to overcome barriers, and to open doors that would be closed to the gam alone. The executive sponsors should not be assigned at random. Ideally, the executive sponsor is someone with specialist knowledge about the industry of the account company, or possibly someone who has a previous relationship with the account company. He or she needs to be a good conversation partner for the customer. Furthermore it is very important that the sponsor be fully committed to the success of GCM. In some companies the executive sponsor also acts as a mentor for the gam, helping him or her to set goals and strategy for the account. This system also works for customers with a global supplier management programme. A global purchasing officer for Royal Dutch Shell said: 'There is endorsement and support for global supplier management from the highest level on. The boss saying "I want it to happen" is not enough, but it does help'.

## Local Account Managers

In general, any company with large, international customers will have different national account managers (nams) dealing with the separate parts of the account. When the large, international customer account becomes a global account, these local account managers will need greater coordination. Also, the nam becomes more than a local sales manager. He or she has to realize that she or he is part of a global team, and that sometimes a global objective will ask for local sacrifices. With regard to global accounts, the main GAM-related task of nams becomes the local implementation of global agreements, in addition to the usual selling and maintenance responsibilities for the local unit of the global customer. Therefore, it is important for the nam to keep informed about activities on the global level. On the flipside, the gam is dependent on the nam for information at the national level, in order to get a good overview of the total situation with the account. In a way, the nams are the eyes and ears of the global account team. They have the most direct links with different parts of the customer, and will gather information that will not be available at the global level. For example, the Unilever gam for Wal-Mart works with about 50 people worldwide to set foundation objectives and operational guidelines.

Some companies have the luxury of having nams who are dedicated to a specific global account, but in many cases, they will have to be spread across different accounts, global and otherwise, as the local business volume with the global account is not big enough to justify a dedicated person. But even though these local managers work for the global account for only a small percentage of their time, it is important that the gam knows exactly who is working on the account. The gam should be able to communicate with these nams on a regular basis. Sometimes one or more nams may even be part of the global account team. As the global account organization, by its nature, is very complex, companies should keep changes to local responsibility for the global account to a minimum. At Unilever, gams complain about the high turnover of personnel on the local level due to the personal career development strategy that Unilever follows. One gam said, 'I have an annual worldwide meeting with all the local managers who are responsible for my account. Every year, half of the people there are new, and I will be outlining my strategy for the account all over again'.

## Global Reporting Structure

The global reporting structure is the backbone of the GAM programme. The reporting structure gives the overall image of what position the gams have in the total organization. The position they are reporting to can say much about the GAM programme and the commitment a company has to making it successful. In general there are three streams of reporting structures, reporting in the geographical organization, reporting in a matrix organization, and reporting in a GCM specific organization. In the first type of reporting structure, the balance of power lies with the country sales managers. The gam will report into the country manager of the country in which he or she is based, often the HQ country of the account.[2]

DMV International works with a regional system in which the global key account managers report to their own regional manager. Many of the global accounts have their HQ in North-West Europe, and therefore a lot of the global key account managers report to the same regional manager, which helps with any local versus global barriers, as this manager is particularly supportive of the GCM project. Having a direct line into the country or region is often the first reporting structure a company starts its GAM programme off with as it is easier to implement than the other two structures. A negative aspect of this structure is the potential friction between benefits for the country and the global account. A country manager might prefer the gam to work on the part of the account that is based in his or her country, as any business with the rest of the account will have no influence on the country profit and loss statement (P&L).

In the second type of reporting structure the gam will be positioned in a geographical area and will report to a geographically defined manager, but will also report to either a corporate executive responsible for global accounts, or a corporate manager of the particular business line the account is active in. This way it is easier to get a power balance between local and global interests. In the third structure, the power balance lies with the global account manager. He or she has authority over local account managers, and might even have them reporting to him or her. The gam will report to an executive manager responsible for GCM, and the global accounts seem to have priority over other accounts. Citigroup Global Relationship Bank (GRB) employees report to both industry groups and country management.

## Global Remuneration System

As remuneration is traditionally based on sales quota, the new GCM structure will create difficulties for the remuneration system.[3] If a gam, who is based in the UK makes a global agreement with the global account about business in Germany, who will be credited with this sale? The gam or the local account manager for Germany? And, likewise, to which country's P&L will this sale be attributed? To avoid discouraging employees from putting effort into global accounts, for many companies double counting of results is the answer. In the example above, both the gam and the German account manager will get credit for this sale. Double counting can be hard to do in some companies, in other companies giving credit for the same sale to multiple entities is a way of life.

A gam at one major multinational company said that every sale averages about 3.5 times in credit attribution!

Bonus systems of companies who decide to double (or triple) count need to be adjusted accordingly, otherwise the company will end up paying out too much in bonuses. A global remuneration system can also be a good way to straighten undesirable situations in reporting structures. Crediting local people or even region managers with a part of the global sales can help motivate them to work on the global accounts. Energy company Shell credits is regional managers with benefits from the business with the global account, even though it might not be part of their targets. This way, the regional manager is motivated to help with global sales in his or her region, while otherwise the focus would have been solely on local business.

Another difficult issue in remuneration systems is how to motivate the gam to act in the long term interests of the account, rather than to go for his or her annual bonus. This is the case in any sales situation in which ongoing relationships are important, but as the success of the GCM programme is dependent on long term partnerships, this problem becomes rather acute. Many companies are moving to a remuneration system in which the salary of the gam is largely fixed, and only a small part of his or her salary is based on actual sales.

## Customer Councils

Customer councils are not reserved for GCM only, but they can be particularly interesting in this situation. As having global relationships is a relatively new situation for most companies, customer councils can help determine what services can be developed to really help the customer create added value. In a customer council relevant executives, ideally as senior as possible, are brought together with the gam and possibly the global steering committee. These events provide an opportunity to understand the customers needs in doing global business. The setting is particularly inviting for the customers to open up about their needs, wants and possibly complaints.

Vodafone runs a testimonial programme in the form of a customer council with six global accounts. A two-day advisory board with two senior representatives from every global account was used to form working groups on different subjects that are relevant to global relationships, like 'global contracts' and 'service management'. Each workgroup has a representative of all the six accounts and is not chaired by a Vodafone representative but by one of the account representatives. Although Vodafone has 50 global accounts in total, it uses this select group of accounts to test new products, services and ideas, and to roll out these products to the other global accounts when they turn out to be successful.

---

### How Royal Dutch Shell Customizes its GCM Programme for Unilever

Establishing a GCM programme is only the start of the process. Suppliers must ensure that their programme's design and implementation meet the needs of their customers. Suppliers must refrain from establishing a GCM programme for its own sake. Real competitive advantage comes from a GCM programme that complements customers' business processes, as does Shell's programme for Unilever. This programme is customized to Unilever's needs, and focuses on helping Unilever to implement its 'total productive maintenance' (TPM) programme at its plants. Both Shell and Unilever see this as a partnership where they can find a synergy that gives them an edge over competitors. While Unilever sees Shell as the ideal partner to contribute to TPM, it is beneficial for Shell to customize its GCM programme for Unilever in this way, as the TPM knowledge gained helps Shell to remain Unilever's preferred supplier for lubricants. As Shell develops a good relationship in more Unilever plants, it can gain greater leverage through global coordination of the entire relationship.

---

# Different forms of GAM Organization

There are many different forms of GAM organization, but they generally seem to be variations on three different approaches: what we call the 'Coordination GAM', the 'Separate GAM' and the 'Control GAM'. When implementing a GAM programme a company needs to find a balance between central coordination and local flexibility. Furthermore, the programme needs to be integrated into the total organization of the company in order to create the informal GCM organization that gets the whole company involved in managing global customers. Whatever organization form is chosen, the GAM programme will have a particular effect on the other account organization in the company as it will often change the responsibilities and communication lines for the national account managers. In companies that have various independent national account structures, it may even lead to standardization among these national programmes. These changes will be less intense with the Coordination GAM, but the effectiveness of this form can be disputed. The typical sequence is for companies to start with the Coordination GAM, then move to the Control GAM, then lastly to the Separate GAM, although few have gone that far.

## The Coordination GAM

The Coordination GAM organization structure takes the existing company organization and adds a coordination layer of gams (Figure 4.1).[4] The main task of these gams is to coordinate with counterparts in the relevant geographical areas when the customer asks for a global deal. Furthermore, the gam will try to develop the account into other areas where the company previously had no

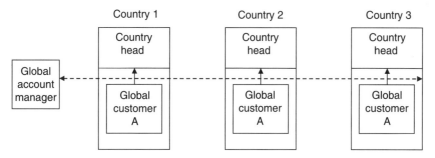

**Fig. 4.1** Coordination GAM

business. In general, the gam in a coordination GAM organization will not have any authority over the local operations but needs to get the consent of local managers for any activity on a global level. Many banks use a Coordination GAM structure because of the importance of local relationships and a relatively low need to globally standardize the services provided to global customers (as discussed in Chapter 2).

---

**Vodafone's 'Coordination GAM'**

Vodafone, UK–based and the world's largest mobile telecommunications company, provides an example of a Coordination GAM approach. The company is relatively young, and has seen strong growth in the last few years, mainly through takeovers. As there is still a high level of autonomy in branches in the different countries, Vodafone finds it hard to work with customers on global deals. Previously, the company took an ad hoc approach to demands for global business, often meaning that the national account manager of the country with the biggest part of the global deal would lead the communications with the branches in other involved countries. As Vodafone grew and global business became increasingly more common, the company has employed an extra coordination level in the form of an international account manager (IAM). The tasks of this IAM differ from those of the national account managers. The IAM negotiates central deals, but the further local implementation is negotiated at a local level by nams. The IAM does not have any control over the P&L of the countries involved. Because of the high level of external growth the different countries have different structures for national account management, which does not help in making the coordination role easier.

---

A benefit of the Coordination GAM is the ease of implementation, as it does not disturb any existing organization structures. The drawback arises from the GAM programme not being as effective as it could be. The lack of authority means there is room for disagreements between local subsidiaries, and it will often be very difficult to come to a global agreement when all local subsidiaries are working for themselves. For many companies, the Coordination GAM programme is the first step, and the programme often evolves over time into a more structured and powerful organization. Managers should take these future developments into account before embarking on global account management, as sometimes it can be hard to change the early perceptions about the position of the GAM programme and the position of the gam. It might be better to incur more disruption in the start up phase of GAM in order to send out the right message—this company is fully dedicated to make global relationships work!

## The Separate GAM

The Separate GAM is in some ways the opposite of the Coordination GAM. In the Separate GAM organization, the company creates a completely new, separate business unit for the global accounts (Figure 4.2). This can be a completely separated unit where the employees are dedicated to the Separate GAM and the GAM business unit operates its own support activities, such as technical support and sales services. The Separate GAM may also run some functions as a separate entity, while sharing other functions with other parts of the company in other geographical areas. In the Separate GAM, global accounts that were previously served by several different geographical areas are moved in their entirety to be managed by the new business unit. The responsibility for the global accounts now rests solely with the new business unit, which operates alongside the existing geographical units that still take care of the non-global accounts. In addition, the global account manager may have some coordinating responsibility for other customers that have not been pulled into the separate, global organization system (as shown in the lower diagram in Figure 4.2).

---

**IBM's and Hewlett-Packard's 'Separate GAM'**

Using a Separate GAM structure for its top 100 or so customers, IBM has three different models in place to deal with account management: territory coverage for smaller customers, an aligned model in which account management is organized around customer industry sectors and an integrated model. In the integrated model, account management forms a business unit in its own right and is used for only very large global accounts. The P&L for these accounts is measured on a global basis, and a global team is in place to manage the accounts. Hewlett-Packard also tried this approach in the late 1990s, breaking out its top 100 accounts. This approach lasted only a short time before it was overtaken by a decision to reorganize Hewlett-Packard into a front-end (customer facing) and back-end (operations) structure.

---

The main benefit of the Separate GAM is the total control the global unit has over the relationship with the global accounts. There is no reason for friction to arise between global and local subsidiaries, and it is easier to manage information on this account. The customer gets the attention it needs from a unit that is experienced in handling global accounts and has employees who

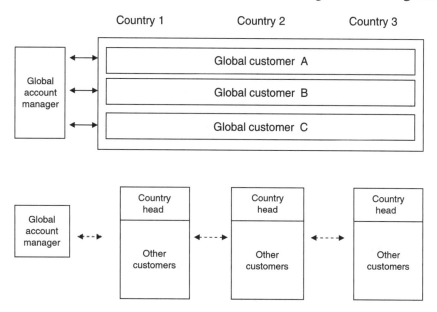

**Fig. 4.2** Separate GAM

are dedicated to global accounts. This structure also makes more clear the interface with the account, so that the customer always knows where to go with questions. However, this approach, which can have 'silo' aspects, also has its disadvantages. Firstly, it is a very expensive solution that can be implemented only by companies that have a substantial amount of global business. Furthermore, the separating out of GAM programme means there is less overlap with other account organizations, which means less sharing of best practices.

## The Control GAM

The Control GAM is the most common organizational form of GAM, and means that the responsibility for the account essentially lies with the GAM programme, and there is some level of authority to enforce that in the local subsidiaries (Figure 4.3). Often the Control GAM is set up in a matrix organization in which all employees who work with a global account on the local level report not only to their geographical line manager, but also to the gam. The gam reports to a senior executive at the corporate level, who is responsible for the whole GAM programme, and sometimes also to a regional manager if this is necessary within the company's organization structure. The reporting lines from the local account managers to the GAM and their geographic managers

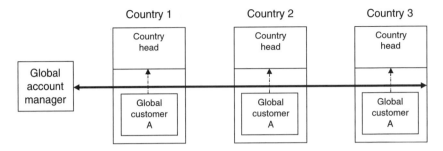

**Fig. 4.3** Control GAM

will differ. Typically, in the early days of a GAM programme the reporting line to the geographic manager will be a lot stronger than the, often dotted, reporting line to the gam. When the programme earns more credibility over time, the balance between those two reporting lines typically moves more in the direction of the gam. In some companies, the regional managers report to the same person as the gams or the GAM general manager, typically a vice president or director for sales. This helps in resolving conflicts, as problems can be escalated to the VP's level.

In the Control GAM, conflict can arise about authority over the local subsidiaries where global accounts operate. The gam needs some level of authority to make sure that global agreements can be enforced on the local level, but most companies try to steer away from taking all autonomy from the local subsidiaries. Enforcing plans on local subsidiaries without any discussion leads to resistance toward the global programme, which damages the programme in the long run. Therefore, gams should involve local subsidiaries with global decisions that affect their local customers. This not only motivates local managers to execute these decisions, but involves them as being a good source of information about the local implications of global decisions.

---

**JWT's and Royal Dutch Shell's 'Control GAM'**

The world's oldest advertising agency, JWT (formerly J. Walter Thompson), now part of WPP, runs a Control GAM programme. The agency has approximately two decades experience with its GAM organization, in which each global client is assigned its own global business director (GBD). This GBD takes responsibility for the qualitative and quantitative results of the business with the client and has executive authority over all business with the client, including any interactions in the different regions. As it will frustrate employees when this authority is used too often, the GBD aims to resolve problems by mutual consent, but if there is real friction he or she has the power to take charge.

Royal Dutch Shell also operates a Control GAM programme. In 2004, Shell had a standard regional approach (EU/US/Latin America/Asia) with regional (zonal) account teams and global account teams for the customers selected to be treated as global accounts. Each global account has a global account manager (gam) who reports to the respective business manager for his or her sector (e.g., automotive). The global key account management programmes are similar across the different business groups with minor differences. In most cases the local account managers are dedicated to one account, but in some sectors (e.g., food producers) this is not feasible, and the local account managers have to serve several customers. The local account manager reports directly to the gam, but has a dotted reporting line to the local commercial manager and the local Shell organization, as he or she depends on local functions such as marketing and supply chain.

Benefits of the Control GAM include the balance between global power and local knowledge, and engagement of local managers. For most companies this seems to be the best way to work with global accounts, and the many benefits outweigh the disadvantages of possible friction and need to make changes in the company's organization structure.

# Global Account Management at Hewlett-Packard

Hewlett-Packard (HP) is one of the pioneers and leaders in the use of GAM. We describe the HP programme in some detail here in order to illustrate how the different elements of a GAM programme can work together and evolve.

In the past two decades HP has developed a globally oriented organization to serve strategic global accounts. The original driver for this development was the globalization of the computer systems industry and the accompanying changes in customer behaviour. Originally, HP's GAM programme covered only certain segments of the its business, but as customer needs became more sophisticated the programme was gradually expanded to involve the whole company. Key to HP's programme is the balance between a single customer interface in the form of the account manager and account team, on a global level, and specialist support for products, service and solutions, on a local level.

## Globalization Drivers Affecting the Computer Systems Industry

Since the late 1980s there has been increasing pressure for globalization in the computer systems industry. A growing number of multinational customers have centralized or coordinated purchasing and vendor selection. These multinationals require vendors to have the ability to serve them as a single entity around the globe. Furthermore, the customer focus has shifted from the product itself to its functionality, which has increased customer demands for global standardization and consistent services. Fast changing technology accelerated the evolution from centralized mainframes to decentralized computer networks that are linked worldwide. Additionally, the importance of continuous innovation and time to market increased because of the opportunities that fast changing technology provided. All these changes led to a revision of the traditional relationship between vendor and customer. Customers expect vendors to be strategic partners who understand their business needs and are able to provide appropriate products, services and solutions to their activities across the world.

## HP Strategy Towards Global Account Management

HP wants to be the trusted information technology (IT) advisor for its global accounts by increasing customer intimacy and satisfaction. This strategy is supported by building a strong competency in higher value-added services and driving HP further up the IT value chain. With the aim of providing direct customer support for key global accounts, HP has been expanding its global account management programme since 1991. Currently the top 200 corporate accounts are classified as global accounts and handled in the HP GAM programme. Important components of this programme include: having unified, empowered corporate account teams combined with strong specialist support; assigning executive sponsors for major accounts; having the look and feel of a worldwide company; and selecting the right accounts to be a corporate global account.

## HP's Account Organization Model

Creating a single interface for the account, HP designates a global client business manager (GCBM) for every global account. This GCBM is assisted by a global account team that comprises members from different HP disciplines. For major accounts, a high-level executive is also assigned to support the account interface. This encourages HP executives to be actively involved with accounts that are considered crucial to the company's long term success. Furthermore, customers highly appreciate this direct connection to upper management. In addition to the global account interface, the customer can also rely on local support. A number of regional account managers are responsible for the local management of the account. Product, service and solution specialists also work at this local level. These specialists can give the customer dedicated support and create a local closeness of experts from the different customer divisions.

To achieve a worldwide company look and feel, HP works with globally uniform commercial terms, infrastructure and company policies. Synchronization of company processes over the different regions ensures the delivery of similar services worldwide.

## Role of the Global Client Business Manager

The GCBMs play a critical part in HP's GAM programme, as they are responsible for the worldwide relationship with the customer. Key responsibilities of the GCBM include:

- identifying and creating 'valued' opportunities that are beneficial to both the customer and HP;
- marshalling and coaching HP and partner teams to pursue opportunities and execute commitments made to the customer;
- measuring and improving customer satisfaction and loyalty;
- meeting HP financial targets;
- providing the primary focal point for managing executive communications and relationships between HP and the customer's management.

To live up to these responsibilities the GCBMs need to understand and communicate HP's capabilities in products, services and solutions. They also need a thorough understanding of the customer's business and business environment.

## Selecting Global Accounts

Obviously, not all of HP's accounts are suitable for global account management. A typical global account would be a large multidivision, multinational company that is one of the leaders in its market; the customer does significant business with HP or shows potential for such; and a good fit with HP's market focus and culture is also necessary to ensure the optimal results from the global account management.

## Value of the GAM Programme to Customers

Customers generally respond positively to the HP GAM programme. Most global accounts have a complex multinational decision-making process. Therefore, HP's single focal point for account communications provides the clarity that customers value in a supplier. As the account team has a thorough understanding of the customer's business, they are able to offer proactive solutions and deliver best practices. The empowered GCBM and account team ensure fast decision-making, which customers also highly appreciate. HP sees the programme as an important differentiator from its main competitors, such as IBM and Xerox.

In line with its strategy, HP aims for long term, mutually beneficial relationships with its strategic customers, and makes major commitments to achieve this. Since its inception, HP considers its GAM programme to be a very successful way to realize these relationships and to develop a truly global organization.

---

### Best Practices

This chapter shows that there is no single best way of organizing GCM. Managers need to find suitable implementation of GCM elements for their own company situation. Some best practices are valid, however, for most companies:

- Find the right balance between global control and local flexibility.
- Get high level executive support for the GCM organization.
- Create a clear, formal GAM programme, that is neither too unclearly defined nor too rigid, and that is visible to the whole company.
- Integrate the GAM programme into the rest of the company organization; it needs to become part of the company culture.
- Choose the right accounts to be part of the GAM programme.
- Have a cross-functional global account team.
- Make sure the balance of power within the GAM programme is workable and effective.

---

# Notes

1. For a discussion of global information management see Michael J. Earl and David Feeny (1996) 'Information Systems in Global Business', in Michael J. Earl (ed.) *Information Management: The Organizational Dimension.* Oxford: Oxford University Press; James Karimi and B. R. Konsynski (1991) 'Globalization and Informational Management Strategies', *Journal of Information Management Systems*, Spring, 7(4): 7–26; Karl Moore and Julian M. Birkinshaw (1998) 'Managing Knowledge in Global Service Firms: Centres of Excellence', *Academy of Management Executive*, December; Julian H. Birkinshaw (2001) 'Why is Knowledge Management so Difficult?', *Business Strategy Review*, Spring, 12(1): 11–18; and Johan Roos, Georg von Krogh and George S. Yip (1994) 'An Epistemology of Globalizing Firms', *International Business Review*, 3(4): 395–409, Special Issue on Organizations' Knowledge, Knowledge Transfer and Cooperative Strategies, November/December.

2. For example, Sun Microsystems set up a financial system called CORONA (Corporate Reporting on Anything) to streamline the report consolidation process. See Mitchell Levy (1990) 'Sun Microsystems Automates Financial Reporting', *Management Accounting*, January, 71: 24–28.

3. For a more complete discussion on global remuneration systems, see John Stredwick (2000) 'Aligning Rewards to Organisation Goals—a Multinational's Experience', *European Business Review*, January, 12: 9–21; Calvin Reynolds (2000) 'Global Compensation and Benefits in Transition', *Compensation & Benefits Review*, January/February, 32: 28–41; Mahmoud Ezzamel and Hugh Willmott (1998) 'Accounting, Remuneration and Employee Motivation in the New Organisation', *Accounting & Business Research*, Spring, 28: 97–110; G. O'Neill (1995) 'Framework for Developing a Total Reward Strategy', *Asia Pacific Journal of Human Resources*, Spring, 33: 103–17; John Smith (1992) 'Reward Management and HRM', in Peter Blyton and E. Turnbull (eds.) *Reassessing Human Resource Management*. London: Sage.

4. Holsapple and Whinston (1996) debate coordination and control aspects of decision support systems in C. Holsapple and A. Whinston (1996) *Decision Support Systems—A Knowledge-Based Approach*. St. Paul, MN: West Publishing Company. For more on coordination see C. Marshall, L. Prusak and D. Shpilberg (1996) 'Financial Risk and the Need for Superior Knowledge Management', *California Management Review*, March, 38; and T. Malone and K. Crowston (1994) 'The Interdisciplinary Study of Coordination', *ACM Computing Surveys*, January, 26: 87–119.

# Part II

## Key Choices

# 5 Selecting and Managing Global Accounts

We fired our largest global customer ($100 million a year in revenues) seven years ago.

(VP Global Sales, one of the world's largest hotel chains)

Part 1 discussed the foundation for managing global customers. In Part 2 we examine the key choices in setting up the global customer management (GCM) programme. In this chapter we first consider how to select and manage global accounts.

The quality of a club depends a lot on the quality of its members. The same holds for global account management (GAM) programmes. Choosing the right accounts to participate in the GAM programme is of vital importance to the success of the programme. That is why the hotel company in the opening quote of this chapter fired its largest customer as a global account. (This decision was not as radical as it might seem. In the hotel business, most hotel choices are still made by individual travellers despite corporate policies. So this hotel chain was able to retain a significant portion of its business with the fired account because of individual travellers' preference for the chain.) This chapter will give some pointers on selecting the right accounts for the programme. After the selection process it is, of course, important that the selected accounts are handled in a way that is most beneficial to both customer and supplier. For example, in order to provide the account with the best global care, it is necessary to gain more knowledge about the accounts. Analyzing the account's situation is a good way to gain more customer insight and to pinpoint the areas where the supplier can provide the account with added value products and services. Furthermore it is important to realize how the account perceives the supplier. This chapter discusses both how to select global accounts company and how to understand them.

---

**BBDO's Definition of a Global Account**

As a global account, an advertising client receives varying levels of service, depending on its needs and on the size of the company. For example, smaller companies may lack market

---

research data and thus request assistance or participation in developing marketing strategy, while larger companies may have performed their own research and can use their own resources to develop a comprehensive marketing strategy. The degree of integration that a global campaign entails also depends largely on the degree of control that a client wishes to exercise.

Advertising agency BBDO (part of Omnicom Group) defines a global account as a customer who wants a campaign that delivers a uniform message to every geographic market. Services offered to global accounts are very similar to those offered to national accounts. The difference lies, however, in the level of complexity that the development and the execution of such a campaign entail. To serve large global accounts, BBDO has established a network of offices in 54 countries worldwide and assigns personnel to exclusively serve each account. Senior level managers—worldwide account directors and worldwide creative directors—coordinate all efforts across market segments and geographic boundaries to support a global customer.

# Selecting Global Accounts

Should every worldwide customer be a global account customer? No. Unlike in normal commercial situations, in the case of GAM, having more accounts is not always better. Neither is there an ideal number of global accounts. Whereas some companies have only three customers with whom they have a global account relationship, other companies, like Hewlett-Packard (HP) or Xerox, have more than 100 global customers. Indeed, HP went as high as having 250 global accounts at one point before cutting back. Instead of focusing on how many global accounts they should have, managers should focus on identifying those accounts where a GAM relationship will add significant value. Because, however, many suppliers are forced into a GAM programme by customer demand, there is not always the luxury of selecting the most suitable accounts before the programme starts. So the risk exists that relationships that would benefit from GAM are overlooked, while others that are not suitable are in the programme, resulting in a very inefficient programme that is likely only to cost a lot in resources without delivering the expected extra volume or added value sales.

To select global accounts effectively, consider the criteria that global managers most commonly use. These are:

- geography;
- organization;
- revenue potential;
- strategic importance;
- strategic, cultural and geographical fit;
- partnership opportunities.

Readers might miss the criterion of 'size' in this list. This omission is deliberate. Although the size of the account will partially determine the global potential and strategic importance of the account, it should not be a selection criterion in itself. As a global manager at British telecommunications company BT said, 'Size is not the only factor, you need to focus on the customers that can bring you more'. Sometimes the biggest customers are the ones that are the least globally coordinated because of the challenges their size gives them in this area. For example, Kraft is one of the biggest food companies in the world. However, as of 2006 Kraft was still working on building effective global coordination, as it is clearly a lot harder to coordinate a big company than a small one. Because of this, having Kraft in a GAM programme will lead only to frustration and unnecessary costs for a supplier, there being no opportunities as yet for any global business. However, suppliers should be on the lookout for any global moves these customers might make, as when they eventually do have an effective global coordination system in place, they are likely to be exactly the customers with the potential a global supplier is looking for. A global account manager for HP agreed, 'Sometimes the largest companies are not the biggest potentials. Smaller companies are often very interesting because they have the ability to grow quickly'.

Not all of the criteria mentioned above are quantifiable. In general, the first three criteria—geography, organization and global potential—can be quantified to some extent, while the other three—strategic importance; strategic, cultural and geographical fit; and partnership opportunities—are softer and require some level of 'gut feeling' from the supplier as selection criteria. Furthermore, these criteria will have different levels of importance for different companies. All depends on the strategy the supplier takes with its global programme, and what customers fit in with its strategy and will add value. Based on this, the supplier needs to choose the criteria that are representative for such a customer. E-business application software provider Siebel includes the following factors in its GAM account selection: account size, account potential, global presence, centralized purchasing decisions, consistent global proposition, whether GAM can add value to the account, and that the customer is not looking to increase discounts or lower price. Research has shown that, in general, the perceived importance of the softer criteria increases with the age of the programme.[1] In the start up phase of a GAM programme, suppliers seem to stick with quantifiable criteria. France's Schneider Electric has just one quantitative criterion for selecting a global account—the client has to offer the potential of sourcing at least 50 percent of its global business from Schneider. The rest of the criteria are soft, such as 'the client has to help Schneider understand its challenges, needs and services', and 'the client has to agree to share early project information and make purchasing commitments'. Other factors that Schneider considers are compatibility of goals, values, styles and time horizons.[2]

## Geography

For most companies, being global does not mean a complete worldwide presence. Most companies will classify a customer as having a sufficient geographical spread to be a potential global customer if it operates and distributes in at least two or three continents and has a growing percentage of its business outside its home market. Obviously, a customer being present in many countries does not do the supplier much good if there is no commercial contact between the two companies in these countries. Therefore, often the number of countries where the supplier and the customer already has a relationship is also taken into account. When there is a particularly good fit between the customer's and supplier's key markets this will help to develop the global relationship and the possible added value that the companies can bring to each other. The Shell global account manager for Unilever sees this as follows: 'Like Unilever, Shell is a global company with global resources and a commitment to delivering a consistent level of service across the world. This gives us a greater understanding of the challenges that impact on such a company'. The importance of a good fit is also recognized from the customer's point of view. The person at Siemens responsible for global purchases at Tyco says, 'There is a good fit between Tyco and Siemens. We are both big global technology driven companies with a large R&D force. The global technological drive for both companies is an important part of the fit. This means that the companies understand each other's drive'.

When a customer is big, but has a less than global spread, for example, they are concentrated in a very large home market and have only a few minor operations outside of the home market, it might be a very important customer volume-wise, but it should not be selected for the GAM programme. It would be better instead to optimize services to this customer through some form of more localized key account management.

## Organization

The global organization of the potential global customer has to be a 'make or break' criterion in the selection process. The customer has to coordinate its activities across borders for it to be an attractive partner in a global relationship. A customer can have a very wide spread of activities, but when it has no global coordination there is no reason to work with it in a global way. The global value will be diluted or lost if the two companies are not able to respond to each other in compatible global organizations. However, the organization selection criterion is also a paradoxical one. On the one hand, it would be best if suppliers selected their own global accounts rather than being forced into global account relationships by customer demand. On the other hand, customers with global coordination and a centralized coordinated purchasing system will probably be exactly those customers who demand a coordinated and integrated response from their suppliers. It is important that the supplier maintains objectivity during the selection process, as it is very possible that the customer demanding a global purchasing deal may, in fact, not be as globally coordinated as it thinks it is. Such a customer may try to get a global price, based on the total potential global purchase volume but in fact it may not have the coordination capability to actually make the local subsidiaries purchase the goods. One global account manager said: 'if you get a global agreement with a non-global customer all you've got is a hunting license!'[3]

The structure of customer–supplier contacts also matters a great deal. As described in Chapter 1, a good global relationship will not depend on the contact between the global account manager (gam) and the global purchaser in a bow-tie structure, in which all of the relationship contacts are channelled via one connection. One of the characteristics of successful global customer management is that there is a diamond structure of contacts between the two companies in which many different geographical areas and departments have direct contact with each other.

Lastly, a customer who also globally coordinates other departments, like R&D, logistics or marketing, will be able to work together with the supplier on so much more than just lowering cost price, to the benefit of both parties.

## Revenue Potential

Whatever criteria are chosen for global account selection, revenue potential, or some variation of it, will be among them. In the end, achieving profitable growth is the main motivation for most management decisions and, therefore, the potential for increasing business volume and profitability is an important selection criterion. Potential revenue is more important than current revenue, unless the supplier is at risk of losing the current revenue if it does not start a global programme with a particular customer. In starting a global relationship with a customer, it is anticipated that this relationship will in time lead to more revenue. This extra revenue will firstly come from combined purchasing. When global deals are made, the customer will want to combine as much volume as possible in one purchase, in order to get a better deal. This will mean that countries that previously bought from another supplier will be forced into the global deal with this supplier. The revenue potential for combined global purchasing is, therefore, the total world demand of the customer for the products involved.

**Key Choices**

Shell Automotive Industry (later re-organized as largely part of Shell Lubricants, Fuels and Bitumen) started its global programme with this objective. Shell saw customers starting to purchase on a global basis, combining all global purchases with fewer suppliers. In response, Shell formed a global team. Shell looked at its biggest customers and asked itself the question, 'Who is poised to start purchasing globally?'

Another source of revenue potential lies in more business in other products that were not previously sold to the customer. A global relationship, if implemented in an effective way, should result in greater trust between the two companies and more insight into the customer's needs and wants. So the supplier will be able to target the customer with products and services that will bring more added value for the customer and more revenue for the supplier. In the extreme form of global partnership, the customer can even be involved in new product development by the supplier, almost guaranteeing sales of the new product to this customer. Another form of revenue potential derives from future growth of the customer's own revenues. When a global supplier obtains similar revenue from two global customers, the customer that has a small but growing market share in its industry may be more interesting than the customer with a large market share but with no real potential for growing. The company with the highest growth in its sector will be a very interesting customer, as it enables the supplier to benefit from its success by 'riding the wave'. Xerox experienced this effect with its customer Siemens. In 2001 Siemens started a period of high growth and sought global suppliers that understood its needs and were able to provide for the requirements that came from this dynamic situation. As a global supplier to Siemens, Xerox had the chance to grow with this customer—the quantities sold to Siemens have grown at an annual rate of 25 percent since the start of the global agreement.

## Strategic Importance of Customer

The strategic importance of a customer to a supplier in general or its global operations in particular can be quite intangible. What is strategic to one company can be irrelevant to another. When is a customer strategically important to a supplier? In general strategic importance is based on three main factors: relative size, product group and image.

### Relative Size

Relative size is determined by the amount of business the supplier has with this customer compared with the total revenue and revenue in the particular product group. For example, when a vendor has a customer that purchases

10 percent of its total production, and 60 percent in a particular strategic product group, it cannot afford to lose this customer, and needs to take extra good care of them, possibly with a GAM programme.

### Product Group

The product group that the customer purchases is important as, for most suppliers, not all of the product groups in which they operate are as strategically important as others. This can be due to the level of profit margin, or perhaps because of its importance within a strategic direction being pursued. For example, for Xerox, customers that purchase just photocopiers are not as interesting as those buying more complex 'office solutions' or 'document management'.

It is advisable to look at strategic importance in relative size and product group from the customer's point of view, also. When a supplier delivers a substantial percentage of the total purchases a customer makes in a specific product group that is strategically important to the customers' operations, it is safe to say that this supplier will have high strategic importance to the customer. If possible this supplier should select accounts in which the relationship is strategically important for both parties. This ensures that the effort and resources that are used on this account will be welcomed and returned.

### Image

The third area of strategic importance is image. Companies like to be affiliated with 'the best', even if 'the best' means other companies. This can mean that 'having a globally recognized brand name' or 'being perceived as a technological leader' become selection criteria. In the example of Shell's relationship with Unilever, even though Shell is the preferred supplier for industrial lubricants, the total revenue from these lubricants is relatively low for Shell. But as Unilever is one of the largest companies in its field, Shell wants to invest in resources to have Unilever in its global account programme and be an industrial partner. Therefore, Shell values the partnership between the two companies more based on the image of the customer than on the actual size of business.

## Strategic, Cultural, and Geographical Fit

For an effective GAM relationship, the customer needs some kind of fit with the supplier in strategy, culture, and geographic presence.

### Strategic Fit

Strategic fit does not just mean that the type of customer fits well within the strategy of the supplier, but that the customer's strategy itself fits with that of the supplier.[4] Although strategies can be sensitive subjects between companies, if they aim to have a relationship that will truly add value to their operations they should open up and share these strategies with each other. In the global relationship between Shell and Wärtsilä, a Finnish producer of marine engines, there is a true drive to create value for the two companies. For example, in the Indian market, Shell and Wärtsilä have a joint marketing agreement in which the two companies market their products together. Also, if Wärtsilä introduces Shell to a project and they are successful, Wärtsilä will earn some commission for this.

Cultural Fit

A cultural fit, or at least cultural empathy, is important because of the many different connections the companies will have with each other.[5] When two companies have a similar culture, for example, they are 'technology driven' or their outlook is, 'agreed is agreed', it will be easier to work together without frustration. Technology and automotive company Bosch has a structure in which many of the worldwide executive positions are filled by German managers. This has led to a very strong German culture in the company worldwide, in which 'punktlichkeit und grundlichkeit' (punctuality and thoroughness) are very important. A company that supplies Bosch worldwide says this German culture does not lead to problems in most European countries, but it does in some other regions where punctuality and thoroughness feature less prominently in the local culture.

Mindset also affects cultural fit. A customer with a global mindset that goes beyond a focus on global purchasing will usually fit better with a global supplier. This mindset will show in global coordination of the rest of the organization. A customer who focuses on global purchasing will in general be in the global relationship for one thing—a lower price. Although for a global supplier this lower price will be made up for by higher volumes, a global relationship could have many bigger benefits that the companies would miss out on by having a solely transactional global relationship. So a customer with a global mindset is more interesting for a supplier to have in its global programme.

Geographical Fit

The third important fit criterion is geography. A supplier has to be able to serve a global customer in most of the latter's key locations. One major British bank complained that most technology suppliers operate in far fewer countries than it does:

Suppliers often have affiliates in countries where they do not operate themselves, but still say they can give you a global deal. Regrettably, the services from the original company and from an affiliate are mostly not the same. Genuine global suppliers are very rare.

However, there is no need to have a complete overlap with the customer, but there should be some alignment in the major strategic markets. For example, when a supplier is aiming to grow in Asia, customers that are also interested in the Asian market will be more attractive than others, as their efforts in the region will give the supplier a piggyback ride.

## Partnership Opportunities

Whether or not a customer is open for partnership is a very intangible measure, but at the same time a very important one. Partnership is what makes a good relationship great, and gives both parties the security to invest in the relationship without doubts. For example, Schneider Electric had to invest in special equipment to design the product for a favoured customer's requirements. In turn, the client made Schneider its sole supplier for that group of products. As trust developed, the relationship became increasingly richer. A perception of partnership also makes it easier to move from a transactional relationship toward a strategic one. A partnership will give the opportunity for value creation, both in the supplier and customer working together on savings, and in the development of new products and services. One company said: 'We are looking at accounts that have a migration path that is parallel to the one we have strategically selected for ourselves. We want customers who, down the line, want us to do more than just provide basic products'.[6]

Strategic partnership seems to be the holy grail of relationship management, but when push comes to shove many companies feel it is hard to be open towards another company. Lack of willingness to open up will prevent the companies from creating the extra value that is locked in the partnership. So openness for partnership should be an important selection criterion if a company wants its GAM programme to be more than just transactional. But how do you determine this openness? There are no foolproof measures that will ascertain the openness to partnership of the customer, but there are some indicators. Accounts where a good relationship already exists will in general be easier to develop into partnerships. When a customer takes the 'old school' purchasing approach of the hard-nosed purchasing manager, who tries to keep the relationship on the transactional level and sees GAM only as a method to lower prices, it will be very hard to transform this relationship into a partnership. 'We have joined strategy discussions with some of our global customers. It is good to have some alignment, openness and trust grow this way', said the global account manager for DMV International. Customers also recognize the importance of this openness in the relationship, judging from a comment from customer Wärtsilä about its relationship with supplier Shell: 'If you are in a long term relationship with another company, you need to give and take. You need more sharing of vision, mission and strategy'.

# The Ongoing Selection Process

Every company starting a GAM programme should have its own set of selection criteria with its own weighed importance for each item. But the selection process should not be restricted to the start of the GAM programme. It is important that the selected accounts are frequently tested against the selection criteria, to see if they are still suitable for the GAM programme. Companies should not be afraid to switch a customer to another form of account management if they no longer fit into the GAM programme, providing this is handled with diplomacy. When Hewlett-Packard found that it had over-expanded its GAM programme to over 250 accounts, it decided to cut back hard. But instead of informing the dropped accounts directly, which might well have offended them, HP simply gradually reduced the services provided.

It may also be possible that due to changing circumstances or strategies, a supplier's selection criteria evolve over time, which consequently means that different customers become interesting for the GAM programme, For example, Shell initially had Delphi, the largest manufacturer of automotive components in the world, in its global programme, because Delphi seemed to be interested in global procurement. After chasing Delphi for three years, Shell decided to drop it from the programme in 2003, as during that time the customer never did go on to buy on a globally coordinated basis. Although Delphi showed interest, it was far from actually having the organization in place for global procurement and, therefore, was not worthwhile for Shell to keep it in its global programme.

# Understanding the Account

One of the most valuable preparation methods of selecting the right global accounts is analysing the kind of relationship a supplier has with its customers. A good way to do this is to get some insight into each customer's perception of the supplier. How important is the supplier for this customer? Furthermore, general understanding of the account, its strategy, problems, needs and wants will give a good foundation for creating a good customer value proposition on which the account relationship can be built. Understanding the account makes the difference between a mediocre GAM programme and an efficient programme that creates value for both parties. If the situation within the account asks for it, it might be necessary to differ from the standard GAM arrangements. For example, in Shell's global account organization for Daimler Chrysler there are two global account managers instead of the one that is usual at Shell's other global accounts. One is based in Europe, a German-speaker focused on Mercedes worldwide. The other is based in the United States, and focuses on Chrysler, Mitsubishi, Freightliner, Detroit Diesel worldwide and Mercedes in North America. This dual gam situation serves to accommodate the internal situation within the Daimler Chrysler organization where the German part of the company works very independently from the Chrysler part.

## Analysing the Account

How does a supplier analyse an account to gain the necessary understanding, and what exactly is it that should be understood? First, it is important to realize that the purchasing manager is not a good representative of the customer company. Even when the purchasing manager is very up to date with the company's capabilities, and its needs and wants, he or she will not be the expert on these issues, and might not want to share this kind of information with a supplier. Furthermore, if the purchasing manager's bonuses depend on the savings made in purchasing, there is no direct incentive for him or her to help the supplier to better understand the company.

So when trying to understand the account, the preferred first point of personal contact, in the customer company, should be end-users of the products or services supplied. These are the people who know why this account company purchases these products, what the positive and negative aspects are for the supplier company, if the service that surrounds the products is up to the account customer's standards, and so on. An end-user will, in general, be glad to discuss these issues with the supplier, as it gives a chance to improve the situation. This is shown in the relationship between Shell and Unilever, where Shell helps Unilever with the latter's new maintenance programme. Information from the employees who will actually work with the new programme is vital for Shell's input into the programme. Both Shell and Unilever see this as a partnership, where they can find synergy that gives them an edge over competitors.

An end-user can help a global supplier gain more understanding about the current use of its products by the customer, but this is not enough for a thorough understanding of the account. Apart from the business unit that is the end-user of the products or services, it is important to gather more information from other areas of the account. For example, a discussion with the marketing department of the customer will help a supplier understand the marketing strategy and future plans of the company. If the products supplied contribute to an end-product, a marketing representative will be able to explain the product life cycle of this end-product and, therefore, the future potential of the supplied product. With the help of available data on the account and its industry, completed with insider information that is gathered from the different contacts with the account, in a good internal information system (of which more in Chapter 8), it is possible to make a thorough analysis of the account. The first thing that should be done is to map the company's activities, both by geography and industry. This should be not just an overview of the account's market segments served and worldwide spread but, if possible, it should include the spread of resources, for example, the number of personnel working in each segment and region. This will give some idea of the basic importance of the different areas to the account, and a rudimentary overview of what areas of potential there are between the account and the supplier. Before Shell started a global relationship with Bosch, there was very little business between the two companies outside of Europe. By taking a global view, Shell determined many new areas of potential sales and succeeded in realizing extra sales in many regions.

The segment analysis will be the foundation for the rest of the account analysis. It will give a good overview of potential areas where projects can be started with the account company, or possible value chain activities that are carried out in both the supplier and the customer, from which both parties can gain some synergy effects. The segment analysis can also help position the account in comparison with their competitors, which will again give more insight into the issues and areas that are important for the account. A supplier that can help an account grow stronger in areas of competition will be very warmly welcomed. As the account company's future will influence the supplier's future, it is a crucial part of total customer understanding. Use the segment analysis to project a possible growth path for the customer, which should indicate its future demands.

Apart from the segment analysis, it is important to know how the account company's decision-making processes work. This can be difficult as, besides a formal decision-making process, many companies have an informal layer of influential people, who may or may not be the same people as those responsible for making decisions. A global account manager at advertising agency Ogilvy & Mather describes how he sometimes sends off little 'probes' in the form of ideas into a customer's network, to see if and how those ideas come back to him. This gives him some insight into the informal influence systems at the customer. However, this is a very intangible area that can only be analysed with a lot of 'gut feel' and instinct. Once a supplier has a good insight and understanding of the account company and its processes, these can be used to determine where there is potential to add value to this account. What problems does the account company have with which the supplier can help? What geographical areas are interesting but have been neglected up until now? In many companies, gathering customer insight and understanding is an ad hoc activity carried out by the global account manager. Ideally, there should be a formalized process both of gathering numerical data about the account and of processing qualitative data that has been gathered by the different employees who have contact with the account company. Unfortunately, for most companies it is hard enough to create a culture in which the internal information system is used to its full potential. Nevertheless, knowledge is power and, therefore, formalizing the customer understanding process can be a good step toward getting real value from managing global customers.

## Purchasing Portfolio and the Consequences for GAM

The customer's perception of the importance of the supplier can be an important indicator of the possible success of a global relationship. Some supplier industries will be naturally more suitable for global account management. This will be the case when the products the supplier produces are important for the customer's business, and are suitable for worldwide purchasing. For example, when a purchaser is buying complicated gearboxes that are vital to his or her company's end product, he or she will be more anxious to have a good relationship with the supplier than when buying pens for office use. Scarcity or complexity of supply also encourage a customer to build a good relationship with the supplier.

The different roles a specific purchasing item can have are illustrated in the purchasing portfolio in Figure 5.1. The portfolio can be represented in a matrix with a vertical axis for the importance to the customer and a horizontal axis for the complexity of supply. This way, four different groups of products exist, corresponding with four different ways of customer perception of the supplier and consequently will lead to four different courses of action for the supplier.

### Commodity Products

The bottom left cell in Figure 5.1 has 'importance to customer' as low and 'complexity of supply' also low. This is typically the case with 'commodity products', where the customer will have many possible suppliers and will want to get the best price for these products. In terms of logistics, these are often the products that get selected for first trials of systems contracting and electronic ordering ('e-purchasing'). As far as the global relationship between the customer and supplier is concerned, the customer will probably not be interested in anything else but to get the best price and terms out of the global agreement and to lower the purchasing costs. Before the customer starts its global coordination, it will in general have different suppliers for these commodity products, many of whom will have a marginal position. The main activity in global coordination

## Key Choices

**(a) Purchasing portfolio**

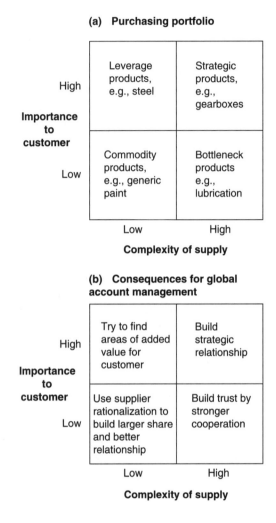

|  | | Low | High |
|---|---|---|---|
| **Importance to customer** | High | Leverage products, e.g., steel | Strategic products, e.g., gearboxes |
|  | Low | Commodity products, e.g., generic paint | Bottleneck products e.g., lubrication |
|  | | Low | High |

Complexity of supply

**(b) Consequences for global account management**

|  | | Low | High |
|---|---|---|---|
| **Importance to customer** | High | Try to find areas of added value for customer | Build strategic relationship |
|  | Low | Use supplier rationalization to build larger share and better relationship | Build trust by stronger cooperation |
|  | | Low | High |

Complexity of supply

**Fig. 5.1** The purchasing portfolio and consequences for global account management

*Source*: (a) Adapted from P. Kraljic (1983) 'Purchasing Must Become Supply Management', Harvard Business review, September-October, 61: 109–17. (b) Adapted from A. J. van Weele (1997) *Inkoop in strategisch perspectief*. Alphen aan de Rijn, Netherlands: Samson.

for this type of product is to reduce the number of suppliers in order to reduce operational costs and to get a better deal because of larger quantities.

When the customer is looking to reduce the number of suppliers, it will mostly look for suppliers who have the capabilities to supply globally. Siemens, which is currently in the process of reducing the number of its suppliers, says that global capability is an absolute requirement, even for areas in which Siemens is not yet ready to buy on a global scale. Therefore, whereas supplier rationalization can be seen as a threat by some suppliers, a supplier with capable global operations should see it as an opportunity to gain more of the customer's business. Once the supplier has gained a substantial part of the customer's business, it is possible to work on the global relationship. Having fewer suppliers means being more dependent on these suppliers, which leads to more willingness to look at global projects that benefit both parties.

Leverage Products

When a product represents a large percentage of a customer's costs, but the complexity of supply is low, and many suppliers are able to offer this product, it is seen as a 'leverage product'. Even a small change in price of these products will have an effect on the cost price of the end-product for the customer. Examples of leverage products are chemicals that are used in large quantities or building materials. Typical for a leverage product is that the customer has a choice of many suppliers, and the cost to keep switching between suppliers is low. This way the customer can get away with squeezing its suppliers and getting the best possible price without the risk of ending up with no products. The best course of action for a supplier of leverage products is to find competitive advantage that will be of value to the customer. Being a global supplier can be one of those competitive advantages, as it gives the customer the opportunity to both lower operating costs and get a better price. Understanding the customer is especially important in this quadrant of the portfolio, as it can make the difference between losing or winning the deal. ABB makes a clear difference in the purchase of 'direct' and 'indirect' products, or those that are critical or not for the continuation of the business. For a supplier that is more strategically important to it, ABB puts more effort into activities such as quality assurance and supplier ratings. So the amount of time and effort that ABB procurement puts into a leverage product is lower than for a strategic product with a greater impact on the company. Therefore, the supplier must find the added value it can offer to the customer, in order to move toward becoming a strategic supplier.

Bottleneck Products

Some products are not very important to the customer in financial terms, but have some sort of supply risk. These are 'bottleneck products'. Often the supply risk comes from the fact that the products can be obtained from only one supplier. This can be because there are no other suppliers (e.g., in the dye industry), there is only one supplier approved by the customer's quality assurance department or because of regulation such as for a monopoly.

In the automotive industry, it is very costly to get a supplier approved for quality and safety issues. Therefore, automotive manufacturers often decide to use only one supplier for specific materials, like lubrication. Another category of products that fall into this quadrant is machine-specific spare parts. The customer will want to secure the supply of bottleneck products, which will give more power to the supplier. In general, the customer will want to lower the dependence on one supplier, by finding alternative products, and even finding new suppliers. When the Volkswagen purchasing department buys a product for which only one supplier exists, it will help other suppliers to start producing this product, in order to create a competitive situation that will lower both price and dependency.

A supplier in this quadrant should not be tempted to take too much advantage of the situation, as this will only decrease trust between the parties, and will drive the customer toward alternative arrangements. The bottleneck quadrant is ideal for building better global relationships as the customer will want a certain level of security, which means it is easier to build trust. A bottleneck supplier should use the existing good relationship to broaden their business with this customer by finding more areas where it can add value to the customer's business.

Strategic Products

Strategic products are those that represent a large percentage of the cost price of the end product, and are also difficult to source. This is the quadrant where the best global relationships are built. For example, products in this category might be gearboxes, for the automotive industry, or factory-specific equipment. Strategic products are often made specifically for a customer, to its requirements. As these products are important to the customer, the latter will probably be interested in greater coordination or even a partnership with the supplier. So a common goal should be to come to a mutual interest based on cooperation between the two parties. Projects can be started to reduce costs, improve quality, enhance the processes and develop new products. This partnership will be beneficial to both companies. Finding itself in the strategic quadrant, a supplier should use the partnership to its full potential, and build a good strategic relationship that will bring the company long term value.

**Best Practices**

When discussing the role of the account in global account management, two issues are important: how to select the right accounts and, when selected, how to gain insight and understanding into the customer's business. Some best practices with respect these two issues are:

- Have a selection process; do not let the customer do the selecting for you.
- Have a set of appropriate selection criteria that are allowed to change over time.
- Do not be afraid to remove an account from the programme if it does not comply with the selection criteria any more.

- Conduct a thorough analysis of the account.
- Gain customer insight through data collection/analysis and personal contacts.
- Try to determine the customer's perception of you as a supplier.

# Notes

1. K. Wilson (1999) 'Developing Global Account Management Programmes: Observations from a GAM Panel Presentation', *Thexis*, 4.
2. 'Schneider Electric Global Account Management', IMD-3-0940, European Case Clearing House, Cranfield, UK, 2000.
3. K., Wilson, S. Croom, T. Millman and D. C. Weilbaker (2000) 'The Global Account Management Study Research Report', sponsored by Strategic Account Management Association (SAMA) and the Sales Research Trust.
4. The role of strategic fit has been studied from various viewpoints in management literature. See, for example, David A. Griffith and Matthew Myers (2005) 'The Performance Implications of Strategic Fit of Relational Norm Governance Strategies in Global Supply Chain Relationships', *Journal of International Business Studies*, May, 36: 254–71; Richard Burton, Jorgen Lauridsen and Borge Obel (2004) 'The Impact of Organizational Climate and Strategic Fit on Firm Performance', *Human Resource Management*, Spring, 47: 67–82; Mikko Ketokivi and Roger Shroeder (2004) 'Manufacturing Practices, Strategic Fit and Performance: A Routine-Based View', *International Journal of Operations & Production Management*, January/February, 24: 171–90; Ruth Aguilera and John Dencker (2004) 'The Role of Human Resource Management in Cross-Border Mergers and Acquisitions', *International Journal of Human Resource Management*, 11 December, 15: 1355–70; Bryan Lukas, Justin Tan and Tomas Hult (2004) 'Strategic Fit in Transition Economies: The Case of China's Electronics Industry', *Journal of Management*, December, 27: 409–29; and Edward Zajac, Matthew Kraats and Rudi Bresser (2000) 'Modeling the Dynamics of Strategic Fit: A Normative Approach to Strategic Change', *Strategic Management Journal*, April, 21: 429–47; J. Harrison and C. St. John (1998) *Strategic Management of Organisations and Stakeholders*, 2nd edn. Cincinnati: South Western College Publishing.
5. On the importance of cultural fit in organizations see Mark Testa, Stephen Mueller and Anisya Thomas (2003) 'Cultural Fit and Job Satisfaction in a Global Service Environment', *Management International Review*, May, 43: 129–38; Thomas Legare (1998) 'The Human Side of Mergers and Acquisitions', *Human Resource Planning*, January, 21: 32–41; Yaakov Weber (1996) 'Corporate Cultural Fit and Performance in Mergers and Acquisitions', *Human Relations*, September 49: 1996; 1181–203; Yaakov Weber, Oded Shenkar and Raveh Oded (1996), 'National and Corporate Cultural Fit in Mergers/Acquisitions: An Exploratory Study', *Management Science*, August,

## Key Choices

42: 1215–28; Datta Deepak and George Puia (1995) 'Cross-Border Acquisitions: An Examination of the Influence of Relatedness and Cultural Fit on Shareholder Value Creation in US Acquiring Firms', *Management International Review*, December 35: 337–60.
6. Wilson et al. 2000.

# 6  Empowering Global Account Managers

A global account manager is much more than a national sales manager with a passport. Among the many requirements, he or she must be comfortable with ambiguity and with dialing long telephone numbers!

> (A director of global accounts at a major US multinational company that was one of the pioneers of global account management programmes.)

After selecting which accounts are to be global, the next key choice is who should be the manager for each account. The global account manager (gam) is the most important person in the account relationship. Therefore, it is important to have a clear view of what the responsibilities of the gam will be, and make sure these are known to all involved. Furthermore, it is important to know what characteristics a good gam should have, and choose a person who has these characteristics. Obviously, these responsibilities and characteristics will differ from company to company. This chapter will discuss the most common responsibilities and characteristics of a gam. Figure 6.1 summarizes the key gam requirements that we discuss in this chapter.

## Roles of the Global Account Manager

The position of a gam is a complex one. The gam functions as a spider in a web of departments and crosses country and company borders. So there are many different roles the gam has with many different people. Often, companies make the mistake of seeing the gam as an upgraded sales manager, but being a gam has much less to do with sales and much more to do with other account issues than those faced by a local account manager. One researcher identified six different roles for the gam:[1]

- boundary-spanning coordinator;
- entrepreneurial strategist;
- team leader/manager;
- information broker;

## Key Choices

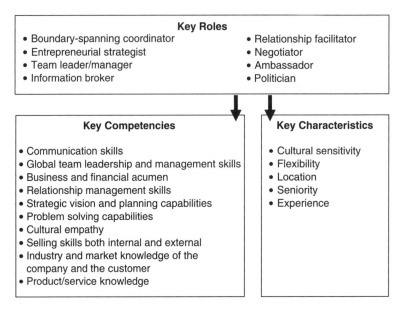

**Fig. 6.1** Key requirements for a global account manager

- relationship facilitator;
- negotiator.

These are all clear and tangible gam responsibilities and roles. This chapter will discuss these six roles, and will also discuss two additional, less tangible, roles for the gam:

- ambassador;
- politician.

Readers may notice that the role of sales manager is missing from this list of roles. Even though some aspects of the responsibilities of the gam will essentially be seen as being in sales, the position of a gam in a company that has truly integrated global customer management (GCM) into its operations will be beyond the transactional responsibilities of a sales manager. For example, at Schneider Electric the gams are expected to exhibit the following behaviours and skills:[2]

1. Clear vision and mission statements.
2. Empowerment in
   - executive global nomination;
   - reporting structure;

- internal awareness;
- cooperation for local implementation.

3. Effective communication network with identified regional managers at several levels and a formalized matrix structure.

4. 'Solution selling' competence.

5. Cultural adaptability.


## Boundary-Spanning Coordinator

The boundary-spanning coordination role is particularly characteristic of the position of the gam and a basic requirement for any global programme.[3] As the gam deals not just with two different companies, but within these companies with different regions and departments, he or she has many different interests to coordinate. Within the coordinator role the gam should bring together different regions and departments to form one globally coordinated proposition for the customer. When a company first starts working with a global account programme, the coordination role is the first part of the total gam position that needs to be developed. Prior to the global programme, the different departments and regions will all have had their own business with the customer, without any formal synchronization among them. When the gam starts coordinating this, there is a high risk of encountering conflicting interests. The boundary-spanning role of the gam means that he or she will have to build bridges between departments, regions and companies to ensure that potential conflicts are kept to a minimum.[4]

The coordinating role is not just for transactional business between the two companies, but is also important when the relationship between the two companies extends into cooperation in innovation and other projects. In these cases more departments which are not sales related will have contact with the customer on a global level, which will mean more coordination effort from the gam. So it is important that the gam keeps a good overview of the network of people involved on both sides of the relationship dyad. In the relationship between ABB and Xerox, the ABB purchasing manager remarked that he does not know exactly what the Xerox global account team looks like, but he does know that the global key account manager is able to represent the whole of Xerox: 'The person or the company, it is the same thing. The GKAM has an extremely good grip, lots of personal contacts. His network is very big, and that is just the thing we need'.

## Entrepreneurial Strategist

Whereas the coordinator role is very hands-on, operational, and with a basic requirement to keep the global programme working, the role of entrepreneurial strategist is to ensure that the supplier gets everything possible out of the global relationship. As the entrepreneurial strategist, a gam needs to take time to look for new opportunities to create value between the two companies. This does not just mean in new sales opportunities, although it obviously will be part of it. As the goal of the global programme is to create a long term profitable relationship between the two companies, the gam will also look for opportunities that help build a stronger relationship. This can be done, for example, by finding synergies between the two companies or by co-developing new products. Improving the processes between the two companies is often a good way to create value for both companies, while bonding them together more closely.

---

**Unilever's Partnership with Suppliers**

Unilever started its E4US (ePartnership for Unilever Suppliers) project to optimize its supply chain processes. Many suppliers look at this suspiciously, as they do not see the benefit in changing all their processes just to please Unilever. However, some global suppliers saw E4US as an opportunity to develop the relationship between the two companies, and were enthusiastic in implementing the necessary changes to enable E4US. Being able to work with Unilever within the E4US system makes the relationship stronger and Unilever prefers to work with the companies that have the system in place.

---

Apart from finding opportunities, the gam as entrepreneurial strategist must make sure these opportunites are converted into actual value for the companies, such as by making and implementing a strategic development plan for the global account. Besides being a long term vision for the account, this plan should record all important objectives regarding the development of the relationship and the actions that need to be taken to reach these objectives. The strategic global account plan is also a good tool to keep all the different people working with the account on the same page.

---

**Global Positions at JWT**

Advertising agency JWT clearly notes that the people who work on a global account need to be entrepreneurial. For its global positions JWT often looks for people who have excelled in a local office, but have decided that being office head or creative director is not the be-all and end-all of their careers, and who realize that the global jobs are the more challenging ones. At JWT the position of global account manager is now seen as being as senior as that of a country office head.

---

# Team Leader/Manager

As will be discussed in Chapter 7, the global account team plays an important part in effective account management. This team often does not have a hierarchical organization, which means the members might report to different people who may or may not be involved with the global account programme. In this case, the informal role of team leader will often belong to the gam. This can be a difficult task, as the lack of formal authority over team members means the leadership style must rely on influencing to urge cooperation. Many gams do this by creating 'team-spirit' so that all members of the team see the global account as being a priority part of their work, and are willing to pull strings to get things done without needing a line manager to tell them to do so.

Ideally, the gam has some say in the selection of team members. Companies that have a formal global account team structure with cross-functional members often have this option. In DMV International, a Netherlands-based global supplier of ingredients for the food and pharmaceutical industry, the global account manager selects a team of employees from different regions and functional departments based on their contact with the account and on the account's specific situation. The team members all report to their own line managers, but they meet with the gam on a regular basis to work on account-specific issues. The gam helps the team members get more and better contacts in the account company, and together they set up a plan of action concerning the account.

Another good way to give the gam higher status as team manager, despite their lack of authority, is to have him or her provide input for each team member's annual review. Even though it is eventually the line manager who will conduct the review, the fact that the gam can give his or her opinion on this aspect of the employee's job gives the gam more weight with the team members. At Xerox, a global account general manager (GAGM) often has to deal with large virtual teams—300 people is not exceptional there. However, the GAGM still needs to be the facilitator for all account issues. He or she takes responsibility for the account strategy. This strategy is created by the GAGM and core team members, which means the former is using the input of the national account managers who will actually implement the account strategy. This facilitates adoption on the local level. Lastly, listening and using local input are important ways of getting local units to willingly cooperate. One of the GAGMs said he tries to keep things simple within the account team, as this means that it is easier to communicate with team members and between team members, and it ensures that everybody is kept up to date.

## Information Broker

As global accounts come with a lot of complexity and vast amounts of information, managing this information is an important task for the gam. The gam will typically have the best overview of the complete account, and be in the best position to collect data from the different local parts of the company that deal with the account. For many gams the information broker role can be a very time consuming activity but cannot be neglected, as information is the key to creating a good customer value proposition. In some companies, the gams have dedicated assistants to deal with the administrative and operational parts of information management but, to date, these are still exceptions. However, managers responsible for the complete global account programme should seriously consider creating the position for a global account assistant for this administrative task, either for specific accounts or for a number of accounts. A valuable employee like a gam could be put to better use than simply to upload information to the intranet or to set up the layout of the account sales report.

To ensure that information reaches the right people, and is used effectively, it is important to have a certain process for information management. The way gams deal with the large quantity of available information differs between companies, but best practices include intranet information systems, global account reports, account specific newsletters and regular meetings or telephone conferences with the involved local managers. Obviously, there will still be the need for a substantial amount of ad hoc communication, but at least people will know where to bring or acquire relevant information for their part of the account.

## Relationship Facilitator/Builder

As the long term relationship between the two companies is key to the success of the GAM programme, the relationship facilitator role is of crucial importance. Again, it is important to keep an overview of the network of people who are involved on either side of the relationship dyad. The gam will have to ensure that enough one-on-one relationships are being built across, and even within, the two companies. As the facilitator for building new relationships, the seniority of the gam can often help local account managers to reach the right people within the local parts of the global account. When the Xerox gam for ABB travels to any of the local regions where Xerox has a relationship with ABB, he always plans a visit to the local ABB office together with the local account manager. His seniority and the fact that he is from 'out-of-town' often gets him access to people who would be out of reach for the local account manager. This way he not only keeps a direct eye on the situation at the local level, but he also helps the local account manager build a relationship that can be used when the gam is back in his HQ country.

---

**Ogilvy & Mather's Use of Gam Location**

The location of the gam makes a big difference to the relationship between the supplier and the global customer. In the relationship between advertising agency Ogilvy & Mather and BP, the main communications traditionally went through O&M's Frankfurt office. When Ogilvy became BP's global agency, however, the global account manager decided to move the business to another office because of expected developments within the future of the BP account that could be handled better there. O&M moved even the communications with BP's parts business, which was located near Frankfurt.

---

## Negotiator

The negotiator role is a small, though important, part of the responsibilities of the gam.[5] The gam generally constructs any umbrella contracts, or possibly even a complete global contract for the account, and is, therefore, the right person to negotiate on behalf of the supplier and its entire group of local account managers with a particular global customer.

In the case of an umbrella contract the basic terms and conditions are negotiated at the global level by the gam and a global representative of the customer. The details surrounding the specific actual purchases will be negotiated by the local account managers at the local level, taking the global umbrella contract into consideration.

With a complete global contract, the total global purchases and all the related terms and conditions are negotiated at the global level. This can be difficult as the actual cost or price of the goods or services purchased might not be similar in all regions. The supplier might choose to compensate certain regions for these purchases, or to give the customer a base price that is complemented by a country specific price addition, depending on real costs. For example, DMV International adds to the negotiated global base price a country-specific surcharge for transport and handling costs.

Even though negotiations are very important to the profitability of the account, they will take only a small part of a gam's time. Global negotiations typically take place once a year, perhaps with some interim changes if the situation requires it. Even including preparations for these negotiation meetings, the time spent on negotiations is very short compared to that spent on finding new opportunities, building relationships, managing communications and so on. Therefore, it is wrong to perceive a gam as an 'upgraded sales-manager'. Obviously, the actual sell will often be part of the gam's role, but the position is so much more than just that. At Marsh & McLellan, a leading risk and insurance firm, the global relationship manager is seen as having worldwide authority and, therefore, the one person who is able to take a global stance that might at times be against the sensibility of a client that is strongly regionally based. This makes him the ideal person to negotiate certain issues on a worldwide basis.

## Ambassador

The gam should be the first point of contact for a customer to the global supplier. He or she is an ambassador for the company to the account company, and in some cases he or she will, like a political ambassador, be based at the account company. When Schlumberger, a French oil and gas engineering company, and BG Group, a British energy company, started working together in a global relationship, the Schlumberger gam actually started by sharing an office at BG Group headquarters with his BG counterpart. The Schlumberger gam works two or three days a week from his BG office, making him a true ambassador of his company to BG. His physical presence at BG headquarters creates easier access for starting projects and discussing problems and issues. He automatically gains more knowledge about the customer and can react immediately with a custom-made response.

Not all customers, however, are happy to have their suppliers on site. A situation like this demands a high level of trust between the companies, and the issue of cost will need to be discussed, but eventually this situation can lead to many benefits for both parties. Most suppliers will not have the opportunity to have such a level of physical presence at their customers. However, a certain level of physical closeness is still desirable. Often, this is obtained by locating the gam in the country where the headquarters or largest operations of the account company are based. This creates a certain closeness and convenience in visiting the account company, and will also help in understanding the cultural background of the customer. Furthermore, the gam needs to be an ambassador for the global account within his or her own company, and to build an extensive network to serve the rest of the global account. As an international account manager for Schneider Electric said:

The main task of an international account manager is the development of a network that will enable him to bring the value of the whole company of 64,000 people to the service of the customer. When I travel to France or the US I spend a lot of time in the engineering centres meeting engineers and software developers—the very people who are crucial in delivering a customized solution to the client. I get to know them and their capacities and they get to understand how I can connect them to customers. For example, while I was in Canada working to expand our opportunities with a Swiss-based company I added several days to my trip to introduce myself to key Schneider manufacturing managers in the US Midwest.[6]

However the company should choose to facilitate the ambassador role of the gam, it is clear that the latter has to have regular visits to both the customer's and his or her company's own foreign subsidiaries. The gam needs to create a large network of relationships with many different employees both internally and with the customer. This way he or she will make the gam position the first point of contact for any issue relating to the global relationship.

## Politician

The politician role of the gam is especially difficult to pin down. It mainly concerns influencing people. The gam should have the power to make things happen both at the account company and at his or her own company. The gam should have influence with the decision-makers in both companies. But in the case of global accounts, knowing who are the real decision-makers can sometimes can be difficult, as it might not be determined by the typical management hierarchic. Having sufficient knowledge of the customer's formal organization is important, but it is at least as important to get some feel for the informal processes in the customer's organization. A gam can use awareness of the internal politics within the customer company to the account's advantage. Indeed, a gam can analyze the internal politics and formal organization to create an organizational map of the customer, in order to use the network in a more efficient way. This way the gam will be able to directly influence the people who are important for the decision-making process.

At his or her own company, the politician gam should ensure that relevant senior managers are engaged in the gam process where appropriate. As the gam often does not have all the authority to get things done in a hierarchical way, he or she must be adept at achieving objectives via the use of persuasion. Senior managers are vital in this process, as they often *do* have the formal authority that is needed. In his relationship with supplier Royal Dutch Shell, the contract manager for Wärtsilä, a Finnish power generation and marine propulsion manufacturer, realizes the importance of the politician role of the Shell gam, '*We don't want an account manager who is weak*', he says, '*We want an account manager with power within his own organization*'. In the past, local networks did not always accept the global account manager as being the leading force in the relationship with Wärtsilä, and went their own way. This situation improved when Shell appointed a new gam. Shell also made some changes in the set up, but a lot of the improvements came from the gam having the political skills that are needed to control such a large account.

# Key Characteristics and Skills

As the position of gam is very complex, companies need a specific breed of managers in this position. The desired characteristics and skills for a gam will differ in each company, and even each account situation, but in general there is a set of skills can be that most companies like to see in their gams. A survey of over 200 companies by the Strategic Account Management Association (SAMA) and the Sales Research Trust (SRT), identified ten competencies of a gam in descending order of importance:[7]

1. communication skills;
2. global team leadership and management skills;
3. business and financial acumen;
4. relationship management skills;
5. strategic vision and planning capabilities;
6. problem solving capabilities;
7. cultural empathy;
8. selling skills both internally and externally;
9. industry and market knowledge of the company and the customer;
10. product/service knowledge.

The desired competencies, added with account-specific desired characteristics would create a rather impressive list of requirements in a job vacancy advertisement. Many companies state that it is hard to find people who fit all these requirements and, therefore, they often have to choose people who need to grow into the position and to develop the required skills after obtaining the position of gam. Even though knowledge of the industry and product are respectively number 9 and 10 on the SAMA/SRT list above, these two points often lead companies to choose an existing employee to fill the gam position.

An existing employee has the benefit of knowing the products, the industry and sometimes, even to some extent, the account. Furthermore, an insider will have the headstart of knowing other people in the different departments of their organization, which will make it easier to create the necessary network of relationships. Obviously, an outside candidate for a gam position could have competencies that far outweigh the benefits of choosing an existing employee. Especially when a company is able to hire, as the gam, a former employee of the customer, there will be similar benefits to appointing an existing employee; but the benefits materialize at the other end of the relationship dyad. Shell's gam for Wärtsilä is a former Wärtsilä employee, who is based close to his former employer's headquarters in Finland. The relationship contact manager at Wärtsilä explained how pleased he was with having an ex-colleague as gam for his company. 'This person speaks our language, not just the Finnish language, but also the company language. He understands what is important for us, and that gives him the opportunity to offer us a customer value proposition that is exactly what we need.' On the other hand, Regus, a leading, global, office rental company uses mainly home-grown gams, as it finds it hard to recruit the right people from outside the company.

Even though it is not always possible to find a gam with all the necessary competencies, some characteristics are particularly interesting when looking at the position of gam, and will be discussed in the rest of this chapter:

- cultural sensitivity;
- flexibility;
- location;
- seniority;
- experience.

## Cultural Sensitivity

Cultures differ not only between countries but also between companies.[8] Due to the border-crossing nature of the position of the gam, both in a geographic and corporate sense, the gam needs some feeling for the cultures involved and a high level of cultural empathy. The gam has to be a person who is at ease working within different cultures and who has the knowledge to handle this in an effective way. Knowledge about the cultures in different countries where the customer operates can make the difference between having a strong relationship and facing a lot of frustration in trying to make a deal but not getting there. Initially, it is most important to have thorough knowledge about the culture of the customer's home country as this culture will to some extent influence the culture of the account itself. Especially when companies work with a large number of expatriates from their home country, the home country culture can have a major influence. A gam serving German technology company Bosch commented that because this customer has many German expatriates at middle and high level management positions in its 50 countries of operations, there is a distinct German culture in the company, which means that agreements should always be observed and work needs to be done thoroughly. So a gam who deals with Bosch needs to be sensitive to this culture, and be able to help the local contacts of the supplier adhere to this German culture, as it might clash with the supplier's own local culture.

## Key Choices

### Flexibility

In order to be able to seize all opportunities that are available with the global account a gam needs to be flexible. Most gams spend a considerable amount of their time outside their home country, especially when they are not based in the customer's headquarter country. If a candidate gam is not willing to travel this frequently, he or she should seriously reconsider applying for the position. Another form of flexibility is being able to stay as a constant factor for the account, even during times of organizational change.

In terms of length of tenure, it is obviously wise not to change the gam for a particular account too often. Many companies say five years is the period they aim to have the same gam on an account. Most companies undergo regular organizational changes, but the customer will have no interest in the internal changes of its supplier. A gam needs to ensure that the supplier's internal changes do not influence too much the way of doing business with the customer.

### Location

The geographic location of the gam is an important strategic decision. Even though the account is supposed to be global, there will be locations that are more important than others and the country of the customer's headquarters will be a particularly important place of having local contact. Some companies do not have the luxury of having local activity and enough sales support in all possible countries, and they have to fall back on having all their gams in one or two central locations. Most companies, however, try to have the gam located as close as possible to the customer's HQ country. This has the benefit of it being easier to have frequent personal contact with the customers global relationship managers. The downside of this is that in some cases the gam might lose direct connection with and, therefore, influence on the central resources of his or her own company. Hewlett-Packard bridges this gap by installing two versions of the gam. Firstly, HP locates the key gam at the headquarters country of the customer, and secondly, HP has a headquarters account manager (HAM) who is responsible for representing the global account at its headquarters in California. This way, there is a good balance between having a local presence with the global customer and having power and influence at the supplier at a central level. Sometimes, economics influences the choice of location. Standard Chartered, a major UK-based international bank, has for cost reasons and because of its Asian heritage, located many of its gams that serve European customers in Singapore.

## Seniority

As a gam will have to influence other departments and colleagues without having actual authority over them, it is a benefit to give the gam some level of seniority. Having a certain level of experience and natural pre-eminence will make it easier for the gam to get other employees on board if something has to be arranged for the global account, even without being their direct line manager. In many cases the desired track record of successful account manager, or experience with the account that are required for this position will ensure the chosen candidate has some seniority, but it helps to keep in mind why this is important. Another reason why seniority is preferable is consideration of the turnover time for gams for any one account. As mentioned, most companies prefer to have a gam in place for each account for approximately five years. Managers at the start of their career mostly aim to change positions much more often than that in order to climb the career ladder and to gain experience. A senior manager will be more likely to stay in the position for the desired five years and to work on the long term development of the relationship, and less likely to be engaged in pursuing more short-term career goals, like the Xerox gam for Volkswagen. With 25 years of Volkswagen related experience under his belt, he has earned the knowledge and seniority that is needed to deal with such a big and important client, and he is less likely to change positions within a short time, than might be a younger less experienced colleague.

## Experience

Experience and the background of the gam is very important in the success of the account management. Even though the gam is essentially an account manager, a sales background is not necessarily required. As mentioned earlier, the actual sales responsibilities are only a small part of the total gam job description. Although many sales skills—such as negotiation skills, and business and financial acumen—will be required to successfully fill the gam position, other attributes might be just as important. Experience of the gam within the industry of the account company or, even better, at the account company itself can be especially beneficial in building the knowledge-base the gam needs to manage the global account successfully. For example, Xerox sees suitable experience and background as an important part of a desired gam characteristics. Xerox's current gam for Volkswagen has been working with and for Volkswagen in different functions and companies for 25 years. This gives him a lot of valuable knowledge about the account's company culture, industry characteristics and key employees. Another example of Xerox's preference for a suitable background is the gam for the British global bank HSBC. His background is not in sales but in finance. His knowledge about the financial industry made him attractive as an account manager for financial institutions. This executive first had a brief stint as UK account manager for Lloyds and then took on the position as gam for HSBC.

---

**Best Practices**

When thinking about the necessary qualities a gam should possess, managers need to focus on more than just excellent sales skills. The gam is not an upgraded sales manager and realizing that some non-sales qualities may be far more important will help in finding the right man or woman for the job. Some best practices with respect to gams are to:

- define a set of criteria for the gam, based not only on the situation of the company itself, but also on the specific global account;
- realize it may be impossible to find someone who meets all the criteria, but aim to find someone who will be able to grow into them;
- both your own company, the account itself and the account company's industry are good hunting grounds to find a gam with the necessary background and knowledge;
- aim to have a gam stay in the position for approximately five years, to ensure continuity and long term benefits for the relationship;
- choose the location of the gam carefully, if possible close to the central operations of the global account company;
- the gam should be a loyal teamplayer, who is not working for short term personal gain but for the long term success of the global account.

---

# Notes

1. K. Wilson (1999) 'Developing Global Account Management Programmes: Observations from a GAM Panel Presentation', *Thexis*, 4.
2. 'Schneider Electric Global Account Management', IMD-3-0940, European Case Clearing House, Cranfield, UK, 2000.
3. Considerable research has explored the nature of boundary-spanning and boundary-spanning roles. The boundary spanning concept was introduced in classic studies by Adams (1976), Aldrich and Hecker (1977: 217–30), and Starbuck (1976). Research in labour relations (Friedman and Podolny 1992: 28–41), banking (Tyler and Stanley 2001: 246–60), marketing (Singh and Rhoads 1991: 328–38), and research and development (Keller and Holland 1975: 388–93) has further described the complex nature of boundary-spanning activities and their effect on the individuals involved (Johlke and Duhan 2001: 87–101; Keller and Holland, 1975; Singh and Rhoads, 1991) and on organizational outcomes (Tyler and Stanley, 2001). See J. Adams, 'The Structure and Dynamics of Behaviour in Organizational

Boundary Roles', in, M. D. Dunette (ed.) (1976) *Handbook of Industrial and Organizational Psychology*. Chicago: Rand McNally; H. Aldrich and D. Herker (1977) 'Boundary Spanning Roles and Organization Structure', *Academy of Management Review*, Vol. 2, April, pp. 217–30; W. H. Starbuck, 'Organizations and Their Environments', in M. D. Dunette (ed.) (1976) *Handbook of Industrial and Organizational Psychology*. Chicago: Rand McNally; R. A. Friedman and J. Podolny (1992) 'Differentiation of Boundary Spanning Roles: Labour Negotiations and Implications for Role', *Administrative Science Quarterly*, Vol. 37, January pp. 28–41; K. Tyler and E. Stanley (2001) 'Corporate Banking: The Strategic Impact of Boundary Spanner Effectiveness', *International Journal of Bank Marketing*, Vol. 19: June, pp. 246–60; J. Singh and G. Rhoads (1991) 'Boundary Role Ambiguity in Marketing-Oriented Positions: A Multidimensional, Multifaceted Operationalisation', *Journal of Marketing Research*, Vol. 28: April, pp. 328–38; R. T. Keller and W. F. Holland (1975) 'Boundary Spanning Roles in a Research and Development Organization: An Empirical Investigation', *Academy of Management Journal*, Vol. 18, April, pp. 388–93; M. C. Johlke and D. F. Duhan (2001) 'Supervisor Communication Practices and Boundary Spanner Role Ambiguity', *Journal of Managerial Issues*, Vol. 13, January, pp. 87–101.

4. Previous research has identified various types and differentiations of boundary-spanning roles and their relationships to the environment (Ancona and Caldwell 1997; Brown and Schwab, 1984). For example, Aldrich and Herker (1977) identified two distinct functions of boundary spanning roles: information processing and external representation of the organization to outsiders. Other researchers added additional features, such as monitoring, scanning, and gate keeping, to the information processing activities (Brown and Schwab, 1984). In a longitudinal study of labour negotiations, Friedman and Podolny (1992) found that over time, representation and gatekeeper roles—although often considered to be performed by a single individual—became differentiated in different individuals. Similarly, advice and trust interactions could be handled by different individuals (Friedman and Podolny, 1992). See D. G. Ancona and D. F. Caldwell, 'Making Teamwork Work: Boundary Management in Product Development Teams', in M. L. Tushman and P. Anderson (ed.) (1997) *Managing Strategic Innovation and Change*. New York: Oxford University Press; W. B. Brown and R. C. Schwab (1984) 'Boundary-Spanning Activities in Electronic Firms', *IEEE Transactions of Engineering Management*, Vol.31, April, pp. 105–12; H. Aldrich and D. Herker (1977) 'Boundary Spanning Roles and Organization Structure', *Academy of Management Review*, Vol. 2, April, pp. 217–30; R. A. Friedman and J. Podolny (1992) 'Differentiation of Boundary Spanning Roles: Labour Negotiations and Implications for Role', *Administrative Science Quarterly*, Vol. 37, January, pp. 28–41.

5. For more discussion on global negotiations see M. Brannen and J. Salk (2004) 'Partnering Across Borders: Negotiating Organisational Culture in a German-Japanese Joint Venture', *Human Relations*, December, 53: 451–87; S. Cavusgil, P. Ghauri and M. Agarwal (2002) *Doing Business in Emerging Markets: Entry and Negotiation*

*Strategies*. Thousand Oaks: Sage; J. Brett and T. Okumura (1998) 'Inter- and Intra-Cultural Negotiations: US and Japanese Negotiators', *Academy of Management Journal*, October, 41: 495–510; J. Brett, D. Shapiro and A. Lytle (1998) 'Breaking the Bonds of Reciprocity in Negotions', *Academy of Management Journal*, August, 41: 410–24; J. Graham, A. Mintu and W. Rodgers (1994) 'Explorations of Negotiation Behaviours in Ten Foreign Cultures Using a Model Developed in the United States', *Management Science*, January, 40: 72–95; S. Weiss (1994) 'Negotiating with Romans', *Sloan Management Review*, October, 35: 859–74; S. Weiss (1993) 'Analysis of Complex Negotiations in International Business', *Organization Science*, April, 4: 269–300; S. Kale and J. Barnes (1992) 'Understanding the Domain of Cross-National Buyer-Seller Interactions', *Journal of International Business Studies*, January, 23: 101–32; R. Tung (1991) 'Handshakes Across the Sea: Cross-Cultural Negotiating for Business Success', *Organizational Dynamics*, October, 19: 30–40; R. Tung (1984) 'How to Negotiate with the Japanese', *California Management Review*, April, 26: 62–77.

6. Fritz Keller.
7. K. Wilson, S. Croom, T. Millman and D. C. Weilbaker. (2000) 'The Global Account Management Study Research Report', sponsored by SAMA and the Sales Research Trust.
8. The role of culture is a widely researched topic in the management literature. See, for example, Geert Hofstede (1980) *Culture's Consequences*. Beverly Hills, CA: Sage; Geert Hofstede (1991) *Culture and Organisations*. London: McGraw-Hill; Y. Weber, O. Shenkar and A. Raveh (1996) 'National and Corporate Cultural Fit in Mergers/Acquisitions: An Exploratory Study', *Management Science*, October, 42: 1215–27; H. Triandis (1994) *Culture and Social Behaviour*. New York: McGraw-Hill; M. Erez and C. Earley (1993) *Culture, Self-Identity and Work*. New York: Oxford University Press; S. Sackman (1992) 'Cultures and Sub-Cultures: An Analysis of Organizational Knowledge', *Administrative Science Quarterly*, January, 37: 140–61; N. Adler and J. Graham (1989) 'Cross-Cultural Interaction: The International Comparison Fallacy?' *Journal of International Business Studies*, October, 13: 515–37; S. Schneider (1988) 'National vs. Corporate Culture: Implications for Human Resource Management', *Human Resource Management*, March, 27: 231–46; A. Jaeger (1986) 'Organizational Development and National Culture: Where's the Fit?', *Academy of Management Review*, January, 11: 178–90.

# 7    Building the Global Account Team

The global account manager for our Volkswagen account is a German national. He lives in Germany, reports partly to the German country manager and may well go back to a purely national job. So I have to be careful in how I integrate him into the global account team.

(Director of global accounts at a US multinational company)

The previous chapter examined the global account manager (gam). But as the relationship with a major account will be more intense than one person can handle, there will always be more employees involved in the relationship besides the gam. The way these employees are linked with each other, both formally and informally, means that they form the global account team (gat). Such teams differ a lot from company to company. Some companies will not have a formal team at all, and rely on the gam for all communication and coordination. Other companies might choose a structure in which the global account team consists of employees who are fully dedicated to the account, and who report to the gam. The type of employees who are regarded as part of the global team can also differ. Whereas some companies look only to sales contacts for these relationships, others have a broader view of global relationships and include, for example, R&D and supply chain management contacts in their global account team.

If a company wants to follow the integrated approach of managing global customers and, therefore, recognize that the relationship with the customer is more than just commercial, it needs to take a formal approach to forming the global account team, and ideally look further than the various sales departments around the world to find members for the global account team.

This chapter discusses the global account team, and focuses on the following issues;[1]

- responsibilities of the global account team;
- who should be selected as members of the global account team;
- organizational structure;
- the team's place in the organization.

# Responsibilities of the Global Account Team

Although the gam holds overall responsibility for the account, the account team has its own important responsibilities in the success of the account. The roles that the gat members play differ, depending on the organization form of the team, but some general responsibilities will be present in most companies. These responsibilities include:

- locating opportunities;
- planning for the global account;
- managing information and communication;
- strengthening the relationship network.

## Locating Opportunities

The global account team members are the eyes and ears of the global account manager and, therefore, have an important role in helping the gam to locate opportunities in the global account. Even though it should be the global account manager who has the best total overview of the global account situation, specific team members can have better inside information on specific parts of the customer's organization. For example, local account managers will have a better view of opportunities within their regions, and a research manager will have better insight about the innovations the customer is working on with which the supplier might be able to help.

In order to locate opportunities, the global account team members need actively to look for them. It is important to keep a clear and open mind when talking to account contacts and to regard all information as useful. Although not all identified opportunities may have a high priority in the global scheme of things, this way the global account manager will get a good overview of the opportunities available so he or she can determine what opportunities will help achieve a stronger and more profitable relationship with the account. The opportunities chosen to be pursued should be clear to all global account team members.

---

**IBM's Global Account Team**

Within IBM the global account team responsibilities are given to very senior people. The global account teams are given three-year targets, instead of the usual one-year target, which recognizes the long term importance of the global relationship over short term sales results. IBM's gat includes a specialist team that deals with global data gathering, as this is one of the things that can be particularly difficult in global accounts. The global account team members are dedicated to the global account. With this system the gat members take prime responsibility

---

for locating global opportunities within the account, In contrast, a local account manager might not realize a global opportunity, as he or she is too preoccupied with the day-to-day sales to the local part of the global account company.

## Global Account Planning

The global account team must assist the global account manager in making the strategic, tactical and operational plans for the account. Input from the different regions and functions are vital for realistic account planning. The global account plan is the place to record all the objectives and actions that are important for the development of the relationship and business with the account.

The global account plan is a good tool to set out long term intentions and to follow the targets reached. Firstly, the global account team needs to help the gam determine what objectives can realistically be achieved and in what time scale. This will often be based on the opportunities that the account team has helped to identify. Secondly, an action plan needs to make clear how these objectives will be achieved, what strategies and tactics will be used, who is responsible for them and who needs to perform what actions to achieve them. The global account plan needs to be a guideline for all team members.

### DMV International's GROW Plan

In the global account teams for food ingredients company DMV International, every member has its own 'GROW' (Goal, Role, Obligation and Workplan), which lays out the specific goals and tasks for that specific gat member. The GROW is updated when necessary, and the workplan part will be checked and updated every meeting. The GROW helps the team members to know exactly what is expected of them, and what they can expect from other team members. It is a good tool to keep the team on track and working towards the same objectives.

## Information and Communication

Managing information and communication are two major tasks of the global account team, working in a two-way stream.[2] Firstly, the team members need to make sure that the global account manager gets all available information in a convenient format. The global account manager needs to develop an information base on the account and the global account team should support this task. Secondly, the team will be the communication channel through which the work with the global account reaches the other departments and regions in the company. In their role of information channel towards the rest of the organization, the team members act as ambassadors for the account within their own organization, to ensure they have the relevant support for specific global account projects. Most companies have some sort of internal information system in place, but a good information *process* is needed to ensure that the system will be used to its full potential. Some discipline is needed if the information is to go into the system in the first place for others to use. This discipline can be enforced by company processes. For example, the local sales people in IBM will get the necessary support to take on projects with an account only if all the information about these projects is present in the information system. This requirement forces the employees to use the system. Therefore, the system is more complete, which in turn motivates more people to use the system as a source of information.

## Strengthening the Relationship Network

As the relationship with the global account will flourish best when there is a good relationship network to build on, strengthening this network is an important task for the global account team.[3] When a company aims to have a truly integrated global account management, it should not have a bow-tie relationship structure, in which the only major relationship contact is between the global account manager and one other person on the customer's side, for example, a purchasing manager. It is advisable to aim for a 'diamond structure' network of relationships in which many different people on the supplier's side have contacts with many different people on the customer's side. Preferably, this means more than just local relations between the local account managers and their counterparts at the local customer company. In a truly integrated approach to global account management, there should be relationships formed between numbers of the global functions of the two companies. For example, when R&D employees of the supplier form a stronger contact with their counterparts at the global customer, this can lead to better insight being gained into opportunities where the supplier can provide added value to the customer, as an R&D employee will have more knowledge than a global account manager about the actual usage options of the supplier's products and services.

# Members of the Global Account Team

The choice of members in the global account team will differ from company to company. Whereas some companies have a sales approach, other companies take a cross-functional approach. Some companies even have the luxury of having a global account team that is completely dedicated to the account. Members of the global account team often include:

- global account manager;
- local account managers;
- cross-functional representatives;
- executive sponsor;
- administrative assistant.

## Global Account Manager

As the person responsible for the global account, the global account manager (gam) cannot be excluded from any global account team. He or she will usually be the formal or informal leader of the team, and in companies where no formal global account team structure exists, he or she will be the initiator in forming one. Especially in structures where the global account team members are not completely dedicated to the global account, the gam will be the strongest link to the global account. Furthermore, the gam has the largest stake in the successful functioning of the global account team, and will, therefore, be driven to support the team members in reaching their individual goals with the account. In this last sense, the gam acts in some ways as a coach for the team members, who helps them get the relevant contacts within the account company, who keeps them on the path that leads to the long term strategy goals, and who helps them stay motivated to work hard for the company's success at this particular account.

Ideally, the gam has some say in who will join him or her in the global account team, but this is not always possible, especially in large global account teams that are formed from national sales personnel. Even though the gam sometimes is allowed to give feedback in the local account managers' annual reviews, it is very rare for the gam to be consulted in the actual hiring of a new local account manager for the account. But companies should start thinking of getting the gam's advice on the selection of local representatives for a global account, as this will be important not only for the local relationship with the account but also for the total global account relationship.

### Wunderman's Multi-Location Teams

Wunderman, a leading marketing communications company that is part of the WPP group, has installed a central international client management group, which is a physically proximate unit consisting of all account managing directors (AMDs) and all other account staff who are involved in the international coordination of the account. The AMD serves as the general manager of the client business, representing the company on a global, regional or functional basis. Responsibilities include directing the operation, being accountable for all client activities, developing the optimum client organization structure and growing business with the client.

Although Wunderman offers global services to its clients, it also puts a strong emphasis on using local inputs in order to better address local requirements and variations. That approach suits the many clients who prefer to buy services not from the cheapest country but from the country in which they are operating. But it is not always possible to source the best resources locally. To avoid this constraint, Wunderman has found a way to provide the highest levels of service to its clients by applying a local/central team focus to its projects. This makes the location of resources irrelevant as the project is managed locally. For example, London-based clients can expect to have a dedicated London-based account manager who coordinates one type of work (e.g., interactive marketing) in Zurich or Amsterdam, and another type (e.g., creative) in Italy. The result is a company that draws cost and quality advantages from this local/central team style of working.

## Local Account Managers

The level of involvement of local account managers in the global account team depends on the type of team that has been formed. If this is a large sales oriented team, usually all local account managers that have some sort of connection with the global account will be involved, as in the virtual global account teams of Xerox. For example, the Xerox global account team for engineering company ABB is a large virtual one that includes more than 300 people working with the ABB account. This team works together mainly via Xerox's Docushare information system, as having team meetings with 300 people is difficult and has no real added value. If a company works with smaller focused account teams not all local account managers will be involved and necessary communications with the local level will be dealt with by other means. This way the account team can work as a team more efficiently, and the local account managers that are included will have the opportunity to get extra value from their position in the team.

The local account manager is the main link to the account company at the local level, and he or she is responsible for gaining insight into the local developments of the account and implementing the global strategy on the local level. Next to information about the local activity of the account, the local account manager will often also be able to give greater insight into local competitive activity and local industry developments. Apart from being the local ambassador for the global team, the membership of the local account manager in a cross-functional team can be very beneficial to the local situation, as it will be easier to resolve operational problems at the local level with the help of the cross-functional global representatives of other departments, like R&D and supply chain management. Wunderman has identified distinct but interdependent responsibilities for the local managers and the international managers.

Local management's prime responsibility is to recruit, coach and manage the in-market resources to deliver to clients, whereas the international client management's prime responsibility is to manage the overall client relationship to maximize profitability.

## Cross-Functional Representatives

When a company wants to manage its global customers in an integrated approach, it helps to have cross-functional representatives in the global account team. These cross-functional representatives can be employees from any department within the organization that has relevant links with the customer. They will act as supporting members for specific projects and problems with the customer that have a link to their function, but they can be a lot more valuable to the global account team. As the cross-functional representatives will form relationships with their counterparts and other employees at the customer company, they will be a valuable source of function-specific information and insight about the customer's situation. For example, when a supplier's R&D employee is asked to help with an innovation project at the customer company, he or she will be able to gain more information about the development process at the customer company, which in turn will help the supplier to make better value propositions to the customer in other areas. Shell has a cross-functional team for its relationship with Wärtsilä, a Finnish power generation and marine propulsion manufacturer. For example, Shell's R&D staff are very much involved with Wärtsilä about new products and to get approvals. Therefore, Shell maintains a central group of R&D people located in Germany which is involved in the global account team. This R&D group develops new oils and has the opportunity to test them together with Wärtsilä at one of their plants in France.

---

**The Power of Partnership is Responsiveness**

From prompt answers to timely loss recovery, the essence of active partnership is action. Anticipating and responding to the ever-evolving risk management needs of customers and agents reflects our commitment to total quality of service. A commitment that distinguishes the power of our partnership from ordinary business relationships ...

To help you handle your risks, we have instituted the Account Team: an internationally experienced expert in risk management leads a group of insurance, financial and technical specialists. This team is dedicated to your industry and will ensure continuity of service for your company. You'd expect that from a global leader who's an expert in change. Both wanted and unwanted.

*Source*: Zurich Insurance Group, extracts from two advertisements in *The Economist* magazine, 1997.

---

## Executive Sponsor

Not all companies have an executive sponsorship programme for their global account management, and the companies that do will not always include the executive sponsors in the global account team. The executive sponsor should be a high level executive within the supplier's organization who is responsible for developing high level relationships with the global customer. In Hewlett-Packard, for example, all the top executives from the CEO downward play such roles, and are called 'assigned executives'. Next to his or her executive contacts with the account company, the executive sponsor will also function as part of an escalation mechanism, and will help resolve issues that occur between different departments or geographical areas. Global account management is prone to barriers and resistance in the organization, as global activities might demand local sacrifices and the global account manager does not always have enough authority to enforce this. As the executive sponsor has both a global scope and enough seniority to make things happen he or she is the perfect escalation point. Even if the executive sponsor is part of the global account team he or she will generally not be involved in all operational activities of the team, but will be predominantly involved in the long term strategy planning of the account to ensure it is in line with the strategy and mission of the company.

## Administrative Assistant

The administrative or global account assistant can be a very valuable addition to the global account team, but not many companies have actually created the global account assistant position within their organizations. The global account assistant is responsible for all the administrative tasks surrounding the management of the global customer. These tasks vary from writing the internal global account newsletter to making monthly progress reports. Often, the global account assistant will be dedicated to more than one account, but companies need to take care not to 'spread the global account assistant too thin', as this will diminish the value of the position. DMV International assigns one assistant for every five accounts. The global account assistant is responsible for the documentation of all information on the global account. He or she will make reports both for internal employees and for the account company. He or she acts as the main information manager and will send relevant documents, such as account highlights and financial reports, to all employees involved. As the same DMV global account assistant operates for five different accounts there are advantages of experience, synergy and best practice sharing. Another company that uses the global account assistant position is document management company Xerox. There, not all global accounts have a global account assistant but in the accounts that do, the global account assistant functions as a sort of personal assistant for the gam, organizing his or her meetings, doing the administrative tasks and so on.

# Organizational Structure of the Account Team

In most companies, the organizational structure of the account team depends on that of the company itself. In general, all global account teams within one company will have a similar set up, with some customization for particular accounts. This customization comes partly from the membership of the global account team, as this should reflect the geographical spread, or operational focal points of the customer. In general, most companies use one of three main structures:

- formal direct global account team;
- formal indirect global account team;
- informal global account team.

## Formal Direct Global Account Team

A formal direct global account team has most of its members dedicated 100 percent to the global account, and has a direct reporting line to the global account manager. In these cases the global account manager is often called the 'global account director' and the global account is managed as a quasi business unit. In this form of global account team the global team members often have a specific role with regard to the global account, such as 'planning director' or 'financial director'. This organization structure of a formal account team means that only a portion of all staff involved with the global account are members of the global account team. This gap can be overcome by using local account teams in addition to the formal direct account team, the latter often being called the 'core team'.

The formal direct global account team structure can exist only when the business with global accounts is large enough to justify this intensive form of management. This is often the case within industries that concentrate on service, in which labour intensive relationships with customers are built.

## Formal Indirect Team

A formal indirect team structure has a formal team all of whose team members also have other functions within the organization, and report to their own line managers rather than to the global account manager. A general structure of this form of team is the global account manager as the leader of the team, complemented by a cross-section of local account managers and representatives of other departments, ideally between four and eight people in total. The team members will not always be 100 percent dedicated to the global account, but might have responsibilities for other global accounts, or have other quite different responsibilities.

The formal indirect team will have frequent meetings in which the progress with specific projects with the global account is discussed, and new opportunities are explored. The formal indirect team is a good organization structure for any company that can not justify managing a global account as a separate business unit, but still wants to have a lot of hands on attention given to the account. The formal indirect team is small enough to feel responsible for the success of the supplier at the account company, which will lead to feelings of 'ownership'. Hence, team members will act as ambassadors for the global account in their own functions or regions, and will ensure that the global account gets the focus it deserves from all who might contribute and not just from the global account manager. It is possible to expand the formal indirect team with extra members when needed, perhaps in the case of a specific project that demands extra attention from a specific department that was not originally represented in the team.

---

**DMV International's Teams**

DMV International works with a structure of a 'core team' and a 'surround team'. The core team has, in general, four or five people from different departments, including the gam. The combination of departments represented is different for every global account, as the makeup of the team must reflect the focus that DMV has for the specific account. Departments that often have representatives in the global account team include supply chain management, R&D, marketing and production. Next to the core team for every account, DMV maintains a surround team. This surround team is less formal and is used only for specific issues. For example, if the core team for an account does not have a supply chain management representative, but a specific project comes up that demands supply chain expertise, the supply chain person from the surround team is asked to join the core team meetings for the duration of the specific project.

---

## Informal Team

The informal team, often called a 'virtual team', is the least cohesive structure for a global account team.[4] In the informal team, all employees who are involved with the global account are team members. Often in this structure, the majority of team members have sales roles in the different countries where the two (supplier and customer) companies have relationships. In this structure the gam still has responsibility for performance of the account, but little or no authority over the members of the informal team. Indeed, the gam has to ensure that he or she knows exactly who all these potential team members are and how best to reach and influence them.

Some companies aim to have the informal team meet face-to-face at least once a year, as in the case of Unilever's global account team for Wal-Mart. This Unilever team comprises 200 people, of whom only five report directly to the vice president (VP) Wal-Mart, as Unilever calls its global account manager. A set of communication tools enables the VP to manage the team members worldwide. Global meetings are held in which about 50 people, mainly account personnel, work together with Wal-Mart to set foundation objectives for the following year. Consistent strategies, objectives and operation guidelines are used and sent out to all personnel involved. A global website enables people to get the latest information and data. In the Unilever–Wal-Mart structure, a local account team has been set up in every country where the two companies work together. There is, typically, a local team leader who runs each local team, and who works closely together with the VP Wal-Mart. This structure enables the global account team to be strategically consistent with the customer within the different countries.

The greatest benefit of having an informal team is that it can be set up and changed however the company and the gam see fit at the time. However, as informal teams tend to be large, it is hard to keep track of all that happens, and it is more difficult for the gam to have a major influence on team members. High employee turnover does not help in forming a consistent team. As Unilever's VP Wal-Mart says: 'Every year at the annual team meeting, half the people there are new. I have to keep explaining the strategy and mission for the account'.

# Place in the Organization of the Global Account Team

When the global account team has a formal and direct structure, it is necessary to think about the appropriate positioning of the team within the total company organization. This is one of the organization issues where companies can take the extra step in managing their global customers on an integrated approach. As with the organization of the total GAM programme, it is important not just to superimpose the global account team structure on the existing organization, but to find a way to integrate it with other departments within the organization. Initially, global account management often develops from within the marketing and sales department, but this does not mean that would be the best location for the global account team. Having a separate global account team organization close to or within the existing selling or commercial organization can lead to friction when the global account team matures. Furthermore, the integrated approach asks for a cross-functional team that is not solely focused on commercial aspects of the account. The formal *direct* global account team should be positioned in the chosen global account organization as described in Chapters 3 and 4. This will often be a 'Control GAM' or 'Separate GAM'. These organization forms lend themselves particularly well to the intensive account management that a formal direct team provides to a customer. For example, IBM has a completely separate business unit for global accounts, and the global account teams sit within this separate unit. This means there is absolutely no friction between local and global interests when operating the global account team. IBM can justify this expensive structure as the customers that are served from within the global account organization are large enough to support this level of dedicated staff.

If the global account team is formal but *indirect* there are more opportunities, as there is more flexibility in positioning. One thing that should be taken care of when working with a formal indirect global account team is that the employees who are official members of the global account team have time allocated for their work with the team, and are rewarded accordingly. Their work in the global account team should be part of their individual annual goals. Therefore, even though an indirect team may give more flexibility, there are additional processes that need to be put in place.

---

**Best Practices**

Almost every company with a GAM programme has some form of global account team, although the cohesion and the composition of these teams differs widely. Some best practices that will help the company come to an integrated approach of managing global customers are:

- have a cross-functional global account team;
- make sure the responsibilities of the team members are clear to all;
- have a good executive sponsor for the team;
- make sure the team members have allocated time for their global account activities, and are rewarded accordingly;
- the global account team needs to have a position in the total organization that allows it to work in a cross-functional manner without causing friction and resistance.

---

# Notes

1. For more discussion on global teams, see Rendel de Jong (2001) *Global Teams*. Pale Alto, CA: Davies-Black Publishing; Gloria Barczak and Edward F. McDonough III (2003) 'Leading Global Product Development Teams', *Research Technology*

*Management*, November–December, 43: 14–29; Michael Harvey and Milorad Novice-vic (2002) 'The Co-ordination of Strategic Initiatives Within Global Organizations: The Role of Global Teams', *International Journal of Human Resource Management*, June, 13: 660–76; Vijay Govindarajan and Anil Gupta (2001) 'Building an Effective Global Business Team', *MIT Sloan Management Review*, Summer, 42: 63–71; Edward F. McDonough III and David Cedrone (2000) 'Meeting the Challenge of Global Team Management', *Research Technology Management*, July–August, 43: 12–19; Michael Hickins (1998) 'Creating a Global Team', *Management Review*, September 87: 6–7; John Grundy and Jennifer Ginger (1998) 'Global Teams for the Millennium', *Management Decision*, January, 36: 31–5.

2. For a review of global communications see Dennis Tourish (2005) 'Critical Upward Communication: Ten Commandments for Improving Strategy and Decision Making', *Long Range Planning*, May, 38: 485–503; Dennis Tourish and Oliver Hargie (2004) *Key Issues in Organisational Communication*. London: Routledge; Nina Wakeford (2003) 'The Embedding of Local Culture in Global Communication', *New Media and Society*, August, 5: 379–99; Oliver Hargie, David Dickson and Dennis Tourish (1999) *Communication in Management*. Gower: Aldershot; Oliver Hargie and Dennis Tourish (1999) 'Internal Communications and the Management of Change', in R. Baker, H. Hearnshaw and N. Robertson (eds.) *Implementing Change With Clinical Audit*. New York: Wiley.

3. For a discussion of social networks see Ronald Burt (2004) 'Structural Holes and Good Ideas', *American Journal of Sociology*, March, 110: 349–99; Ronald Burt (2001) 'Attachment, Decay, and Social Network', *Journal of Organizational Behaviour*, December, 22: 619–43; Ronald Burt (1997) 'The Contingent Value of Social Capital', *Administrative Science Quarterly*, March, 42: 339–65; Ronald Burt (1992) *Structural Holes: The Social Structure of Competition*. Cambridge, MA: Harvard University Press. There is also a significant body of research related to organizational networks. See, for example, Ranjay Gulati and Nihil Nohria (2000) 'Strategic Networks', *Strategic Management Journal*, March, 21: 381–404; Ranjay Gulati (1999) 'Network Location and Learning: The Influence of Network Resources and Firm Capabilities on Alliance Formation', *Strategic Management Journal*, March, 20: 397–420; Ranjay Gulati and Maurice Gargulio (1999) 'Where Do Interorganizational Networks Come From?', *American Journal of Sociology*, October, 104: 1439–93; Ranjay Gulati (1998) 'Alliances and Networks', *Strategic Management Journal*, March, 19: 293–317; Ranjay Gulati (1995) 'Social Structure and Alliance Formation Patterns: A Longitudinal Analysis', June, 40: 619–52. For a discussion of networks from a global perspective, see N. Nohria and C. Garcia-Pont (2002) 'Local versus Global Mimetism: The Dynamics of Alliance Formation in the Automobile Industry', *Strategic Management Journal*, February, 23: 307–21; N. Nohria and R. G. Eccles (1992) *Networks and Organizations: Structure, Form, and Action*. Boston, MA: Harvard Business School Press; N. Nohria and C. Garcia-Pont (1991) 'Global Strategic Linkages and Industry Structure', *Strategic Management Journal*, January, 12: 105–24.

## Key Choices

4. For a discussion of formal versus informal groups, see Michael Armstrong (2003) *A Handbook of Human Resource Management*. London: Kogan Page; Simone Kauffeld (2006) 'Self-Directed Work Groups and Team Competence', *Journal of Occupational and Organizational Psychology*, March, 79: 1–21; Stacie Furst, Martha Reeves, Benson Rosen and Richar Blackburn (2004) 'Managing the Life Cycle of Virtual Teams', *Academy of Management Executive*, May 18: 6–20; Bradley Kikrman, Benson Rosen, Paul Tesluk and Cristina Gibson (2004) 'The Impact of Team Empowerment on Virtual Team Performance: The Moderating Role of Face-to-Face Interaction', *Academy of Management Journal*, April, 47: 175–92; Elizabeth Kelley (2001) 'Keys to Effective Virtual Global Teams', *Academy of Management Executive*, May, 15: 132–5; J. DiStefano and M. Maznevski (2000) 'Creating Value with Diverse Teams in Global Management', *Organizational Dynamics*, January, 29: 45–63; Richard Becherer, Fred Morgan and Richard Lawrence (1982) 'Informal Group Influence Among Situationally / Dispositionally-Oriented Consumers', *Academy of Marketing Science Journal*, Summer, 10: 269–81; George Moschis (1976) 'Social Comparison and Informal Group Influence', *Journal of Marketing Research*, August, 13: 235–42.

# Part III

## Supporting Tools

# 8    Managing Knowledge

> If IBM only knew what IBM knows.
> (Anonymous saying)

In Part 3 we now discuss the key supporting tools that help companies to implement global customer management (GCM). In this chapter we will examine tools for managing knowledge, while in Chapter 9 we will examine tools for rewarding and motivating the GCM team.

We all now know that knowledge provides a major competitive advantage. Keeping track of knowledge is particularly hard for global accounts, given the geographic nature of this beast. Having larger and more geographically spread out accounts means having more and geographically spread out knowledge about these accounts. So the global demands of the accounts increase the necessity for global knowledge management capabilities.

All the executives whom we interviewed agreed on the importance of a good knowledge management system and most of their companies had some form of management information system in place. However, when asked about the accomplishments of this system, many interviewees disclosed that although the system seems to be state of the art, at present it does not operate to its full potential. Why is it so difficult to manage knowledge effectively? When mentioning knowledge management, most people will immediately think about information systems. However, whatever high-tech information system a company implements, eventually it is the people in the company who will determine if a knowledge management process fails or succeeds. Therefore, it is important to have some form of formal or informal communication structure, surrounding the use of information systems, that encourages and enables staff to use the system to put in and take out relevant knowledge about customers.

## Importance of Good Knowledge Management

Knowledge management is important in any customer situation, but in the case of global customer management it becomes absolutely crucial.[1] As the contacts with the global account are spread over many different regions and departments, knowledge about the account will be scattered throughout the company. Whereas in a local account situation, the account manager might be able to get by without a good formal knowledge management system, a global account manager will not be able to count on all knowledge on the account naturally coming his or her way

Having a single point of contact who can deal with all customer queries is an important part of GAM. Therefore, it is important that at least this person, usually the global account manager (gam), has all the available information about the account. In many companies, the gam resembles a customer-specific information manager, as he or she will need to combine all available knowledge about the customer to become the ultimate customer expert within the company. Firstly, the members of the global account team, and other employees who work with the customer, will count on the gam to have the necessary knowledge, but often customers will also depend on the gam to have a perfect overview of their global business and projects.

---

**How the Xerox Gam Manages Knowledge**

As Xerox works with large virtual teams, the information role of their gams is of vital importance. All information from and to the virtual team goes through the gam via Xerox's Docushare system. In general, a gam will send out a frequent newsletter and perhaps a couple of notes in the meantime. The main reason for these newsletters is to build greater customer understanding by all team members. Although the gam works with the virtual team, it is possible he or she will never meet some of the members. Therefore, the Xerox Docushare system works as a source of information for all team members.

---

In order to deliver the global capabilities that the customer demands, a gam needs to have a good overview of sales, shipments and returns in the different countries where the two companies do business. Furthermore, it is important to have some sort of knowledge on the other interactions there are with this customer, e.g., sales calls and technical visits. Ideally, the gam will have a better overview than the customer representatives with whom he or she deals, as this will give the relationship some added value for the customer. In one of our interviews, a customer of ingredient company DMV International said, 'When I need to know something about our dealings with DMV in other regions, I call [a particular DMV gam] as she knows everything. So it is much quicker than calling my own colleagues'. It is essential that this balance of information is not the other way round, as dealing with a global procurement officer who has the advantage of having more information than the gam, basically means giving him or her the means to squeeze the supplier's profits.

Having an overview of all the sales figures and other basic customer information is not enough if a company wants to follow the integrated approach of global customer management (GCM) as set out in this book. In order to develop the sort of relationship with the customer that GCM requires, it is important to have deeper knowledge of the customer than merely of the business and interactions between the two companies. As the aim of the relationship is to build a mutually profitable partnership, a supplier needs to find opportunities that will deliver these benefits. To locate these opportunities, there needs to be real customer insight. This latter requires active knowledge generation by all employees who touch the business with the customer, something that requires a lot of discipline and motivation. An item of local information might not look very important to the local account manager, but combined with other information from another region it might shed light on a new business opportunity with the customer. Therefore, it is important to train all involved personnel in the why and how of gathering and analysing information.

## Obstacles to Good Knowledge Management

Even though knowledge management is widely seen as crucial to the success of GCM, many companies seem to struggle with it. In one survey, 50 percent of the respondents mention lack of an integrated IT system as being a major difficulty in global account management.[2] It is hard enough to find or build the right information systems to fit perfectly with the company and the management demands of GAM, but it seems to be even harder to integrate the use of these systems into everyday work for the involved employees. Therefore, if a knowledge management system fails to succeed, there are two main areas to look at: the information systems and the employees. The knowledge management system needs to allow for a broad view of the concept of knowledge—just collecting all sorts of factual data will not necessarily lead to the collection of valuable management information. The systems used to streamline knowledge management will need to allow for a broad sense of knowledge. Furthermore, the knowledge management system and its use need to be embedded in the informal organization, as without the interaction of employees with the system, it will be useless. In Shell, for example, a global account specific report would generally consist of 85 percent of information gathered from the MIS reports while the rest is supplied by a business analyst based on other information gathered from the involved employees.

## Knowledge for Managing Customers

Knowledge is often mistakenly confused with information, but it is more than just that. One view is that knowledge is made up of both information and know-how.[3] This shows that knowledge is not just a collection of facts, but the less tangible know-how is required to turn information into knowledge. Whereas the collection, analysis and dissemination of information are reasonably easy to deal with by management information tools, the management of know-how is a lot more difficult. As know-how is softer knowledge, it is not likely that it can be collected automatically unlike, say, sales figures. For the management and dissemination of know-how a company needs engaged people and a good *qualitative* communication structure. It is possible to have some form of internal system in which employees can try to share certain areas of know-how, but as it is often hard to identify and categorize know-how it is best transferred by informal social processes. Therefore, companies need regular, 'live' contact between different people working on the account to provide opportunities for the dissemination of this know-how.

## Knowledge Management and Information Systems

Information systems are vital for good knowledge management. Although having a good information management system will not automatically mean there is good knowledge management, not having a good information management system will surely mean that the knowledge management system is under par. Firstly, the basic corporate systems, such as for revenues and shipments, need to be set up to allow for the global, not just multilocal, collection and analysis of data. This information needs to be available for each account. This may sound trivial but it can be difficult to achieve, because a company does not always use the same software in all subsidiaries, nor are all the geographical areas automatically connected to a global corporate system. And even if the technological systems do match up globally, there can still be some obstacles to gaining a global view. For example, a customer may have different subsidiaries purchasing from the supplier under different names. So these subsidiaries might be recorded in the supplier's system as separate accounts. Such barriers to good global information need to be removed.

It is important to have a global overview of the basic figures, as this will be the information most used to control the development of the account. A gam will not be able to be a good business partner for the account if he or she does not even know what is being sold to this account. Some companies resort to customer-specific financial reports that are created manually. In this case the gam, or another designated employee, collects all data on the account, both from the existing system and, if necessary, directly from the local subsidiaries. He or she combines this information into one tailor-made report that is created on a regular basis. This approach provides a reasonable solution but means getting this information only periodically. It would be better if this information were available with a few strokes on a keyboard, at the time and in the format needed at that point.

This globally integrated, basic information stands as the basis of any good GAM programme. It is essential when trying to determine which customers are suitable for GAM. It is then vital for managing the relationship with the selected account companies. As we said, sometimes there can be manual solutions to these requirements, but as GAM will be a structural part of the corporation, these will be costly and ineffective. In one example, when a multibillion dollar computer company was trying to take its first steps into GAM, it spent three months trying to identify its top 100 customers, and finally resorted to doing it manually. This shows that it is not a task that can be taken lightly.

The two main sorts of information systems that need to be geared up for collection analyses and dissemination of information are enterprise resource planning systems (ERP) and customer relationship management systems (CRM).

## ERP Systems

Enterprise resource planning (e.g., a SAP system) is an important part of the general information systems of most companies.[4] Whereas a CRM system assists a company with the front end of its business—the relationship with customers—ERP systems deal with all back office information related to all company resources. A typical ERP system will keep track of all raw materials, manufacturing, inventory, logistics, shipping and accounting and is, therefore, a major tool in the control of many business functions. As, for many companies the ERP system is the main information source, it is also the backbone of the most important steering information for the managing of the global accounts. However, the collection of information on a global scale is not always part of these systems. They are often set up in a national or site-specific format that does not allow for a global overview.

Traditional corporate information systems focus on collecting data related to transactions with customers and suppliers, and focus on individual transactions without providing a global overview. A key reason for this local focus is because companies usually calculate profit at the country level for tax and accounting purposes. So creating globally integrated data for specific global customers usually means having to provide an extra set of accounts. When starting a GAM programme, it is vital that these problems are dealt with—either structural manual solutions need to be in place or the system needs to be aligned globally. The last option is preferable, as it will give more flexibility in use of the system, and though possibly expensive to implement, it will save time and money in the longer term.

## CRM Systems

A key theme of this book is the need to go beyond GAM programmes into a global customer management (GCM) relationship. Customer relationship management (CRM) is an important tool in using knowledge management to achieve GCM. When the customer and supplier embark on a global relationship, the customer expects the supplier to have a single interface with them. A global customer will want to save costs by combining previously separate communication lines, and will not want to have extra costs due to a supplier not being as globally coordinated as expected. Global customers will choose from a limited number of suppliers and in order to qualify as one of this group, a company needs to offer good global coordination. As a CRM system collects all data regarding the relationship with the customer, it can help in delivering to the customer this global coordination. In particular, a good CRM system enables the supplier to provide a single point of contact (usually the gam) who has all necessary information to be a good global business partner.

As relationship data means, however, not just financial data but also more intangible qualitative information, a CRM system can end up being a bit fuzzy and incomprehensible—and not being used. The initial system that Schneider Electric implemented, based on Lotus Notes, was far too heavy and complicated, and resulted in many account managers avoiding it as much as possible. The motivation to update these managers' own data was completely lost.

Implementing a CRM system has shown mixed results with corporations across the globe. Some companies have spent large amounts of money without getting a tangible result from these investments into CRM. The success of these systems has just as much to do with their integration into everyday use, as with the configuration of the systems themselves. Firstly, the set up of the system needs to cater for the different sorts of data that can be collected about the accounts. This can be anything, varying from standard business data to very qualitative information about pending organizational changes. In one company, the gam could even show us personal information about the key people within the account, such as the buyer's hobbies and what charity his wife was involved in. Whether or not it is important to have all this data, it definitely is vital that all data are stored in a conveniently arranged manner. Many CRM systems tend to be overloaded with transactional information and other qualitative data, which is hard to categorize, leaving the system cluttered and unworkable.

Employees need to know exactly where to leave or find certain items of data. Xerox, for example, has specific rules with respect to its Docushare system, allowing only certain people to upload data, to ensure that everything is in the right place, and the system does not become a data landfill.

One specific sort of data that is often forgotten when implementing a CRM system, is feedback from the account company. Whereas sales calls will mostly be recorded, an unexpected call from the customer with a question or a complaint often is not. This is regrettable, as it is this kind of information that gives greater understanding about the customer.

Ideally, a CRM system should be more than just a collection of data. When a strategic analysis can be done on the information in the system, a CRM system can help the supplier to gain greater customer insight into the account, which in its turn can lead to the development of new business opportunities.

## Knowledge Management and Employees

There are two reasons why employees are key to the success of any knowledge management system. Firstly, they are the carriers of know-how that is too intangible to put into a system. Secondly, they have actually to use information systems for these to be successful.

In order to disseminate the existing know-how it has, a company needs to create an environment that is favourable to the exchange of knowledge. There need to be many opportunities for real life communication. Employees from different regions should be able to share best practices, methods and even gossip about common global accounts. Many companies organize regular global sales meetings at which local sales representatives from different countries get the opportunity to meet. An example is the global meetings that the Unilever gam for Wal-Mart organizes to share strategy and action plans with all relevant account personnel. Meetings of this kind are often costly, and sometimes difficult to organize, but the results, intangible as they may be, are definitely worth the effort. It is advisable to ensure similar opportunities for direct communication and knowledge exchange for other, non-sales, employees who are in contact with the global customers, e.g., R&D personnel.

An information system is nothing if employees do not use it. Employees need to input data into the systems, and employees need to find information in the systems that they can use in their relationship with the customer. A new system can end up as a chicken-and-egg situation—there is no information in the system, so nobody uses it. But as long as nobody uses it, there will be no information in the system. A company, that starts using an internal information system which requires employee input but nobody uses it will need to break this negative cycle. Things are easier with ERP systems, where the input is largely automatically generated by the normal company processes, but here too employees need to be conditioned to use the system for more than is usual.

Training is one of the prime methods to enhance the use of the information systems. When implementing a new system, there needs to be some basic training for all people using the system, and some extra training for specific 'key users', who are usually scattered throughout the company. Knowing how to use the system, and what benefits it can provide in their jobs, will encourage employees to use them when they return to the workplace. Furthermore, it is important that all users have the same perception as to which data goes where. The key users will advocate the use of the systems in the workplace even further. Additionally, they will be the first port of call when an employee has a problem using the system, making the threshold for asking questions lower, and therefore increasing everyone's use of the systems.

Besides training, companies need to create a culture in which using the system is completely natural to the employees. Some companies enforce this by demanding certain information is available in the system before any resources can be claimed for a specific project. Other companies try to make the use of the system more usual, by linking it to other day-to-day systems, e.g., linking the CRM and ERP systems in one.

---

### Siebel's FileNet Information Solution

eBusiness application software provider Siebel believes that globally shared sales information is the foundation for global account management. Siebel's FileNet solution (Web content management solutions), deployed by 700 global sales users within Siebel (90 percent of its use being via a mobile client server) enables worldwide collection and visibility of customer information. FileNet is enabled in five languages and ten currencies. In addition, the FileNet provides quotes and forecasts opportunities in three different currencies, which offers each sales representative the ability to operate in his or her own currency while reporting to management in US dollars. FileNet also defines account-based selling objectives; identifies revenue opportunities; maps solutions to customer needs; and includes an account map and account plan reports.

---

## Knowledge Management—Rules and Procedures

It is clear that making knowledge management work requires both having the right systems and having the right employee behaviour. However, there needs to be rules and procedures that link these two together into a successful system. These rules and procedures should be followed at least in the handling of any communication and information on one particular global customer. Even better would be if these rules and procedures were followed for all communication and information management across the entire (supplier) company. As some employees within the company will be working with more than one global customer having a cross-company set of rules and procedures will obviously make their work easier and more effective.

Simply said, the rules direct employees in what they are expected to do in certain situations, and the procedures direct them in how to do it. The rules for handling customer knowledge will work as a guideline, and will ensure that all employees deal with both information and know-how in an effective manner that is aligned with their colleagues. These rules will differ from company to company, based on a particular situation, but they always need to be clear and concise. Naturally, it is also of vital importance that all relevant employees are actually aware of these rules and comply with them. Typical rules cover the types of reporting that are expected for particular contact situations with the global customer and where information should be stored.

Procedures that surround knowledge management prescribe the courses of action that need to be taken. As with rules, the procedures must be clear and give no room for unnecessary discussion or flexibility. For most companies the procedures take the form of particular forms, reports or systems that need to be consulted or completed before and after a contact with the customer. Typical documents to be found in the relationship management systems include: account plans, presentations made for and by the customer and visit or contact reports.

## Philips' Account Management Information System

Philips works with an account management information system that provides all relevant employees with a common reference point and a single point of entry for all account relevant information. The system includes a number of standard information mechanisms that help the employee find and store their available knowledge. Among other items, there are account plans, presentations, project files, regular reports and a multilevel contact network that does not just show who is who, but who *knows* who, within the customer–supplier relationship. Furthermore, a simple one-page contact report form has been created that needs to be completed and distributed after all customer visits. This way Philips ensures that all relevant information will be communicated effectively.

It is also important that the company culture is one that fosters the sharing of knowledge. If there is a public acknowledgement of, and a strong group identity for, the GAM programme within the company and people know why it is important, it will be easier to share knowledge for the greater good. Employees need to look beyond their own responsibilities, and realize how they can help their colleagues in other areas, and therefore support the overall account. For its global accounts, Shell started using template documents and an intranet tool where all account plans are available for all account managers. The monthly report also works within a template. This gives the entire account communication process a standard feel that gives the individual local managers more sense of being part of the total global team for this account. As we discussed in Chapter 3, changing a company's culture can be a very difficult task, but potentially a very worthwhile one.

# Global Account Information Manager

A good knowledge *management* system needs to have a *manager*. Just collecting vast amounts of knowledge about the account is not enough. Although a good system will ensure some analysing and dissemination of the knowledge through use of the system, it helps to have somebody who is responsible for the end-management of this knowledge, be it for the complete GAM programme or only for specific accounts. It is not unheard of for the collection of knowledge to spin out of control. Too much data, usually qualitative and possibly overlapping, is uploaded to the system, there is no clear overview left, and nobody will read new information appearing on the system anymore, if they can even locate it! Even though it should be part of the employees' responsibilities to check out any useful new data in the systems, there are only so many hours in the day. So some people will just not find the time to regularly access and update the information system. As a solution, many companies appoint a manager who is responsible for information management for specific accounts. In a lot of cases it is the global account manager who is responsible for this, but sometimes this task lies with the gam's assistant, or it is covered by a separate employee dedicated to that specific role. IBM even has a specialty team that deals with global data gathering.

A global account information manager needs to generate a separate, globally combined, report on the global account at regular intervals based on information in the systems, and on information collected directly from employees who touch the global account in the different regions. This report needs to be concise and practical for those who read it. If the information manager decides to work with highlight bulletins, he or she must take care that it is exactly that—just the highlights. As with the systems, when too much information ends up in the bulletins they lose their impact, and employees stop reading them. Some companies go one step further, allowing only the information manager to upload information to the systems. In this case all employees are approached for their knowledge by the information manager, who then decides if and how this knowledge ends up in the system. Although this channelled approach will make the content of the information system relevant and usable, a drawback is that taking away from the users one sort of interaction with the information system might harm their willingness to use the system at all. As always, the best way to deal with these situations will differ from company to company, and will depend on the specific situation and sorts of data with which the company deals.

**Best Practices**

When companies deal with global accounts there will be a bigger strain on their knowledge management capabilities. As a global customer demands to be dealt with as one single entity, this asks a lot of the global account manager in terms of information management. When dealing with large accounts and, therefore, having many different employees touching this account, a company cannot rely on all knowledge of the account being disseminated among the right employees by only natural communication processes. At the same time, the traditional quantitative information systems might not facilitate a global overview, as they are not globally linked. Some best practices that will help companies in building an effective system for knowledge management are:

- ensuring that you are not less informed about the global relationship than the customer;
- enabling a global overview of all sales figures and other basic customer information;
- enabling the collection of deeper, more qualitative, information on the customer globally;
- building a global insight into the customer;
- when working on knowledge management, not to forget that knowledge is more than information alone;
- enabling and encouraging informal communication between employees who work with the same customer;
- investing in effective and efficient global information systems;
- ensuring that ERP systems are globally integrated;
- not implementing a CRM system without thinking of how your employees will use the system;
- ensuring the CRM system has a clear classification structure so employees know where to bring in and take out specific data;
- devising a clear and concise set of rules and procedures for handling customer knowledge;
- building a culture of knowledge sharing;
- training employees to use the knowledge systems;
- having 'key users' for the systems who are spread throughout the company;
- appointing a person responsible for knowledge management either for the whole global programme or for specific accounts.

# Notes

1. For key readings in knowledge management see D. Teece (2000) *Managing Intellectual Capital*. New York: Oxford University Press; R. Axelrod (1997) *The Complexity of Cooperation*. Princeton: Princeton University Press; K. Conner and C. K. Prahalad (1996) 'A Resource-Based View of the Firm: Knowledge Versus Opportunism', *Organization Science*, October, 7: 477–501; N. J. Foss (1996) 'Knowledge-Base Approaches to the Theory of the Firm: Some Critical Comments', *Organization Science*, October, 7: 470–6; R. M. Grant (1996) 'Towards a Knowledge-Based View of the Firm', *Strategic Management Journal*, Winter Special Issue, 17: 109–22; B. Kogut and U. Zander (1996) 'What Firms Do? Coordination, Identity, and Learning', *Organization Science*, October, 7: 502–18; J. Spender (1996) 'Making Knowledge the Basis of a Dynamic

## Supporting Tools

Theory of the Firm', *Strategic Management Journal*, Winter Special Issue 17; J. Quinn (1992) *The Intelligent Enterprise*. New York: Free Press; W. Starbuck (1992) 'Learning by Knowledge-Intensive Firms', *Journal of Management Studies*, November, 29: 713–40; I. Nonaka (1991) 'The Knowledge Creating Company', *Harvard Business Review*, November–December 1.

2. K. Wilson, S. Croom, T. Millman and D. C. Weilbaker (2000) 'The Global Account Management Study Research Report', sponsored by Strategic Account Management Association (SAMA) and the Sales Research Trust.

3. Martin P. Arnold, Christian Belz and Christoph Senn (2001) 'Information and Know-how: The Two Pillars of Knowledge', *Thexis*, 1.

4. For a discussion of Enterprise Resource Planning Systems see Jacky Swan (2003) 'Knowledge Management in Action', in Clyde Holsapple (ed.) *Handbook on Knowledge Management*. Berlin: Springer, pp. 286–9; Arun Madapusi and Derrick D'Souza (2005) 'Aligning ERP Systems with International Strategies', *Information Systems Management*, Winter, 22: 7–17; David Gefen and Arik Ragowsky (2005) 'A Multi-Level Approach to Measuring the Benefits of an ERP System in Manufacturing Firms', *Information Systems Management*, Winter, 22: 18–32; Sue Newell, Carole Tansley and Jimmy Huang (2004) 'Social Capital and Knowledge Integration in an ERP Project Team: The Importance of Bridging and Bonding', March, 15: 43–57; Theodore Grossman and James Walsh (2004) 'Avoiding the Pitfalls of ERP System Implementation', *Information Systems Management*, Spring, 21: 38–42; Cindy Stevens (2003) 'Enterprise Resource Planning: A Trio of Resources', *Information Systems Management*, Summer, 20: 61-70.

# 9 Rewarding and Motivating the Team

The main challenge with the reward systems is that we need to encourage both global account managers and local sales forces to look for a win-win situation.
Francois Leblanc, Head of Global Strategic Development at Schneider Electric)

The success of the global customer management (GCM) programme depends mostly on the efforts of the employees of the company who deal with the global accounts—in other words, not just the global account manager (gam) but also the global account team (gat) members and any other employees who deal with the global accounts. So it is vital that all employees know about the importance of the GCM programme for the company, and that they have a positive attitude toward it from the start. Incentives and compensation constitute two critical tools for building such a positive attitude that helps implementation of the GCM programme. After all, the compensation system is what directly touches every employee and has to be carefully designed to reduce any resistance toward the GCM programme.

This chapter will discuss the difficulties in constructing a compensation structure that is fair to all involved and that remains effective in achieving the objectives of the GCM programme. This includes remunerating the right people for the right results, and using the right criteria to measure these results.

Another way to create a positive attitude toward the GCM programme is through knowledge. All employees need to know that the GCM programme exists, why the global accounts are so important to the company and how the programme might affect them. In the second part of this chapter, we will discuss the information tools that can be used to create this knowledge.

## GCM Related Remuneration Systems

Setting up a fair and effective compensation system that does not lead to resistance among employees is hard enough in any situation, but GCM brings an extra level of complexity, and possible source of discontent, to the compensation system.[1] While nearly all employees will be paid in a single country, both the sources of income and the determinants of performance will cross country borders. So a company operating a GCM programme needs to keep in mind the situations in the different countries involved. Furthermore, the fact that a large number of employees are responsible for the same account, albeit to different extents, makes it hard to determine which people should be rewarded, and to what extent, for the performance of a GCM account. Siebel has a complex compensation calculation system which is based on both global and regional sales performance. Its performance measurement system includes data on global and regional revenues, profitability and targets. IBM has put in place a process called Setmap. This sets the level of expectation of the customers. Once the projects or the products are delivered, the performance of individuals is measured against the set expectations, and the result affects compensation.

In general, the compensation system should focus on three different types of employees who touch the global accounts business: the gam, the global account team members and other personnel dealing with the account or the total GCM programme.

## Remuneration of the Gam

Having the right compensation system in a GCM situation is probably most important for the gam's position. The total compensation needs to be competitive enough to attract the highly skilled, globally multitasking, senior manager who would, ideally, fill the gam position. At the same time, the gam's pay should not be out of line with other managers of similar seniority and geographical location. A good start for getting a competitive yet internally fair compensation for the gam position is by making a detailed description of the position, its responsibilities and its objectives. Having a good job description makes it easier to measure the activities of the gam against other senior management functions within the company and against gam positions at other companies. In some companies the activities of the gam even differs between different global accounts, making the drafting of a fair GCM compensation system yet more difficult.

Another issue is the mix between the fixed and flexible part of the gam's compensation. The head of the strategic global business development organization of Schneider Electric commented on this issue, as follows:

In countries where sensitivity to quotas and incentives is very high (such as in the US) international account managers can receive an additional 20% to 50% of their salary as bonus. In general, I consider that the amount tied to local turnover is still too high relative to global turnover. The main challenge with the reward systems is that we need to encourage both global account managers and local sales forces to look for a win–win situation.[2]

The position of gam has traditionally evolved from a commercial account management position, and it is customary for most sales positions to have a substantial part of the compensation flexible and based on direct sales successes. However, this is not necessarily the right structure for the compensation of the gam. One of the objectives for the GCM programme should be the long term development of the relationship with the global account companies. Pushing short term sales can possibly be in conflict with that objective. Therefore, having a significant flexible part of the remuneration, based on the annual business with the account company will not always be in the best interest of the relationship with the account company, and therefore not representative of the gam's position and objectives.

In addition to the conflict with long term objectives, the gam is not always in a position to directly influence sales to the global account. In most GCM programmes the role of the gam is more strategic and his or her focus is on relationship development. The actual selling will be done by lower level, local account managers. Therefore, even though the efforts of the gam should in the long term be translated into more profitable business with the global account, in the short term this is not the best measure of the effectiveness of the gam. Nowadays, many companies choose to have a large part of the gam's salary fixed, with only a small part depending on business and other measurements. The head of the GAM programme at Hewlett-Packard believes that the variable portion of a gam's salary should be much less than that for a national salesperson, as the gam has to make strategic investments for the longer term.

The development of the gam's compensation should depend more on the year-to-year realization of strategic plans for the global account as these plans are a more representative measure of the actual objectives that the gam has. This way the gam has a say in setting feasible goals for the development of the account relationship, and can work with objectives for issues that he or she can actually influence.

---

### Royal Dutch Shell's Aligned Targets

To ensure support for the global business on all levels, Shell started aligning scorecard targets. Before that change, the country managers might have had different priorities to those of the gam and, therefore, would not always be willing to lend the support needed for good key account management. Now, there is clear commitment from the cluster business management team. There is clear alignment of targets and tactical actions. All targets are in line with the global targets of the company. The new organization is a global organization with a global scorecard, the effects of which cascade down into the rest of the organization. The template is the same for the global account manager and the local account manager, and the targets are filtered down.

## Remuneration of the Global Account Team

Developing a fair compensation system in a border crossing situation becomes very difficult in the case of global account teams. For example, where the global account team for a specific account has representatives from China and Germany among its members, how can you explain the difference in pay that is likely to occur due to local standards? Furthermore, the members of the global account team will not always be working on a dedicated basis with that specific global account. Even though it is difficult to arrive at a fair compensation system, it is vital to do so. Especially when global account team members spend only a limited amount of their time on the global accounts, it is easy to overlook the efforts the team members have to make for the global account, when deciding on remuneration.

One global account team member, who was a representative from the company's marketing department, told us;

My personal targets and objectives focus on the market development of a specific product group but the account, for which I am in the global account team, does not even need this product group. Therefore, all the work I do for the global account team does not show up at my annual salary review.

A situation like this can be highly demotivating, and should be prevented. Some companies like to build on the team work aspect of the global account team by rewarding all team members with a fixed bonus when a certain goal with the global account is reached. This goal is often sales related. However, as with the global account manager, the global account team members, or at least the non-sales related team members, often do not have a high level of influence on the direct sales with the account, nor is a short term rise in profitable sales the most important objective for having a global account team in the first place. Ideally, the global account team members should have personal objectives, linked to their remuneration, that take account of their presence in the global account team and the share of their time on global account issues. For the non-sales related members of the global account team these will often be qualitative objectives. For example, a global account team member who is a representative for the research and development department, and who spends 20 percent of his on her time on a specific global account, may have a bonus objective that accounts for 20 percent of his or her annual salary review. But this objective would be stated qualitatively as follows: 'the company and the global account should have started one combined project for improvement of a product, and one combined project for a complete new product innovation'. This way the team members will be remunerated on issues that they can actually influence and that accord with the long term objectives of the GCM programme.

## Remuneration of Other Employees

As the relationship with a global account company is a far reaching one, the gam and the global account team members will not be the only people working with the global account. Naturally, employees will have to be paid for the work they do and, therefore, the work for the global account has to be included in the remuneration. As this means remunerating people from many different departments and geographical locations, it can be difficult to align this across the organization. Furthermore, how does a company know exactly who is involved in the global account, and how much work does an employee need to do for him or her to qualify as working with the global account? The remuneration of employees other than gams and global account team members can be divided into two groups, those who are on a fixed salary, (often non-commercial, e.g., logistics) and those who are on a (partially) flexible salary, (often commercial, e.g., sales).

### Remuneration for Other Employees on a Fixed Salary

For employees on a fixed salary who are in contact with the global account company, it is important that the work they do forms part of their job description and targets. This can be either specifically for the global account, or there can be a general job description that contains the work that is done for the global account. For example, a quality assurance employee might have in his or her job description: 'Research and respond to any complaint filed by a customer within seven days. If the customer is a global account the process should be completed within five days'. This way, the employee can work for the global account within his or her own job description. In general the deciding on remuneration for employees on a fixed salary does not present a major difficulty, as long as everything is well documented.

### Remuneration for Other Employees on a Flexible Salary

Employees on a flexible salary are usually partially remunerated for quantitative results, these often being sales related. In a global situation this can lead to problems. If a local account manager in Canada helps to get a global contract signed, for which the actual revenue ends up in Germany, which is the headquarter country of the global account, who will get remunerated for this contract? The German local account manager, the Canadian local account manager or the gam? One step further in the same example: should the country manager for Canada be remunerated for this global contract, as the employee working on it directly reports to him or her? If not, he or she will surely not support the fact that the local account manager is spending his or her time on a contract that will not end up in adding to the manager's national revenue. These can be very tricky situations. Because the remuneration is so directly linked with the way the revenue is recorded, this can easily lead to resistance if not handled in the correct manner. Many companies choose to work with so-called 'double counting' of the results. Obviously the financial results of a global contract will not themselves be double counted, but they will be considered in the remuneration of more than one person.

As for the line managers of the local account managers, it is important to either have a good understanding of the fact that work for a global account is not included in the yearly targets, or there should be some kind of remuneration for these regional managers. In Shell, any revenue will always go to the local unit. Therefore, all benefits from the business with the global account will go to the regional organization, even if they were not initially part of the regional manager's targets. This way, global business becomes a bonus activity in which managers are more willing to invest time. In whichever way the flexible salary dilemma is solved, it will always be prone to conflicts and resistance, so it is wise to pay close attention to how the attitude of local and regional personnel towards working on global accounts changes over the years.

## Measurements

When linking remuneration to results, the measures to rate these results need to be chosen wisely.[3] As discussed, the long term objectives of the gam do not match particularly well with the short term results related to sales volume or revenue. Therefore, when reviewing the success of the gam, measurements other than annual sales are likely to be more representative. However, sales results are quantitative and, therefore, an easy measure to use when conducting annual reviews. Although most companies still include sales results in their reviews, more and more interest is shown in other measurements such as customer satisfaction, profit development, and achievement of account company plans. By using other, often qualitative, measures to rate the success of the global account relationship, a clearer image of the situation with the global account can be seen. Obviously, the measurements used for annual reviews should differ from position to position. For more sales oriented positions, it can be completely rational to use direct sales results as the primary measure. The important thing when choosing measures is to match the criteria for measuring results with the objectives of the position.

## Personnel Perception of the GCM Programme

A good GCM programme does not just have the cooperation of a set of thoroughly informed and highly capable gams, and an effective global account team for every account, but has the support of the whole organization. After all, the level of care and attention that the global accounts deserve cannot be provided by the global account manager and his or her team alone. Furthermore, it is necessary that all interactions with the account company, including one-off encounters with employees who normally do not have anything to do with GCM, are in line with the chosen strategy for the account. It is important that the whole organization knows exactly how the GCM programme is constructed, which global accounts are part of the programme, which people are responsible for these accounts, and what the company's objective is for the global accounts. As implementation of a GCM programme is often prone to resistance at all levels of the organization, particularly at the local parts of the company, it can be difficult to get all personnel in a positive mindset toward the programme and its accounts. Even though GCM is a special and important programme for the company, it is important not to create an 'elite' part of the organization that all other employees will love to hate. The most important tools for achieving a more positive attitude toward the GCM programme are:

- basic knowledge about the GCM programme;
- ongoing information;
- executive support.

## Basic Knowledge about the GCM Programme

When the GCM programme is first implemented, it is important that it is not just the directly involved personnel who know what global customer management is and why and how the company is investing in it. As with any organizational change, all employees need to be informed about the basics of the GCM programme and how it might influence their day-to-day work. This is often done by company meetings or 'cascade' presentations (explained below). It is important to choose the right information to disclose, to prevent the situation that arose in one company where the lower level staff dismissed the GCM programme as 'another wild executive idea that will be here today and gone tomorrow'. This is a difficult task, and will depend on the company culture and the level of impact the GCM programme will have on core company processes.

Furthermore, the medium that is chosen for the presentation of the new programme is important. Company newsletters, for example, will not be read by everybody, and should not be the only way of disseminating this information. Big company meetings have a tendency to be very one-sided, in that it is usually executive management presenting something to the staff where there is little opportunity to detect and then handle possible scepticism or negative feelings about the organization changes.

Some companies choose to use cascading presentations, which seem a suitable tool to discuss a far-reaching organizational change like global customer management. In a cascading presentation the knowledge 'cascades' through the ranks. A general presentation is prepared at corporate level, after which each line manager will discuss the presentation with staff who report directly to him or her. These employees will in their turn discuss what they have learnt with the staff who report to them. This sequence will repeat itself throughout the whole company. By using a cascading presentation, the groups in which the organizational changes are discussed at any one time are relatively small, which allows for more interaction between the person disclosing the information and the persons receiving the information. Furthermore, the information will be given by the employees' direct line manager, with whom employees ideally should have a better acquaintance, and therefore should find it easier to ask questions and air doubts about the programme. Cascading presentations, therefore, have a more direct effect through each manager's own endorsement, and are a good way to reach more people in a more concentrated manner. However, it is important to ensure that all managers who will be giving this presentation to those directly reporting to them are positive towards the organizational changes, and are thoroughly informed, as there is a risk of misinforming employees or, even worse, passing on a negative attitude towards the GCM programme. Whatever method is chosen for providing information to the employees, it is important that it is done at an early stage, thereby nipping any negative rumours in the bud.


## Ongoing Knowledge

After the initial disclosure of information about the GCM programme, it is important that the whole company keeps up-to-date about the status of the programme. The GCM programme should be an integrated part of the company, not a separate part with which the rest of the company has minimal dealings. Especially in the early stages of the implementation of the GCM programme, it is important that employees get used to the existence of the programme and its objectives. Personnel should not feel excluded, as this will fuel a negative attitude toward the programme at a later stage. A regular update on the successes of the programme in company newsletters can give some basic information on progress. Another good method of having a more organic integration of the new programme into the company organization is to have employees whose roles are partially dedicated to the GCM programme. If people from many different organizational parts of the company are, for example, 50 percent dedicated to the GCM programme and the other 50 percent to another department, they will automatically transport knowledge about the new programme to the rest of the organization. Another benefit of having these 'shared time' people in the GCM programme is that they will be able to help better align the programme with the rest of the organization, as they will know what works in relation to the other departments.

## Executive Support

Executive support is important, not only for external success, but also for internal acceptance of the programme. Companies should show executive endorsement of and involvement with the programme to the rest of the organization. This way it is clear to the employees that this programme is something the company is serious about and so should get everyone's support. A senior manager at a major bank told us: 'If there is a change in policy, or any other need for important communication, I will write it, but it will be signed at the top. This shows the sponsorship the executives give this programme, and gives the employees more confidence'. Xerox also recognizes the importance of using the knowledge of senior executives. On Xerox's intranet, gams can find information on the senior 'focus executives' (Xerox's name for its assigned top executives) and can book some of their time to engage a global customer. These focus executives can offer up to four hours of their time a year for meetings with a global customer. It is also possible to engage more than one focus executive per client.

**Best Practices**

The quality of employees' efforts are a critical part of the success of the GCM programme. Due to the all-embracing nature of the relationship between the company and its global customer, it is likely that the global account will need treatment that is not always within the standard processes. In order to ensure that the global relationship gets the care it deserves, it is important that all employees have a positive and can-do attitude toward the GCM programme in general and the global accounts in particular. There are many ways to gain this attitude but, even more important, there are at least as many practices that will cause employees to develop a negative attitude and therefore create resistance in them toward any global business. Some best practices with respect to motivating and rewarding employees involved with global accounts are:

## Supporting Tools

- The gam's salary should be competitive enough to attract highly qualified candidates, yet comparable to other managerial positions of similar seniority in the same geographical location.
- There should be a detailed description of the gam's objectives and responsibilities.
- The gam's responsibilities and salary should be benchmarked against competitors and within the own company.
- The global account team members must be fairly remunerated for the work they do for the global account.
- The job descriptions of other employees on a fixed salary must include the work they do for the global accounts.
- Local resistance should be avoided by remunerating local employees for work done on global accounts.
- Managerial support should be encouraged by acknowledging the work done on a local level for a global account by national and regional managers.
- Suitable measures must be used when reviewing results; this does not always mean looking at sales revenue, but the criteria will differ among different positions.
- The GCM programme should not be allowed to become an 'elite' part of the organization from which other employees feel excluded.
- All employees should know how the programme is organized, why it is important and how it will effect them.
- Executive support could be used to give any communications necessary weight.

# Notes

1. For a more extensive review of compensation systems, see M. Armstrong (2003) *A Handbook of Human Resource Management*. London: Kogan Page; E. Lawler (1990) *Strategic Pay*. San Fransisco: Jossey-Bass; E. Lawler (1981) *Pay and Organisation Development*. Reading, MA: Addison-Wesley; Lucy Newton McClurg (2001) 'Team Rewards: How Far Have We Come?', *Human Resource Management*, Spring, 40: 73–92; K. Bartold and L. Haqmann (1992) 'A Key to Effective Teamwork', *Compensation and Benefits Review*, 24: 24–9; G. Akerlof and J. Yellen (1988) 'Fairness and Unemployment', *American Economic Review*, May, 78: 44–52.
2. Francois LeBlanc.
3. For a discussion of the effects of measurement on managers' behaviour, see André de Waal (2001) *Power of Performance Management: How Leading Companies Create Sustained Value*. Chichester: John Wiley & Sons; R. Simons (2000) *Performance Measurement and Control Systems for Implementing Strategy*. Englewood Cliffs, NJ: Prentice-Hall; C. Holsapple and W. Luo (1996) 'A Framework for Studying Computer Support of Organizational Infrastructure', *Information and Management*, January, 31: 13–24; Sean Nicholson-Crotty, Nick A Theobald and Jill Nicholson-Crotty (2006) 'Disparate Measures: Public Managers and Performance-Measurement Strategies', *Public*

*Administration Review,* January–February, 66: 101–14; Barbara DeSanto and Danny Moss (2004), 'Rediscovering what PR Managers do: Rethinking the Measurement of Managerial Behaviour in the Public Relations Context', *Journal of Communication Management,* March, 9: 179–95; Andre de Waal (2002) 'The Power of World-Class Performance Management: Use It!', *Measuring Business Excellence,* August, 6: 9–22; M. Armstrong and A. Baron (1998) *Performance Management: The New Realities.* London: Institute of Personnel and Development; G. Gooderham and B. Maskell (1998) 'Information Systems That Support Performance Management', *Journal of Strategic Performance Measurement,* February / March, 12: 23–35; A. Rucci, S. Kim and R. Quinn (1998) 'The Employee–Customer–Profit Chain at Sears', *Harvard Business Review,* January / February. 34–56.

# Part IV

## Process

# 10 Developing for Ongoing Effectiveness

> Changing a global account programme is like changing the tire on a car while driving at 70 m.p.h. down the freeway.
>
> (Alan Nonnenberg, originator of the global account management programme at Hewlett-Packard)

Once the global customer management (GCM) programme has been implemented, the work is not over. Managers of the GCM programme have to realize that it is an ongoing process, not a project. So in this section of the book we review how to continually develop the GCM programme, and we also provide a summary of the critical factors for ongoing success.

In order to achieve the best results from the GCM programme, it needs to continue running as smoothly as possible. Once the implementation phase is over, GCM managers will find some need to customize the programme for the different accounts. Also, barriers and resistance appear that may not have been apparent during the implementation phase. To make the GCM programme a valuable addition to the company, managers need to transfer the effort taken in implementing the programme into its ongoing development. This chapter will discuss the support that the programme needs and especially why relationship management is key for ongoing success. Furthermore it will discuss the planning process and possible barriers that a company can encounter while working with a GCM programme.

## Supporting the GCM Programme

The level of support for the GCM programme has a large influence on the successful development of the programme. Part of this support, as discussed in Chapter 9, comes as less tangible support from all the employees and management involved in one way or another. This less tangible support is particularly seen in employees' attitudes towards the programme, powering their motivation to assist when needed. More tangible support, however, from personnel and systems that have a direct function within the GCM programme also have an important effect on success. Advertising agency Wunderman (part of the Young and Rubicam group within WPP) realized that it needed to invest in specific GAM-supporting systems. For example, Wunderman set separate profit-and-loss accounts for 50 global customers. This system is expensive but having previously managed on the basis of industry groupings, Wunderman had used too many resources on smaller accounts and not enough on larger ones.

Companies might be reluctant to use many resources on the global programme, especially if they perceive the global relationships as being mainly part of a sales-related programme in which the customer will try to obtain lower prices. In this situation the company is afraid the costs of the global programme will outweigh the benefits. If, however, a company wants to transform a global sales-related programme into an integrated approach to managing global customers, it will have to allocate extra and specific resources. In the selection process for GCM accounts, described in Chapter 5, a company needs to ensure it chooses only those customers for whom the benefits will outweigh the costs of providing the special support functions that the GCM programme requires. These critical support functions include:

- infrastructure support;
- personnel support;
- executive support.

## Infrastructure Support

GCM infrastructure comprises all the basic facilities, services and installations needed for the functioning of the programme. Like any other part of the organization, a GCM programme will draw from the corporate infrastructure for the majority of its needs. However, some infrastructure elements are especially important for GCM success and from which the GCM programme will demand much more than do the normal corporate functions.

### Information System

The company's information and communication systems have to be standardized and globally linked for them to be effective for the global operations. As also described in Chapter 8, the ability to gather, combine, analyse and distribute information from all the different areas (both geographical and divisional) affected in the relationship with the customer, is key to being a valuable global supplier for the customer.

Measurement System

Next to the knowledge management part of the information systems, the measurement systems need to have a global aspect. It is surprising to see how many companies that call themselves global do not have a system to measure account profitability on a global scale. Often, companies use different accounting systems in different geographical areas. But even companies with one global system can have difficulties: a given customer is often present in the system as many different entities, as it operates under different company names in different regions and divisions. So a global supplier needs to develop a system to combine all of this information in one place, providing clear account information, which is vital for the global account manager.

## Personnel Support

A large part of the costs in resources for a GCM programme will be spent on extra employees. Of these, the most visible form of personnel support for GCM comes in the global account team (as described Chapter 7). Ideally, the global account team has members from different geographical areas and departments. That way, the team members will form a good first line of support that stretches into the most relevant parts of the organization. But apart from the employees who work directly with the global accounts or in the global account team, GCM also needs supporting roles, often on a central or headquarters level. Examples of this type of personnel support include: a central order desk, special project support for global accounts and central account administration. It would not be cost efficient to have these functions covered at different locations, but when centralized it is feasible to offer these resources as support for the GCM organization.

---

**Hewlett-Packard's Headquarters Account Manager**

Another form of personnel support that can help develop the GCM programme is an assigned manager who will provide support to the global account at headquarters. In its original global account organization Hewlett-Packard (HP) created the position of the headquarters account manager (HAM). While there was also a regular global account manager who was ideally based close to the headquarters of the global account, the HAM was the advocate for the account at HP's headquarters. The HAM's mission was 'to champion the critical needs and significant opportunities of the global account within HP headquarters and to establish HP as a strategic vendor of Cooperative Computing Systems through long term sales growth and customer satisfaction'. The HAM worked together with the gam on the strategic development of the global relationship and reported both to the gam and to the product divisions' headquarters. Next to being a very valuable resource in the support for the global account, the HAM positions increased the visibility of the global accounts on a corporate level.[1]

---

## Executive Support

We have mentioned before the importance of executive support for the GCM programme, but we cannot stress this enough. Firstly, companies need a board level executive who has the final ownership of the whole GCM programme. As well as holding overall management responsibility of the GCM programme, this executive should send out all corporate-wide communications about GCM in order to show top management commitment to the programme.

Secondly, most companies with a successful GCM programme have some form of executive sponsorship programme. In this, all global accounts are assigned to a specific high level executive (e.g., a board member) who is the corporate sponsor for this account. Each executive sponsor develops a personal relationship with a high level executive on the customer side in order to strengthen the corporate relationship between the two companies. This executive relationship should not be used to discuss trivial problems between the companies, but rather to focus on the future of the strategic relationship. For example, when the executive sponsor at Shell for the Bosch account has a meeting with this customer's executive level counterpart, the gam will write a two-page briefing. This guides the executives to talk about general items and strategic business issues. Furthermore, by developing the high level relationship, the executive sponsor might be able to open doors for the global account manager that had previously been closed. In some companies the executive sponsor also works as a sort of mentor for the global account manager, giving advice on strategic planning and other critical issues for the global account company. Obviously, the executive sponsors should be executives who are positive and enthusiastic about the GCM programme, and if there are existing relationships between particular executives and any global customers, it would be a waste not to take these into consideration when allocating global customers to executives. Whereas executive *ownership* of the programme works to show commitment to *internal* stakeholders, executive *sponsorship* works mainly to show commitment to *external* stakeholders.

# Relationship Management

The long term success of the global customer management programme depends largely on the extent to which the customer will be happy to expand the relationship and, therefore, business with the global supplier. Hence, relationship management is an important part of the ongoing process of global customer management. Relationship management should not be taken for granted as being part of the gam's responsibilities, to decide on and deal with on his or her own. Companies have to set up processes that ensure effective relationship management with *all* account companies. Chapter 8 discussed knowledge management and CRM systems. Here we will discuss the more organizational and individual aspects of relationship management:

- relationship management processes;
- customization;
- mirroring of the customer's organization;
- educating the customer;
- balance of power.

## Relationship Management Processes

Relationship management processes should function as a backbone to the relationship with customers. Ideally, the processes cover everything that needs to be organized for the relationship from starting up to shutting down. The selection process, described in Chapter 5, should apply not just at the start of the relationship, but as a continuing exercise where every global account is evaluated on a regular basis against the selection criteria. A company that was a very suitable candidate for global account management can turn out to be less desirable a year later. In one example, a big pharmaceutical concern had shown its interest in a global relationship to a supplier who was starting up a global programme. As the pharmaceutical company seemed to be offering a lot of potential global business, and met the selection criteria based on the knowledge the supplier had about them at the time, it was added to the supplier's global programme. However, after 18 months of approaching the relationship as part of the GAM programme, none of the assumed potential had materialized, and as the supplier had gained more knowledge about the customer by this time, it could conduct a better evaluation against the selection criteria. Based on this information the customer did not comply with the selection criteria any more, and was removed from the global programme. Obviously, removing a customer from a global programme can be potentially harmful for the relationship. When explaining this to the customer the gam needs to take extra care to ensure the message does not come across as: 'We just think you are not that important to us any more'. After all, you do not want to lose the customer's business altogether. Hewlett-Packard once took the approach, when taking a large number of customers out of its GAM programme, of simply not informing the customers but gradually withdrawing the GAM services.

Apart from the selection process, some guidelines for relationship management need to be set up and documented for all involved. This process can involve making a set number of visits each year to different parts of the customer company, or outlining specific plans that need to be made and followed.

## Customization

When a supplier customizes its account organization for different customers, this provides a better fit and demonstrates dedication to the global relationships. Customization can be used on many different levels, the possibilities largely depending on the characteristics of the product or service provided. Some companies customize the entire account organization and the way that the company works with the customer. Generally, full customization will be possible only in the situation where the product or service is unique to the customer. For example, most advertising agencies might have a structure in which an account team is completely customized to the account and works in the way that best fits with the customer. In these cases, only very basic processes, such as financial administration, can be handled in a standardized way.

Many companies provide only superficial customization. For example, the gam may include the name of the account in his or her job title—'Global Account Manager XYZ (customer)'. Another good example of providing the appearance of customization is the customer intranet, provided by Xerox, which develops a customer portal for each global account. These web-based portals are customized for the account and include information, for example, about existing contracts and which account managers are responsible for the account in each country. The basic set up of these Xerox portals is similar in each case, but the layout and content will be based on the specific account. As we mentioned, extensive customization is easier when the offered product or service is itself highly customized, such as with advertising services. Companies that have fairly standardized products or commodities are better off providing customization at a superficial level that does not interfere too much with the standard operational processes, as this will only increase base costs, which is definitely not desirable in a global relationship.

## Mirroring

Mirroring is a form of customization in the sense that it is done to have a smoothly aligned working relationship with the customer.[2] By mirroring the customer's organization, a global account organization ensures there is a perfect fit with the organization of the customer. It is not necessary or wise to copy the complete organization of the customer in detail, as this would be a very difficult and costly solution. The main idea of mirroring is that the supplier knows exactly how the customer is organized globally, including the key contact positions for the relationship, and ensures that every key contact has a counterpart at a similar level of importance at the supplier company who will act as the main link between the two companies at that level. For example, when a customer has three main procurement points in Japan, the USA and Germany, a global R&D department in Japan, and a global marketing department in Germany, the global account organization of the supplier should contain global points of contact in these regions, and divisional global points of contact, if possible, in the respective regions. Mirroring can make relationship management a lot easier and more effective but, as with all customization, the extent to which a company can mirror its customer's organization depends on its own flexibility and the type of products and services offered.

## Educating the Customer

What use is it to have an advanced relationship management organization in place that can handle any customer query, if the customer does not know it exists? Customers need to know what the supplier is willing to do for them—not just to show dedication but to further the actual relationship. One of the main objectives for GCM from the supplier's perspective is the expansion of the relationship to eventually lead to more profitable business. This will not happen if the customer does not know about the new opportunities for cooperation that the supplier is willing to offer. The gam needs to ensure that all the key people at the customer company know exactly how the supplier can help them reach their goals. In other words, the message given to the customer should not be focused on 'why you should buy from us', but on 'how can we help you to achieve your objectives'. This means informing the customer about not just different services and products, but also about the global account process. The customer needs to know who to turn to with specific queries, and what is and is not possible in the new global way of working together.

## Balance of Power

As a global account relationship can have a very strong effect on the actual profitability of the business between the customer and supplier, it is important that there is a good balance of power between the two parties. Firstly, the two companies need to have a similar level of global coordination. If this is not the case, it is often the customer who benefits most and, therefore, the supplier needs to ensure it does not end up in an unbalanced relationship. As shown in Figure 10.1 a situation in which both the customer and the supplier are globally coordinated will provide great potential for the global relationship, but if one of the two parties is not as globally coordinated as the other party, it is the less well coordinated one that loses out. In the case where the customer is better coordinated, the supplier will inevitably end up in a price squeeze in

## Process

|  | | Low | High |
|---|---|---|---|
| **Customer's international coordination** | **High** | Price squeeze (low potential) | Global fit (high potential) |
|  | **Low** | Country-by-country relationship (non-existent potential) | Hollow agreement (low potential) |

Low        High

**Vendor's international coordination**

**Fig. 10.1** Vender–customer fit

Source: Adapted from David Arnold, Julian Birkinshaw and Omar Toulan (2001) 'Can Selling Be Globalized? The Pitfalls of Global Account Management', *California Management Review*, 44(2): 8–20.

which the customer plays different geographical sections of the supplier against others. In the case of a customer that is not as globally coordinated as the supplier, the relationship will end up with a hollow agreement, in which the supplier offers a better deal for a global contract, but the customer does not have the global capability to keep its end of the deal. In one example a US-based computer manufacturer had a global agreement with a major global financial services company. For some reason the German subsidiary had been offered a price below the specified minimum. As a result, all other subsidiaries lost the motivation to keep to the contract, and the global deal fell apart. To add insult to injury, the German subsidiary bought less than originally agreed, and some of the cheap systems found their way to Eastern Europe.[3]

Difference in size of the customer and supplier does not necessarily mean an unbalanced relationship, as it can be easier for smaller companies to coordinate internally, which offsets the possibly more extensive global organization of the larger company. Another type of power is the importance the customer has for the supplier and vice versa. For example, when a global relationship is based on the purchase of a particular chip-technology, the customer needs to determine what percentage of the total purchases are made with a particular supplier, and how many other global suppliers could deliver the same specifications. On the other hand, the supplier needs to know what percentage of the total sales of this chip-technology is being sold to this particular customer, and how many customers for this product there are in total. This way it is possible to determine the dependence between two parties, which can help in determining the importance of the relationship.[4]

**176**

# Planning

In order to continue developing the GCM programme meticulous planning at different levels is essential. From the objectives to the strategies used to obtain those objectives, the planning process should provide a frequently updated roadmap for the development of the programme and the separate account relationships. The strategic plan for the whole programme should be carried through the different plans for the separate accounts. The following types of planning are important for the ongoing development of the GCM programme:

- GCM planning;
- global account planning;
- planning with the account company.

## GCM Planning

GCM should be a process not a project, so the strategic plan for the GCM programme should have a long term outlook. Most companies' plans give a more detailed vision of the development of the programme within the first two years and a more general objective for the next five years. The long term strategic plan should state how the GCM programme contributes to the long term strategies of the whole company. Therefore, the GCM plan should be updated as frequently as is the corporate strategic plan. The GCM plan should set out the general guidelines of the GCM process such as the approximate number of global accounts with specific characteristics, and the expected amount of business generated through global business. The highest executive level should endorse this GCM strategic plan. Good GCM planning will also ensure that the necessary resources for the programme will be allocated.

## Global Account Planning

As GCM is a long term programme, account planning should be seen as a rolling exercise. In the initial start-up phase, a global account plan should have been written by the gam, assisted by the global account team. The Shell gams write their own global account plans. There will be input and feedback from the different Shell companies, based on a fixed template that is completed by all local account managers, and the gam will combine that into one big key account plan on a global level. This includes the potential for the account, a plan of action and a contact matrix. Focus has to be on the biggest opportunities. The global account plan is a bottom–up planning instrument for Shell.

## Process

When engaging in a global relationship the global account plan should be regularly reviewed and updated. Furthermore, to work on the long term strategic objectives and the development of a strong relationship with the account, the global account plan should be reworked into a global account *development* plan. Obviously, the global account planning should be in line with the overall GCM planning, and for this reason most companies have an annual meeting during which corporate executives and global account managers measure the achievements against the last global account plan, and discuss the plan that has been devised for the coming year. In general, the account plan should contain global account objectives that are challenging yet feasible, and the strategy and tactics the gam is proposing to use to achieve these objectives. It is also important to mention the available and required resources for this plan. After agreeing on this plan with corporate management, the gam should face fewer problems obtaining these resources when needed.

## Planning with the Customer

If the relationship is strong enough, and there is sufficient trust between the two parties, making a combined plan with the customer can be very rewarding. The two companies can make a strategic outline of the kind of relationship they propose to have, and mention an achievable number of projects they can work on together. They will also inform each other of plans in their own company that can influence the other party. For example, in the case of a raw materials supplier that works on a global basis with a global producer company, the two parties will have a combined planning process. They will line up a plan that says that they will start a combined project to try to make the ordering system easier and more cost effective for both parties. Furthermore, the producer company will provide the supplier with the timings of innovation plans on which it is working, and for which the support of the supplier's R&D people might be necessary later in the year. This way the supplier can use this information when allocating the required resources and give the customer support when needed without having to upset any existing plans. UK energy company BG Group and US engineering company Bechtel even set up a joint steering committee to nurture, maintain and oversee their relationship. The committee comprises three people from BG Group and three from Bechtel. Within the committee there is a high level of trust, which enables the two companies to plan together in order to speed up their combined projects.

# Overcoming Barriers and Avoiding Pitfalls

The way in which a company handles possible barriers and avoids possible pitfalls is paramount to the success of the GCM programme. Any GCM programme will encounter friction with other existing organization structures and all sorts of obstructions both in the supplier's own organization and in the customer's organization. Therefore, it is important for the ongoing development of the programme that these barriers and resistances are dealt with in an effective manner that does not upset relationships with other departments in the long term. There are many different possible barriers and pitfalls:

- local versus global attitudes;
- global capabilities being unavailable;
- barriers on the customer's side;
- downward pricing spiral.

## Local Versus Global

The friction between local and global interests is one of the most common barriers in global customer management. When implementing the GCM programme, local managers often worry that they will lose part of their responsibilities. Perhaps they will even have to report to a global representative on a relationship with a customer for which they used to have complete ownership. As an international account manager for Schneider Electric remarked about negative reactions from account representatives:

The local service and sales engineers are essential to our local presence. With the GAM approach, they are afraid of losing power and independence, and tend to resist its implementation in their area. My job is to help them understand that I bring with me the resources of the whole company to support their needs.

Resistance toward the global programme has to be overcome by good communication and by building a global corporate culture. It is in no one's interest if good local managers end up with less responsibility than they can handle; companies must ensure that these people are allocated other challenging local accounts or some responsibility within the global account team. However, the local versus global friction is potentially an ongoing problem, even when the programme has been running for some years. National or regional managers will not always agree on activities at the local level for a global account, especially if the benefits of these activities go to the global level or a region that is out of their jurisdiction. The best way to reduce this type of friction is to have a fair compensation system that rewards any effort benefiting the global programme.

## Process

This idea has been discussed in Chapter 9. Another way to limit the local versus global conflict is to build a company culture in which the importance of the global account is clear to all employees. This way, employees will be more likely to go the extra mile for the global account, even though this might not directly influence their personal targets.

Another local versus global barrier is friction between different cultures internationally. One Shell gam described how he has frequent problems due to the difference in mentality among countries like China, Brazil and Germany. This can be especially difficult regarding issues of responding and being on time. Sometimes it is hard to convince colleagues in certain countries of the demands that the global account has in these areas. The only way to overcome this barrier is to convince the local people of a customer's expectations. Furthermore, the gam, himself or herself, must also show exemplary behaviour in these aspects.

---

### Citicorp's World Corporation Group

Loss of internal support, stemming from conflict with national account managers, can be another problem. Citicorp (now Citigroup) used a global management system for nearly 500 of its largest multinational customers from 1974 to 1980.[5] Citicorp grouped these accounts, representing about 20 percent of the bank's worldwide loan volume, into a new unit—the World Corporation Group (WCG). This global unit was given primary responsibility for all activities on these accounts around the world. For each of the companies assigned to the WCG, a parent account manager located in the company's home country was designated to handle relationships with the parent company. This global account management system worked well for Citicorp. Between 1974 and 1977 profits on the global accounts increased by 63 percent, and total borrowing increased by 85 percent.

But problems arose despite this success. Traditionally, the bank had placed a strong emphasis on local autonomy for each country. With the WCG approach, country managers had a reduced role for the global accounts—setting guidelines rather than making decisions. By 1980, internal conflicts induced management to eliminate the WCG as part of a corporate-wide reorganization that had the objective of simplifying the organization structure. Although Citicorp continued with the other aspects of the global account management system, such as the global planning and budgeting, the loss of a separate organization structure soon put the emphasis back on local management. But this disbanding of the WCG adversely impacted on Citicorp's relationships with its customers, and complaints from them increased. It took the bank about five years to realize what its customers were saying. In 1985 Citicorp re-established the WCG as a 'bank within a bank'. The re-establishment of the initiative, and its subsequent success (which led to the creation of the Global Relationship Banking (GRB) business), has been an object lesson for both Citicorp and its corporate customers in the mutual benefits of a close relationship.[6]

---

## Global Capabilities

In our research we found that many companies do not have the global capabilities they seem to think they have.[7] This can lead to very serious pitfalls for companies starting a GCM programme. Having global presence does not automatically mean a company has global capabilities.[8] At the outset, the company needs to have enough global authority over local parts or the organization to get them to cooperate with global account management. More complicated is having enough authority over independent agents and subsidiaries in countries where the company does not have its own presence. When making a global deal, the customer will expect the same service and conditions from representatives of the company in all the countries involved. An independent agent will not always be able or willing to deliver this. Companies that want to be a global partner to their customers will have to find a way to deal with this. In one example the Malta agent of a global electronics company was not willing to give an account the price that was agreed at the global level, as the agent had previously charged a much higher price to the Malta division of the some customer. In this particular case, the supplier decided to pay the agent the difference in price, just so it would have the global capabilities that were needed to do business with this account on a global level, and therefore win more business in regions that were initially not in the global account portfolio.

## Barriers on the Customer's Side

Just as the supplier can lack global capabilities, so can the customer. This can be a big barrier in having a global relationship. A typical situation is where the customer is globally very well coordinated for the procurement function, but has no real global cohesion anywhere else. In this situation a global contract will be made, but the customer has no capability to enforce the conditions of the deal with its divisions. One global manager at a major advertising agency remarked:

We need the client to be more global. It drives us up the wall because the problem is the customer is ill disciplined. Quite often, a local marketing manager will still buck the system. So much time is spent reinventing the wheel, i.e., local staff doing their own thing. Then the agency has to be the cop and blow the whistle. We complain that the customer's global brand directors do not have authority.

Similar stories are heard from Shell, 'if the customer does not have a lot of global coordination, account management takes a lot more effort', and DMV International, 'if a customer reacts in a fragmented way, he often is not ready for a global relationship. This is not positive for the GCM programme'.

Other barriers at the customer end can include reluctance to take the global relationship beyond global procurement. For the supplier, the true value of GCM does not lie in the global contract itself, in which a higher volume of sales is often offset by a lower selling price, but in the improved relationship which will in the longer term lead to more profitable business. When the customer is willing to talk about transferring only the current business into a global contract, there is not much benefit to be gained in keeping this customer in the global programme. If this is the case for more than one customer, it might be worth identifying an extra category of global customer that need only coordination on pricing and logistics, so that the supplier does not waste valuable resources in trying to develop the relationship.

## Downward Pricing Spiral

It is reasonable to give the customer a certain price reduction if a larger volume of sales comes with a global contract. However, the supplier has to ensure that this reduction is in fact a reasonable reduction, in line with the reduction in selling costs that the supplier achieves. It is very easy to fall into a downward pricing spiral, in which the customer will want to negotiate a lower price at every opportunity, because the volume involved is so much larger than in any local deal. Especially when the customer is globally better coordinated than the supplier there is the potential for the customer to play different parts (geographically) of the supplier against each other to get the best price. Therefore, the first step in avoiding this downward pricing spiral is to ensure that there is good financial coordination within the company between the different local regions.

From the onset of the relationship, the supplier will have to ensure that the customer knows the programme has been set up to create a win–win situation for both parties, and not just to create lower selling costs and therefore achieve a lower price. Pricing issues should not dominate in the global relationship. If a customer would like to achieve a cost price reduction, the supplier should propose to start a project together to find price reductions in other areas than in its own profit margin. Companies could start a project to streamline the ordering process, or the logistical situation, therefore lowering costs and creating a profitable situation for both parties.

# Evolution of a Global Relationship

In our research we did a detailed case study on the evolution of the global relationship between the Star Alliance of airlines and advertising agency Young and Rubicam.[9] This case study, summarized here, illustrates many critical issues in how to develop a global account relationship.

## Creation of Star Alliance

Driven by the wave of global alliances in the aviation industry, Star Alliance was founded by five airlines in 1997. Lufthansa, United, Air Canada, SAS and

Thai Airways expanded their already existing bilateral cooperation agreements into multiple partnerships. The airlines, all with different geographical areas of strength, moved from having a reciprocal code sharing system to the coordination of flight schedules, joint advertising, integration of frequent-flyer programmes and common purchasing programmes.

## Role of Young and Rubicam

In the early days of Star Alliance, advertising company Young and Rubicam (Y&R) in New York was chosen to launch the brand into the global market. Y&R was an international advertising group which worked with many global accounts and customers. Wunderman, part of the Y&R group of companies, took responsibility for all below-the-line (i.e., non-media advertising) activities of Star Alliance.

As Star Alliance was a virtual organization, without the corporate departments in place to deal with marketing, it formed a marketing and communications committee (MCC) to work with Y&R. Each airline member had one representative in the MCC with one vote regardless of size, and the committee adopted a unanimous approach to reaching decisions. With all five members having the same passion and enthusiasm for the potential benefits that the Alliance could bring, progress within the MCC was swift.

## One Global Account but Many Masters

Y&R mobilized its global force to deliver on Star Alliance's needs, though the account was centrally controlled from its headquarters in New York. Working with Y&R meant Star Alliance had access to the talent and expertise in this supplier's 539 offices in 80 countries, plus the wider network of WPP, Y&R's parent company.

However, Y&R faced a steep learning curve. It had never before worked with a client that was both global and virtual. The traditional client–agency model proved ineffective for this account. With the lack of physical structures at the client company, such as offices or headquarters, the agencies had to earn the trust of each of the Star Alliance partners. The demands of the Star Alliance project—creating a global brand from scratch, working with different cultures and languages, transacting across different time zones—required the utmost creativity, flexibility and persistence of the whole Y&R organization and network. It was not going to be an easy ride.

Each airline had a vision for Star Alliance, and these visions were sometimes hard to reconcile. The agency responded by getting the Star Alliance members to a consistent platform worldwide. They did this by agreeing on a common target audience—the international business traveller. Y&R also assembled a team that had a thorough understanding of the different cultures represented in the Alliance. This way, any cultural sensitivities and nuances were carefully considered before putting together the marketing campaigns for Star Alliance.

Y&R had to evolve internally to work better with Star Alliance. Gradually, new processes were put in place within Y&R that not only improved client servicing but also addressed the client's concerns about this supplier's centralized organizational set-up and Western inclinations. The agency took very seriously, for instance, suggestions that its work was too New York-biased, and revamped the composition of its team so it achieved greater international representation. New initiatives were developed, for example, a global creative council, but when the 2001 terrorist attacks of September 11th happened, the consequences for the aviation industry resulted in a decrease in the marketing budget for the Star Alliance from $59m to $5m, which meant these initiatives had to be shelved.

Y&R later evolved from being the central base and originator of ideas and activities to having the role of international coordinator and strategic planner. Input from local partner agencies brought greater participation, as Y&R set objectives and strategies and then passed them on to the local markets to comment on how the ideas would work, as well as on their implementation. The local client and Y&R agency often worked together to agree the right execution of a strategy or idea.

The biggest test the Y&R agencies faced in working with this global client was the diversity of cultures within Star Alliance. The agencies were mostly tasked to prepare the agenda for the regular conference calls among the MCC representatives where discussions and approvals on marketing initiatives would take place. After the calls, Wunderman executives always noticed the lack of participation from some Alliance members (who came from particular national cultures), and took this to signify agreement with the proposals. Later on, however, the whole group would experience delays with campaign sign-offs because the members who had not participated in the discussions had some issues that they wished to clarify. This meant that Y&R and Wunderman had to constantly balance the delicate task of getting consensus on marketing campaigns with not sacrificing the creative and emotive elements of the group.

Members often played the 'culture' card ('you can't do it this way in my country') to delay things when actually issues were born out of their own personal interpretations.

It was important to distinguish between the national characteristics versus personal interpretations of the MCC members because at some point we risked being paralyzed by national cultures. Sorting out the cultural diversities was my greatest challenge, but also the most enriching,

said Louise McKenven, who was the committee chairman at the time.

But thanks to the combined efforts of Y&R and its members to overcome all these challenges, Star Alliance had a successful global launch in May 1997.

# Expansion within Star Alliance

For Y&R, the importance of keeping projects on track and having an efficient coordination system became even more improtant as work progressed and membership within the Alliance grew. The MCC found itself transformed from being a lean machine to becoming a bureaucratic organization, as it grew from five airlines and their five representatives, to 15 airlines and 30 representatives, supplemented with committees and sub-committees. At one point, meetings had over 50 people in attendance, and all with their own point of view.

'It was like being in the UN', recalled Carl Hartman, Y&R Account Director for Star Alliance. 'We at the agency realized we were also starting to create unnecessary people infrastructure for the project'. Motivated by the desire to serve its client's needs as best it could, Y&R recognized that putting more and more human resources on the project was not the way forward, as it only slowed processes further.

Due to the virtual nature and committee structure of Star Alliance, many functions that would normally lie with the client were filled by Y&R. The agency acted as the marketing department and virtual project manager for Star Alliance. 'There was a lot of pressure on us to keep everything on track. It came to a point when we were even involved in setting up the MCC's quarterly meetings, making phone calls to book dates into people's diaries', commented Hartman. To ensure timely delivery of projects Y&R and Wunderman employed a process management system. The system itemized each stage of the project, listed key timings and deliverables and colour-coded them to indicate which airlines had made decisions or complied with deadlines. But all this responsibility initially led Y&R to feel that its relationship with Star Alliance lacked the necessary tension of the client writing a brief and the agency delivering, 'Things were too one-sided in the beginning. To be so reliant on an agency like that was not to Star's advantage', said Hartman.

## Y&R as a Global Supplier

As a global supplier to Star Alliance, Y&R had to put all the necessary measures in place to keep communication lines open between them and their client. They did this in a number of ways.

First, the Y&R agencies made sure that their internal structures mirrored those of their client where relevant. Star Alliance was a global client. Therefore,

## Process

Y&R and Wunderman needed to have a global account management structure in place.

Second, because the Star Alliance account was incredibly demanding from a resourcing point of view, the account managers needed a strong support team. People who worked on the Star Alliance account had to work on it virtually full time. This presented challenges in terms of fulfilling their other responsibilities on other projects, as it was the norm in an agency environment to have responsibilities for more than one project at any one time.

Third, to ensure constantly open communication with its client, Y&R initiated a biannual client satisfaction survey conducted through a third party company, to rate the agency on eight criteria that dealt with building client relationships. The study enabled Y&R to determine existing client satisfaction levels; assess individual Y&R offices as well as the effectiveness of the network; and determine the level of value and loyalty the agency was creating. The study also allowed Y&R to benchmark its performance across its clients and year on year. Results of the study were presented internally and to clients. Hartman revealed,

We literally had our to-do list for the year coming out of the surveys. On the whole, the comments were fair, and by learning firsthand what the clients wanted because sometimes they won't tell you face-to-face, we were able to always evolve our management of the account

## A Mature Relationship

The relationship between the MCC and Y&R changed gradually as Star Alliance evolved from virtual to real, and as global economic climates changed. In January 2002, Star Alliance registered under German law as a limited liability company with 65 permanent staff at its world headquarters in Frankfurt. The new company, Star Alliance Services GmbH, had a full time marketing department that was headed again by McKenven. The strategic planning that the agencies used to conduct became the task of McKenven's team. Wunderman also took over handling the Star Alliance account from Y&R in New York. But whereas Wunderman's former role was that of partner to Star Alliance, it evolved back to the more traditional role for an agency.

From Wunderman's perspective, Star Alliance was a success story, 'It started from nothing, and within five years, it has managed to build a brand and be the leading airline alliance in the world. It has won the battle over other alliances'.

**Best Practices**

The development of the GCM programme needs to be seen as a process, not a project. Therefore, it is important that the ongoing management of the programme has the resilience to overcome barriers and resistance, and is adroit enough to ensure the right level of support for the programme is in place. Issues that are particularly important in the development and ongoing management of the GCM programme are:

- There needs to be effective information and communication systems that have the global capabilities necessary for GCM.
- The accountability systems need to be globally aligned.
- There needs to be a certain amount of personnel to support the gam in operational tasks.
- There needs to be someone to support the gam in strategic tasks: either a representative at corporate level or an executive sponsor (or both).
- After selecting the right accounts for the programme, it is important to frequently check if they still answer all criteria to be in the programme.
- Customize the global organization to the account, as far as the company's flexibility allows.
- Ensure the customer knows what you are doing for them.
- The best relationships will form between two companies that have retained a even balance of power.
- Have a planning routine for both the GCM programme and the specific accounts.
- If at all possible, involve the customer in the planning process.
- Be sensitive to friction between local and global interests.
- Ensure the company has global capability potential before offering it to the customer.
- Show the customer that the global relationship is not about price, but about working together for a better future for both parties.

# Notes

1. Greg Mirhan (1993) 'Advantage: Hewlett-Packard', *Global Executive*, March–April: 10–13.
2. Mirroring can be viewed as a form of organizational isomorphism. For classic readings on this topic see J. Meyer and B. Rowan (1977) 'Institutionalised Organisations: Formal Structure as Myth and Ceremony', *American Journal of Sociology*, September, 82: 340–63; M. Hannan and J. Freeman (1977) 'The Population Ecology of Organizations', *American Journal of Sociology*, September, 82: 929–64; P. DiMaggio and W. Powell (1983) 'The Iron Cage Revisited: Institutional Isomorphism and Collective Rationality in Organizational Fields', *American Sociological Review*, January, 48: 147–60; W. Powell and P. DiMaggio (1991) *The New Institutionalism in Organizational Analysis*. Chicago: University of Chicago Press; R. Scott (1987) *Organizations: Rational, Natural, and Open Systems*. Englewood Cliffs, NJ: Prentice-Hall. For more recent discussion, see D. Deephouse (1996) 'Does Isomorphism Legitimate?', *Academy of*

*Management Journal,* August, 39: 1024–38; G. Davis (1993) 'Agents Without Principles? The Spread of the Poison Pill through the Intercorporate Network', *Administrative Science Quarterly,* August, 38: 583–613; D. Palmer, D. Jennings and X. Zhou (1993) 'Late Adoption of the Multidivisional Form by Large US Corporations: Institutional, Political, and Economic Activity', *Administrative Science Quarterly,* January, 38: 100–31.

3. Example from David Arnold, Julian Birkinshaw and Omar Toulan (2001) 'Can Selling be Globalized? The Pitfalls of Global Account Management', *California Management Review,* 44(2): 8–20.

4. Bargaining power relative to suppliers and customers constitute two of Porter's five forces. See Michael E. Porter (1980) *Competitive Strategy.* New York: Free Press.

5. Robert D. Buzzell (1984) 'Citibank: Marketing to Multinational Customers', Harvard Business School case No. 9-584-016, revised 1/85, Harvard Case Services Boston, MA.

6. *Corporate Finance* (1995) 'Citibank's Object Lesson in Relationship Banking', July, p. 8.

7. For more on global capabilities and global strategy, see George S. Yip (2003) *Total Global Strategy II: Updated for the Internet and Service Era.* Upper Saddle River, NJ: Prentice-Hall; J. Dunning (1993) *The Globalisation of Strategy.* London: Routledge; S. Ghoshal (1987) 'Global Strategy: An Organizing Framework', *Strategic Management Journal,* January, 21: 425–40; G. Hamel and C. K. Prahalad (1985) 'Do You Really Have a Global Strategy?', *Harvard Business Review,* July–August, 63: 139–48; B. Kogut (1989) 'A Note on Global Strategies', *Strategic Management Journal,* April, 10: 383–9; and K. Ohmae (1989) 'Managing in a Borderless World', *Harvard Business Review,* May–June, 67: 2–9.

8. One definition of global capability says: 'The global company does not have to be everywhere, but it has the capability to go anywhere, deploy any assets, and access any resources, and it maximizes profits on a global basis'. See Yip (2003: 7).

9. A. Andal-Ancion and G. S. Yip (2004) 'Star Alliance (A): A Global Network', in C. A. Bartlett, S. Ghoshal and J. Birkinshaw (eds.) *Transnational Management,* 4th edn. New York: McGraw-Hill/Irwin, pp. 618–45; A. Andal-Ancion and G. S. Yip (2004) 'Star Alliance (A): A Global Network', European Case Clearing House, No. 304-566-1; and A. Andal-Ancion and G. S. Yip (2004) 'Star Alliance (B): A Global Customer', European Case Clearing House, No. 504-128-1. See also Angela Andal-Ancion and George Yip (2005) 'Smarter Ways to do Business with the Competition', *European Business Forum,* Spring, 21: 32–6.

# 11 Winning with Critical Success Factors

Align your measures to the customer's measures. For example, that means not the cases sold in but the revenues sold out.

(Tom Johnson, VP Global Customers at Diageo)

In the previous chapters, we discussed many different features that affect the success of global account management (GAM). In addition, we covered how to use these features to progress from a GAM programme to a more beneficial global customer management (GCM) programme. This last chapter combines the most important of these features into an overview of the most important critical success factors.[1] These fall into four main areas (Figure 11.1):

- the infrastructure of the company and the GCM programme;
- GCM roles;
- the relationship with the customer;
- an integrated approach.

## The Supporting Infrastructure

As described in Chapter 10, a major critical success factor for GCM is *having a good support system*. The support system provides the infrastructure through which the GCM programme can function to its full potential. This infrastructure also enables the integrated approach needed for GCM, so that the normal company processes and systems can interact smoothly with the GCM activities. *This way, GCM becomes part of regular company processes rather than standing apart from them.* Two elements of the infrastructure are particularly critical for a good GCM programme: good support in terms of people and good support in terms of information systems and processes.

### Good Support System—People

People can be a major strength for a GCM programme, but only if the right ones hold the right, critical positions. The supporting employees are just as

**Process**

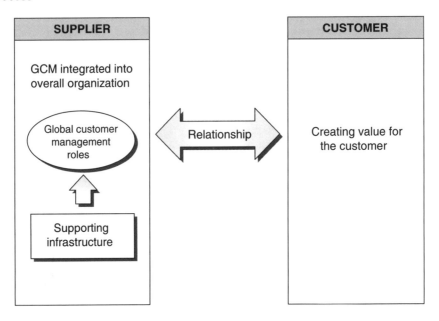

**Fig. 11.1** Critical success factors in global customer management

important, albeit less directly so. A good supporting network at the company headquarters and other important locations will ensure that the global account gets the esteem it deserves. This supporting network consists of two parts: operational and executive.

The operational supporting network comprises any *central service organization within the company that can be used by the GCM programme.* It would not be cost effective to have these services, such as desk support and account administration, at every location where relationships with the global customer exist. The GCM programme must, however, have access to this support for the company to be able to provide a professional and global service to the customer. For example, Schneider Electric allocates central marketing resources that are dedicated to the global programme, from which the global account manager can obtain support. Furthermore, it has industry expert teams in various relevant geographic locations (e.g., Silicon Valley for the microelectronic specialists). Both sources of support are extremely important for an effective people network for GCM.

The second necessary aspect of the people network is to *have executive commitment.* Most companies provide this executive commitment by having an executive sponsorship programme in which every global account has a sponsor on the executive level. This executive sponsor has occasional meetings with a senior executive on the customer's side, and helps the global account manager gain access to new parts of the customer's organization. When the executive sponsor is used to communicate information about the global programme within his or her own company it shows internal staff that the programme has the commitment of top level management, which will motivate them to help the programme succeed. Again, in the case of the people support at Schneider Electric, there is a corporate sponsor for the global accounts. He or she will meet with senior executives from the customer to discuss the strategic aspects of the relationship. Bringing these very senior people from both companies together ensures that the relationship is reinforced at all levels of both companies and that common goals are achieved.

## Good Support System—Information Systems and Processes

Another critical factor in support is *having good information systems and processes* that the GCM programme can use. The global account manager (gam) works with a diverse group of people and has to keep track of developments in many different parts of the customer company. Having the right information is key to progressing the relationship with the customer toward a partnership in which new initiatives can be taken that will lead to mutually beneficial situations. However, as the total network of the relationship between the global supplier and global customer is very complex, it is equally complex to keep track of all the corresponding data.

Just having an information system is not enough. All of the companies we studied had some form of information management system in place but, when asked, many of the gams admitted that the system did not work to its full potential. This is often the case when employees see the system as something they can get information out of, not something to put information into. Companies need to have a process of data gathering in which employees are motivated actively to provide data and information about their part in the relationship with the customer.

The IBM global programme works with an information system that deals with all project data. No customer project that is not in the system can expect to get any service support, which means that employees are trained to be diligent in uploading project information, and this is turn makes them more likely to upload other customer information. Another example comes from a large financial institution that actively encourages its employees to visit the internal information system at least once a day. This way the employees are confronted with the value of the information in the system regularly, which leads to higher use, and eventually to higher upload of information. Another option is to use advanced systems that are integrated with information that is available from other company systems, like the ERP system. Siebel has a system that does just that, which automatically leads to higher usage by employees, as they are able to find all the relevant information in one place. Again, higher usage will eventually lead to a greater number of employees who upload information themselves.

# GCM Roles

Next to the supporting network of employees, some particular GCM positions have a direct influence on the success of the programme. Working with global customers requires a new skill-set, and often the exact boundaries between the different roles within the programme are not completely clear. Therefore, the most important success factors relating to the GCM roles are that the roles are clearly defined and those who will fill the different GCM positions are chosen carefully.

## Clarify the Roles

As the implementation of a GCM programme brings new positions it is important to *clearly identify all responsibilities and duties of each GCM related role*. Whereas originally a customer was served by different local account managers who were each responsible for his or her own part of the business, in the new situation more overlap will exist, not least between the global and the local account managers. This can lead to misunderstandings as to who is responsible for certain activities, and can also lead to demotivation on the part of the local employees, as they feel all of their duties have been taken over by the global part of the organization and they are left with the, possibly uninteresting, part of the work. Therefore, it is important to make a job description for each GCM related position that does not give room for any confusion about duties. Furthermore, for other positions that only touch on the global business, a clear description of the global responsibilities needs to be written. For example, if there is an executive sponsorship programme, it has to be clear what responsibilities the executives have within the global programme and for the customer. Finally, all of these descriptions need to be transparent to all involved. Every employee working within the global programme needs to know exactly what to expect from his or her colleagues.

# Choose GCM Employees Carefully

For the key positions in the GCM programme it is important to *choose carefully who will fill the positions*. The position of global account manager can be especially hard to fill. First considerations will go to the sales part of the position, and many companies initially see the position as that of a glorified sales manager. But if a company wants to move its global programme beyond sales, it needs to look further than that. Admittedly, sales and negotiations are part of the relationship with the customer, but just a small part. If the company wants to progress the relationship with the customer toward partnership, it is important that enough emphasis is placed on relationship management, finding opportunities, entrepreneurship and long term strategy. Therefore, it is important to look further than simply upgrading a sales manager to global account manager, but rather to look for other qualities and skills. Prior knowledge of the customer or the customer's industry can be beneficial. Companies have been known to hire a former employee of the customer as global account manager. The Xerox gam for Volkswagen has 25 years of experience of working with Volkswagen, both within the company itself, and in other related companies. The Xerox gam for HSBC has a sound background in financial services, making him very knowledgeable about HSBC's industry. The Shell gam for Wärtsilä switched directly from Wärtsilä to Shell.

# The Relationship

The relationship between the supplier and the customer is crucial to any GCM programme. The better the relationship, the more opportunities arise to add value to the relationship and so enhance the GCM programme. However, the value of the relationship depends on more than just the global account manager and the global procurement manager getting along. Firstly, it is important to choose the right customer. Besides the customer needing to have the global potential sought by the supplier, there should also be some level of 'fit' between the two parties. Secondly, the relationship with the customer should not be on one single level, rather it should be a multichannel relationship. Finally, in order to reap the most benefits from the global relationship, a partnership between the supplier and customer should be built.

## Choose the Right Customer

In order to get the most out of the GCM programme, it is important to *choose the right customers*. Primarily, the customers chosen to be in the GCM programme need to have enough global potential to justify the extra cost that will be incurred. But beyond the global profitability of the customer lies the disposition of the customer. There needs to be some kind of *strategic* fit between the supplier and the customer for the two companies to see real benefits for both parties. The two companies both need to regard global business as a way to progress the relationship, not just to save on selling costs or to realize a lower purchasing price. Furthermore, there has to be a certain level of *organizational* fit. This can mean geographical organization, as GCM does not work well if the supplier and the customer do not operate in the same countries or have corresponding departmental organizations. Lastly, there can be other softer, qualitative measures of fit, such as having similar corporate cultures or opportunities for partnership, that are harder to evaluate. Many companies use a set of criteria to determine which customers will be part of the GCM programme. Just remember to include some 'soft' criteria measures in the process of selecting global customers, as this will help in selecting the partnerships that will be profitable in reality and not just on paper.

## Multichannel Relationship

When looking at a global relationship on a superficial level the main contact point will be between the global account manager and his or her counterpart at the customer company, often a procurement person. If, however, a company wants to create a GCM programme that goes beyond sales, it is important to *create a multichannel relationship*. A relationship that works on multiple levels will deliver more value to both parties. It is this approach that will enable a company to arrive at the right fit with the customer company, to find and seize opportunities, to create management commitment and to achieve good overall integration. A multichannel relationship does not just mean that the gams are based in different relevant countries, although it is important to keep up good local contact. The multichannel approach advocates more contact between non-sales related departments in both companies. For example, a representative from the supplier's corporate R&D department would be in direct contact with the corporate R&D department of the customer. Furthermore, the global account manager would not just have contact with his or her purchasing counterpart at the customer company, but preferably also with the end-customer within the account. So it is often a sign of a good relationship if the main contact at the customer company is with the end customer rather than with the procurement manager. For example, if the company supplies the customer with lubricants for its factory, the gam should develop a relationship with a senior person in charge of maintenance. This relationship will provide the gam with more information on the actual needs of the customer than would a relationship solely with the person responsible for purchasing the lubricants (with whom dialogue will mainly be about requesting lower prices!).

## Build a Partnership with the Customer

The last major critical success factor relating to relationships is to *build a partnership with the customer*. To get the most benefit from the GCM programme, it is important to lift the contact with the customer beyond a sales oriented relationship toward a partnership oriented one. The necessary trust between two parties for a partnership will enable both to be more open toward each other about future plans, needs, wants and problems. If both parties know where the other party is going, it will be easier to find opportunities for cooperation. For example, if a supplier of ingredients knows its customer is planning to start a whole new product line, the supplier can start developing the right ingredients for these new products. This way the supplier will innovate with a certain level of expected sales behind it, and the customer will achieve a shorter time to market, as the supplier is developing the ingredients parallel to the development at the customer company. However, for a relationship to be transformed into a partnership both parties need a belief in the capabilities of the other party, and a high level of trust. An example of such a partnership is the relationship between energy company BG Group and engineering company Bechtel. Their global agreement includes having a steering committee for the relationship with members from both companies and with the intention to treat each other as being their preferred customer and supplier. The openness and trust between the two companies have helped shorten lead-times and lower risks.

# The Integrated Approach

Throughout this book, the integrated approach of managing global customers has been outlined. It is, therefore, not surprising that *integrating the GCM programme into the normal corporate organization* and processes provides the final set of critical success factors.

## Integrating GCM into the Total Organization

By using the integrated approach, a company ensures that the GCM programme works smoothly within the rest of the organization. There will be no negative feelings towards what could be seen as an elite part of the organization, and the GCM programme can draw on support from all departments in the organization. Having people both within and outside of the GCM programme working side by side will generate more awareness of the global programme throughout the company, which will eventually help in promoting staff to give more support and to offer that little bit extra for these very special customers.

## Look Beyond Sales Activities

Nobody will deny that global account management relates to sales, but it is important to realize it can be so much more than just another sales strategy. In the integrated approach, GCM is a long term programme. It has to be seen as a process—here to stay—not just as a project with a start- and end-date, or the latest top management whim. Whereas sales traditionally focuses on the short term, trying to get that deal clinched just before the year-end cut off point for bonuses, GCM will have to look beyond that. Therefore, it is not advisable to have a large part of the gam's remuneration based on sales results. This might conflict with his or her objective to develop the relationship with the customer to bring more structural, value-added business. The focus on value-added activities can mean anything from providing the customer with products that have a higher profit margin, to starting projects that will decrease costs for both parties, such as working together on a more efficient ordering process, leading to smaller stocks and lower order costs. Trust is an important asset, and it will be gained only if the gam is not focused too much on the quick sell. *Having a relationship that goes beyond sales activities*, but is more focused on the added value that the two companies can give each other is more likely to lead to trust. A gam from Intel recognized the importance of the end user: 'The end user within the customer's company is very important. Even though this is not the person you are directly selling to, you need to know what they need, and how to influence them'.

## Seize Opportunities

It is important that GCM is more than merely 'minding the store'. The best reason to start a GCM programme is because it will open the door to bigger opportunities with the customer. However, if GCM gets stuck in the global coordination mode, it is not likely that these opportunities will be taken. If a company wants to get the true value out of its GCM programme, it needs to have people (the gam comes to mind) *actively looking for and acting upon opportunities*. To do this it is necessary to have a thorough knowledge of both the capabilities of their own company and the situation at the customer company. A good information management system will be necessary for this.

## Leveraging your Competitive Advantage

Every company needs to know why the customer prefers them to its competitors. Armed with this knowledge it is possible to *leverage a competitive advantage*.

It might be possible to build on the advantages with this customer, creating an even better position compared with competitors. For example, Shell develops a customer specific customer value proposition (CVP), in which it outlines the value that it can bring to the customer. A CVP can, for example, say that Shell is willing to invest in any new power plant initiatives of the customer. This will give the customer more security and, therefore, it will be more willing to do business with Shell than with competitors who cannot make such propositions.

## Evolving the Programme over Time

The GCM programme will not be flawless from the day of implementation, and even if it were, situations change. Therefore it is important to *keep evolving the programme over time*. The programme should fit well with the rest of the organization, as there has to be good integration. There should be a regular review of the programme to determine if any changes need to be made or if any customers need to be added or taken out. However, even though it is important to keep the GCM programme fitting seamlessly within the total organization, the GCM programme should not experience frequent big changes. As the GCM programme is a long term strategy, the relationships formed with the customer should have a long term orientation. If the company decides to make changes in the GCM programme, it is important that this has little or no effect on the relationship with the customer.

## Continuity

Implementing GAM takes time. Avoid pressures for short term results. The majority of companies that are new to GAM seem to struggle a great deal with resistance from the local level within the company and the lack of directly attributable results. However, the majority of companies that have had a GAM programme for over ten years say that they had these same problems in the beginning but that now GAM is a completely accepted and profitable part of their organizations. Continuity in the personal relationship is also important. Most companies agree that a global account manager should preferably be in this position for at least five years. This means the company does need to keep the position interesting. The short term goals for GAM should be well balanced and probably emphasize more qualitative goals. Be wary of constant organization changes within the company that affect the GAM programme. The customer will not appreciate this.

# Summary of Critical Success Factors for Managing Global Customers

## Infrastructure

- Build a good support system.
- Create central service organization that can be used by the GCM programme.
- Enlist executive commitment.
- Implement good information systems and processes.

## GCM Roles

- Clearly identify all responsibilities and duties of each GCM related role.
- Choose carefully who will fill the GCM positions.

# The Relationship

- Choose the right customers.
- Create a multichannel relationship.
- Build a partnership with the customer.

## The Integrated Approach

- *Integrate the GCM programme into the rest of the corporate organization.*
- *Create a relationship that goes beyond sales activities.*
- *Focus on added value activities.*
- *Actively look for and act on opportunities.*
- *Leverage a competitive advantage.*
- *Keep evolving the programme over time.*
- *Ensure continuity in the programme; GCM will become more rewarding, give it time!*

# Note

1. The concept of 'success factors' was first developed by D. Ronald Daniel of McKinsey and Company. See D. Ronald Daniel (1961) 'Management Information Crisis', *Harvard Business Review*, September–October, 39: 325–31. Jack F. Rockart was first

to coin the term 'critical success factors' in John Rockart (1979) 'Chief Executives Define Their Own Data Needs', *Harvard Business Review*, March–April, 57: 81–93. Also see J. Rockart (1986) 'A Primer on Critical Success Factors', in J. Rockart and C. Bullen (eds.) *The Rise of Managerial Computing: The Best of the Center for Information Systems Research*. Homewood, IL: Dow Jones-Irwin. For more recent discussion please refer to L. Mendoza, M. Pérez and Anna A. Grimán (2006) 'Critical Success Factors for Managing Systems Integration', *Information Systems Management*, Spring, 23: 56–75; H. Barrett, J. Balloun and A. Weinstein (2005) 'Success Factors for Organizational Performance: Comparing Business Services, Health Care, and Education', *SAM Advanced Management Journal*, Autumn, 70: 16–28; J. Goodbody (2005) 'Critical Success Factors For Global Virtual Teams', *Strategic Communication Management*, February–March, 9: 2005, 18–24; L. Ho and G. Lin (2004) 'Critical Success Factor Framework for the Implementation of Integrated-Enterprise Systems in the Manufacturing Environment', *International Journal of Production Research*, October, 42: 3731–42; S. Huang, Y. Hung, H. Chen and C. Ku (2004) 'Transplanting the Best Practice for Implementation of an ERP System: A Structured Inductive Study of an International Company', *Journal of Computer Information Systems*, Summer, 44: 101–10.

# Appendix
# Case Studies

In this Appendix we provide summary case studies that describe the approach to global customer management by four companies (DMV International, Royal Dutch Shell, Unilever and Xerox), and global supplier management by a fifth (Siemens). We have used some of the information in these cases in different chapters earlier in this book. As every company's global management programmes change often we give specific dates as to when we collected the information about these programmes.

## DMV International (as of 2004)

### Introduction to the Company

DMV International develops and produces functional and nutritional ingredients for the food, nutrition and pharmaceutical industry worldwide. DMV International is the industrial ingredients division of Campina b.v., one of the largest dairy cooperatives in Europe, with annual sales of €3.7 billion. The DMV headquarters are in Veghel, the Netherlands, and production and R&D facilities are based in Europe and North America. There are also 16 sales offices spread over Europe, Asia-Pacific and the Americas.

### History of Customer Management

DMV global account management started in 2000 with one pilot customer. When a major reorganization of the commercial structure of DMV was planned in the following year, it was decided to apply the best practice set up from the pilot account to other accounts. A customer segmentation project identified four types of customers: key accounts, core accounts, large transnationals and others. This selection process determined the key accounts as the ones that would be part of the new key account management programme. The set up in the pilot account was copied for the other key accounts, where each account had a key account manager (KAM) responsible for the account, and a key account team (KAT) supporting the KAM to develop a key account plan and to execute it. In July 2003 a training programme was set up for the KAMs and core KAT, and in October 2003 the surround KAT members were enrolled in the training. Since then the KAM and KAT have worked together on key account plans for each account.

## Objectives and Importance of Global Selling

The customer segmentation project is based on the objective to give the right level of attention to the right customer. This project identified the companies by which DMV wanted to be viewed as a valued supplier in order to make it easier to utilize internal resources in an effective manner. Next to identifying the right accounts to spend the resources on, another objective was to gain more openness and trust with these companies. For DMV, key account management means putting itself in the account's position to get a better knowledge of what the customer needs. KAMs enable DMV to occasionally take a look behind the scenes at customers and find out what motivates them.

A big driver to initiating the management of accounts on a global basis was the fact that customers were becoming better coordinated. Internal communication within major customers has become increasingly better organized, and each year there are more requests for global pricing. DMV always had an edge in global communication as it is a relatively small company and, therefore, internal communication was less challenging for them than for some of their customers who are larger companies. However, to keep this edge, as their customers become better coordinated, it is important for DMV to stay informed and to use any acquired knowledge to enhance the global customer experience.

## Designing a Global Customer Management Programme

The structure of DMV's key account management is built on having a key account manager and a key account team for every account identified as a key account. The KAM is responsible for the margin and business of the whole account. The budget is set up with worldwide input and feedback, and the target of the KAM is based on the overall budget margin. There are no dedicated key account managers. They all have more than one account. Because there are no KAMs dedicated to a single account the person chosen to be KAM for a position will often operate from the region where the majority of the business with a specific customer takes place.

## Appendix: Case Studies

The key account teams (KAT) consist of a core team and a surround team. The core team of every account consists of four or five people from different departments, including the key account manager. This combination is different for each key account, as the numbers of the team must be representative of the focus DMV has for each account. Departments that are often represented in the KAT are supply chain management, research and development, and marketing and production. Next to the core team for every account, a surround team is identified. The numbers of this surround team are less clearly named and will only be used for specific issues. For example, if the core team for an account does not have a supply chain management representative and a single project comes up that could use some supply chain expertise, then the supply chain person from the surround team is asked to join the key account team meetings for the duration of the specific project.

A special function in all the KATs is that of the key account assistant (KAA). The KAA makes sure that all information on the key account is well documented. He or she will produce reports for both internally involved people and the key account company. The KAA is the main information manager and will send out relevant documents such as highlights and financial reports. The same KAA operates in all KATs, therefore offering the advantages of experience and best practice sharing. Recently the position of KAA has gone. A new role for the key account coordination manager has been put in place. He is responsible for a proper execution of KAM and best practice sharing.

Roles have been described for all relevant parties for the key accounts, so that everybody knows what to expect from each other. What does the management team do? What does the business line manager do? What does finance do? Everyone knows what is expected in terms of support and implementation.

The KAM is the main point of contact for the account, but DMV tries to avoid a bow tie structure in the relationship with its account companies. A diamond structure where different DMV people have communications with different people from the account is seen as ideal. To have this on a global relationship, the customers need to have other global departments too. For example if the customer has a global R&D structure, this makes it easier to work together with the global DMV R&D people. There is no separate key account management department. Currently all KAMs happen to work in Europe, and therefore all report to the regional manager of Europe and the Middle East. This is more a coincidence than planned, but it does help. Both this regional manager and the MD are strong supporters of key account management. Local sales people working with the same account are on the same hierarchical level as the key account managers. They will report to their own regional managers, but have a dotted communication line to the key account manager. In some cases they are in the KAT.

Apart from the KAA, there are no people dedicatedly working on the key account management. For some of the KAT members, key account management feels like something they do 'alongside' of their actual job. It would be good if key account management could be more embedded in the whole organization.

## Selection and Customization

Initially the key accounts were identified in the customer segmentation project in 2001. The key accounts are not just selected based on size, they have to be strategically interesting and have potential for more added value sales.

Customization mainly occurs in the composition of the KAT, which is based on the issues and needs of the account. Apart from the difference in composition, each KAT member will have his or her own GROW (Goal, Role, Opportunities, Workplan) plan that is customized based on the situation of the account and the expertise of the KAT-member.

## Tools

The most important strategic information tool is Radar, a live link programme that works as an intranet information system. Radar was introduced in 2000 and rolled out in all the different DMV geographical areas over the following year. Although it seems that not all Radar capabilities are being used to their full potential within the company, it has proved to be a useful tool for key account management. Next to all the general documents that are available for all DMV departments, the key accounts have their own folder. In this account-specific web space, all relevant documentation on the account is gathered. Besides all the internal and external reports that the KAA is responsible for, Radar is also used to keep track of the progress in the 'GROW' of each KAT member. Although the Goal, Role and Opportunities are more or less fixed items, the Workplan is being updated at every KAT meeting. The achieved targets in the last Workplan are discussed and new targets for the next few months determined. The 'GROW' is an important guidance tool for DMV's key account management as it ensures that all relevant people are working with the account in a customized manner that is in line with the total key account plan. Another tool that was used during the start-up phase of DMV's key account management programme was specific training for global account personnel. The first group to be trained were the key account managers, then core members, followed after a few months by the other KAT members.

The KAT meetings for most teams are once every two months. Foreign colleagues who are part of the KAT core or surround team will not always be physically present, but video-conferencing equipment is available at all major DMV sites. Once a year the complete KAT will take a day together to work on the key account plan. This plan should give direction with the account company for the next year, and helps plan the 'GROW' of each team member. It is possible that the KAT members change because of a change of focus for the key account. The surround team is changing more frequently as members move in and out, due to the variety in current projects and issues. All team members will get the reports and minutes of the KAT meetings. Other information tools for all people involved are the regular booklet of highlights of all key accounts, combined by the KAA and the international quarterly report per key account.

## Company Influences

The fact that DMV is relatively small helps to overcome most barriers. Short communication lines help in having everybody well informed about all out-standing issues with the account. The standard friction between global and local targets that exists because of the matrix structure for global account manage-ment is therefore not as strong as in most companies. Most problems can be overcome by talking directly to the people involved.

Although DMV is a relatively small company, the key account management does not yet seem to be fully integrated in the day-to-day business. The internal mindset at DMV is not always positive towards changes. Sometimes there is some operational resistance because people do not understand why these accounts should be more important than others. The KAM programme needs to be part of a cultural change, and people need time to adapt to it. Aligning the KAM targets with the company targets and the personal targets of employees will help integrate the KAM programme.

Supplying 'service products' can sometimes raise some internal resistance. These are products—although not profitable in themselves—that are supplied to key accounts as part of the total service DMV wants to give these companies. As the current DMV structure means that an account can be supplied from two different business lines, these 'service products' can be the cause of some friction. One business line has to supply a product that is not profitable for them, while the other business line will reap all the benefits of the good relationship that is created with the account company by providing this service. Again, DMV's size allows for good communication and this helps to overcome these problems most of the time. However, it is important to ensure there are no conflicting targets within the company, and if DMV decides to supply a 'service product' the customer should not be made aware of any resulting internal friction.

The executive support is good. The roles of the management team for the key account management have been described and are visible for everybody in the information system. A letter from the management team was sent into the organization to endorse the key account management programme and to show everybody that top management is very supportive of the programme. There is a formalized executive sponsorship programme. DMV does want to have contact with its global customers on an executive level. Some global account personnel believe that a structured meeting with the key accounts on an executive level could strengthen the relationship, provide a better understanding of the customer's strategy and needs, and open up more opportunities.

## Performance

The key performance indicators for the global accounts are margin, the number of projects running and their position in the project-pipeline, and vendor rating (how the customer perceives DMV). Four times a year the KPIs are reviewed by the commercial management team.

As DMV is relatively new to working with global account management it is hard to really see performance changes, although small positive changes are starting to emerge. Customers seem to be more willing to start a partnership that will end up beneficial to both parties. Although customers will always demand a competitive price from a supplier, this type of relationship often leads to companies becoming preferred suppliers, which leads to a higher success rate in new business opportunities and more security in the supplier position. However, even with a partnership, getting all of a customer's orders is not a certainty. Good relationships should never be taken for granted.

DMV notices an increase in projects coming from the key account companies. Over time these projects will lead to more sales and an improvement in performance. In the case of the pilot key account, the good relationship that DMV had with the European part prior to the start of the programme, seems to have rubbed off to its American part. The KAM believes that valuable information reaches him faster than it used to.

## Future

As DMV only recently started the programme, the future will show a maturing of the programme organization. There have already been some changes in selected accounts and at this time all account teams have started to work on projects on a regular basis.

Based on the first experiences some changes in the programme organization might be made. One of the most repeated comments is that the programme should be 'better imbedded in the total organization'. Especially for the KAT members it can feel like something they do next to their job. Aligning job objectives throughout the organization is an important factor in achieving this.

## The AA Account—Interviews Conducted in April 2004

The relationship between DMV and AA has existed for approximately 20 years. Good personal contact is key to the relationship, as the Nutritional part of AA is strategically dependent on DMV's products. The core team for AA consists of a key account manager, the key account assistant, the sales person for the US, a representative of R&D and a representative of marketing. Regular surround team representatives are supply chain, application & development and sales people from other regions.

In 1999/2000, AA was the pilot for DMV's key account management. DMV noticed that for them AA Europe and AA US were two different companies. While there was regular communication between the account managers for the US and the EU, they felt they were missing something. Furthermore, the communication with AA's global R&D and marketing was not very good. DMV decided that it might be beneficial to take a global approach to the company.

After initial training, the designated KAM formed a key account team and wrote a key account plan based on input from the key account team members. He tried to structure the relationship on a more global basis. When AA first heard of these plans, they thought it would create a difficult situation, as they have a split between their US and Europe operations, but in the last few years they have started to see the benefits. A fixed point during every meeting with the AA EU part is the question, 'Please tell us what is going on at AA US'. AA appreciates DMV having this knowledge, but it is important to be careful with it.

AA is the global market leader in medical nutrition (with a market share of 15–20 percent), a market that is strategic to DMV's business. Therefore, it is a company that needs to be in the global customer portfolio. As AA wants to be innovative in this market, it is an excellent company to work with, to show them new DMV developments, and to learn from them what is important in the medical nutrition market. On the other hand, DMV as a supplier is also very important for AA. DMV is the market leader in strategic products for AA. AA also needs DMV because of its innovation strategy: DMV can help AA innovate with new products and R&D service.

R&D is a very strong part of the relationship. The direct contacts, between the AA and DMV R&D departments, help them to have a strong working relationship. They fully utilize their experience and knowledge in R&D. The AA EU purchaser would like to be more in this R&D loop. Historically, R&D would have the final say in what needs to be purchased, therefore disabling the purchaser's negotiation position. In recent years this power has moved more to the purchaser.

There is no hierarchical connection between the US and EU purchasers. Therefore, decisions made between the two of them can be jeopardized by local issues. Most of the time, the word 'global' stands for a theoretical approach. There is no coordination between the divisions. AA does see the advantages of possible global coordination, but the practical operations are far from being at that stage.

Executive sponsorship of the relationship between these two companies mainly comes from the DMV side. While the AA purchaser knows the commercial director and region manager of DMV, he said that the CEO of AA 'possibly doesn't even know where this factory is'.

## The BB Account—Interviews Conducted April 2004

BB is a little over a century old, and a leading presence in the clinical and baby food markets. It is present in 100 countries and has 12,000 staff. Six years ago BB started to consolidate procurement, starting in Switzerland with raw materials and packaging materials. A global department took over purchasing from the factories, mainly for Europe. The communication had not been very smooth. Therefore, it was decided that all the purchasing people would be grouped together. There is a global purchasing team in the Netherlands, managed by the vice president for purchasing worldwide. Global purchasing is definitely an important issue for BB, mainly for economic reasons.

For BB the key success factors to be a world supplier are:

- good economic performance (being competitive);
- quality;
- ability to bring value through innovations;
- security of supply.

A vendor rating exercise showed that BB rates the DMV performance as 'good'. They welcome DMV's step toward global account management as it enables the two companies to take a strategic view and to create success stories together. The appreciation of DMV as a global account was demonstrated by the 'BB Booster Awards' that were founded to recognize and encourage BB's top tier suppliers. With this ceremony BB emphasizes the importance of its suppliers in providing outstanding value adding performance and contribution to BB's strategic objectives. DMV was awarded the Booster Award for the Dairy, Proteins, Oils & Fats category.

BB thinks there is potential for extra business between itself and DMV, but DMV has to understand its needs, understand the strategy and deliver the objectives that the strategy aims to achieve. For example BB would like to see some innovation in the supply chain that would save money. But when this information is given to DMV through the procurement person it is hard to know what they mean by innovation. DMV needs more insight into what BB needs, wants and what its current situation is. One of the objectives of the DMV key account team for BB is to extend the diamond contact structure with BB. This way, they will gain more customer insight, learn about the needs and strategy of BB and be better able to provide the necessary products and services.

Sometimes the relationship falls back to common price negotiations, which undermines the partnership. There are times when there are talks about strategy and mission, but when the annual contract comes along its focus is on price. BB has a company culture where there is prestige in having purchasing skills. On the other hand, BB managers complain that DMV is not always as transparent as they want them to be. They feel if the two companies had more trust and openness with each other to work together on cost improvements, discussions on price would be more constructive than just being about claiming more of a margin. However, the BB purchaser feels that the relationship is moving in the right direction due to increased communications between the companies.

## The CC Account—Interviews Conducted April 2004

The DMV–CC global relationship grew in line with CC's needs. When CC wanted to start streamlining its contracts, DMV had just started the KAM programme. Therefore the consolidation of the CC contracts was not forced upon DMV, they were ready for that request. The CC core key account team consists of the key account manager, the key account assistant, a market development manager, a supply chain manager, and an R&D manager. The objectives for starting the key account approach with CC were building a good relationship, gaining more knowledge about the company past the procurement stage, and, therefore, being able to anticipate CC's needs and requirements. Even though CC is not buying on a global basis yet, the fact that DMV can offer global services gives them a competitive edge. CC knows they will want to move to a more global approach in the future, and supplier capabilities are surely taken into account at this time.

The KAM negotiates on all products that CC buys from DMV in Europe; coordinates the price in the Americas and the Far East; and makes sure there is one single strategy for working with CC. The latter is not very advanced in global procurement yet, and the negotiations in the Americas and the Far East are being done by the relevant geographical DMV sales people. For this, the KAM is in close contact with them. For existing business, after the KAM has set the contract, the day-to-day business of executing the contract goes back to the customer service personnel or the area sales managers for the relevant area. For new business the KAM is the first point of contact for the CC development team. They will bring in DMV experts to support them in this.

The KAM would like to see the customer service role dedicated to a key account. At this time several different customer service people work with CC, according to the geographical location. Having dedicated customer service people would improve the flow of information.

Both companies are very important to each other. They need to work together in the supply chain, as continuity is important to them both. Both parties realize that the way forward in a supply chain is openness. The more the two companies work together, the more tied up they will become and the harder it will become for CC to change supplier. An example of tying up the two companies is the E4US supply chain project that CC has been running for the past few years. DMV has been actively implementing E4US and has it running in four countries now. As the main competitors are not geared up for E4US yet, this binds CC even more closely to DMV.

CC is investing heavily in DMV as a supplier. The TPM (Total Productive Maintenance) programme that CC is working with worldwide is currently being implemented at DMV. The latter has acquired a new operations manager who previously worked for CC and has experience with TPM. CC also has an internal TPM consultant that helps DMV in the implementation. By implementing TPM, it is the objective that DMV products will become more economical, from which CC benefits. Some DMV personnel see this as CC taking over their factory and trying to squeeze them out of more margin. However, by implementing TPM the cost for all products will go down, not just for the products sold to CC. In a way this is a win–win situation.

The main concern in developing the global relationship to its full potential is the level of trust between the two companies. Especially where new innovations are involved. It is important to ensure that this does not escalate into a block on communication at other levels between the companies.

The main CC contact is very pleased with the current DMV KAM, as he perceives her to have a very accurate view both of CC's needs and requirements, and of DMV's capabilities in these. He says: 'If I want to know something about CC I call the KAM at DMV. That saves me calling all my colleagues around the world'. Furthermore, he is impressed by the level of global coordination and communication at DMV. Points of improvement that he mentions are a lack of entrepreneurial activities at DMV, and the legal barriers with new innovations.

# Royal Dutch Shell (as of 2004)

## Introduction to the Company

Royal Dutch Shell is a global group of energy and petrochemical companies whose activities include transporting and trading oil and gas, marketing natural gas, producing and selling fuel for ships and planes, generating electricity, and providing energy efficiency advice. The Shell companies are engaged in exploration and production, gas & power, oil products, chemicals and renewables as well as other activities, in over 145 countries and territories around the world.

## History of Customer Management

The global customer account management (GCAM) programme started in 1999. All global accounts were part of the Shell unit Oil Products (OP). Shell has a standard regional approach, (EU/US/Latin America/Asia) with regional (zonal) account teams, and global account teams for the customers selected to be global accounts. At the start there were five business groups for the global accounts; Automotive Manufacturing, Gas and Power (e.g., ABB, Siemens), Automotive Components (Lubricants, e.g. Bosch), Food, and Mining. During the set up, 12 customer groups were determined as global accounts, based on criteria such as size, importance, impact on business and regional spread. Over the years more global accounts were added—often by their own request—and some accounts were taken out of the programme, as they no longer qualified. In 2004 there were approximately 35 accounts in the global accounts programme.

At the start of 2004, Shell made some organizational changes in OP, which influenced the position of the global accounts. In the new situation there were two streams of business: fuel (retail) and lubricants. Lubricants consisted of consumer lubricants and industry lubricants. The global accounts are spread across the different business streams. For example the automotive accounts are part of consumer lubricants while the food accounts are part of industry lubricants.

## Objectives and Importance of Global Selling

There used to be a relatively low percentage of business with the major customers. Shell saw itself as the global market leader in lubricants, which showed in the amount of business it had from large companies. Shell noticed companies beginning to purchase on a global basis and in response formed the global team. It looked at its biggest customers and asked the question, 'who is poised to start purchasing globally?'

Three levels of key account management (KAM) were determined:

- real international accounts;
- regional key accounts;
- national key accounts.

The leverage of KAM should be that Shell grows into the opportunities the key accounts provide. They would appoint local people to a certain sector to help in zonal and global accounts. Shell would identify potential accounts and determine how many sites they have in a certain country, and how many Shell FTE's there should be for that country.

## Design of Global Customer Management

Each global account has an international key account manager (IKAM) who reports to the respective business manager. An IKAM is supposed to stay in his or her position with a customer for at least five years. The IKAMs have a team of local key account managers (LKAM) who are responsible for the customer in a certain country or region. The number and location of the LKAMs depends on the amount of business in the various locations. In some cases the LKAM has only one customer to attend to, but often he or she is responsible for multiple customers in a certain region. There are similar global account programmes across the different business groups with some differences. In the consumer lubricants group the LKAM reports directly to the IKAM, based on the majority of business, but will have a dotted line to the local commercial manager and Shell organization, as he or she is dependent on local marketing, local supply chain, etc. The LKAM's salary is paid for by the global account organization, as are all their expenses. In most of the other business groups, the LKAMs are reporting into their local line manager and have a dotted line to the IKAM. In these groups the salaries for the LKAMs are paid for by the local organization.

As the countries are P&L responsible, all the Shell local operating units are in charge of their own products and margins and they have the final say in pricing. All margins stay in the local country, even in the case of consumer lubricants where the wages of the local account managers on global accounts is paid for by the global accounts organization. The GAMs are remunerated on the total global business and the local account managers on their part of it.

In the old situation there was no alignment on scorecard targets. The country managers would have different priorities from the global account organization, and therefore would not always be willing to lend the support needed for good key account management. Now, there is clear commitment from the cluster business management including clear alignment of targets and tactical actions. All targets of people involved with global accounts are in line with the global targets. The new organization is a global one, with a global scorecard which cascades down into the organization. The template is the same for the IKAM or the LKAM and the targets are drilled down.

## Customization for the Global Accounts

The GCAM organization is the frontline to the customer, and deals with all the different elements the customer seeks from Shell. The customer value propositions (CVP) and, therefore, the elements that need to be offered are different for each industry, and sometimes even for each customer. For example, for the aviation industry risk management is very important, whereas the marine industry requires more time availability. In the automotive industry there are often CVP elements tailored to each customer as each company wants to improve their competitive advantage. The CVP is the perfect way to customize the accounts. This way the account knows its needs are understood by the IKAM and LKAMs.

## The IKAM and Account Team

The global account manager operates as an independent entity. Many of the IKAMs work from a home office, and are not directly involved in local operations. The account team does not take a fixed form for all the accounts, as it depends on the business and potential with a specific customer in a particular country. The LKAMs often work for more than one account. The IKAM does not have influence on who is appointed LKAM for a specific account, and he or she often has to negotiate on the amount of manpower in the different countries. This way it is hard to make a cohesive team, as you need the cooperation of the country managers to get people involved, and they will normally work on the things they are paid for (i.e., on local targets—not necessarily with the global account). The recent organization changes and alignment of goals have helped to improve this.

## Tools

As the global account organization is fairly new, Shell is still looking for the best way to handle internal communications. A first trial with teleconferencing took place, but with 50 people participating, it ended up with one person doing most of the talking. A better communication tool is a regional meeting, which takes place frequently. During these meetings everyone working with global accounts in the region is present, as are all the IKAMs. This way there is one face-to-face meeting between the IKAM and the LKAMs on a regional basis once a year. For regular information, a monthly 'highlights' document is produced with input from all the IKAMs. Some of the accounts also have an account specific newsletter.

Another tool that is being developed is a website for the global account management group. This website will hold all the relevant information needed by anyone involved with global accounts, such as: vision and goals, people directory, news and recommended training. The different global accounts will have their own tab in the website, with account specific information like the CVP and the account plans. These sites are not to be used for upstream information, and only the IKAM's are able to change the content of the site. For communication of results a management information system is in use, but not all countries have access to this. Business analysts will create monthly reports that take 85 percent of its input based on the MIS, and the rest combined manually. These reports help managers see at the click of a mouse what the current business status is. One of the tools that most IKAMs rate as very useful is the key account plan template. These templates cover everything about an account and are drilled down through the account team. This helps making account plans easy and coherent for everybody involved.

Apart from the general global account tools, each IKAM decides on the day-to-day communication tools that are most suitable for the account.

## Company Influences

During the start of the programme many conflicts were seen, mainly on the local level. Over the last five years things have settled down, although the system structure occasionally causes friction between local and global interests. The aligning of goals will aid this, and in the business group, Automotive, where the LKAMs report directly to the IKAMs it is less likely to occur. When Shell works on joint ventures, conflicts of interests will very likely always exist.

There is currently no formalized executive sponsorship for the global account organization, although the perception is that the executive level is supportive. As the new organization is being rebuilt some IKAMs have expressed the hope that some form of executive support will be formally set up. This would give the global accounts more power to climb the first barriers in business, open up initiatives and create more options to speak to the global account companies on a strategic level.

## Performance

It is hard to tell how much revenue comes from global accounts, as tax is included in the revenue records and can differ a lot over regions. However, most of the IKAMs can point out parts of a business that Shell received as a direct result of the global account structure. Sharing best practices and being able to duplicate projects from one country to another are good ways of enhancing the business.

The P&L responsibility is at the country level and the benefits of the business with the global account will therefore go to the local organization. This helps the country managers see the benefit of working with global account companies.

## The Future

As the new organization for oil products has just been implemented, there will be some minor changes in the near future to help things run more smoothly. No major changes to the global account organization are foreseen in the near future.

## The Wärtsilä Account

Wärtsilä started as a global account for Shell in 2001. The objectives were to grow the business as much as possible but also to become Wärtsilä's number one supplier, replacing Mobil Oil.

Wärtsilä is involved in power, marine business and the after-sales service market. Shell has been mainly dealing with power and Wärtsilä has a similar global organization to Shell, but only in around 50 countries. Wärtsilä has a matrix organization with geographic- and business-defined areas. In terms of sales, when one geographical area is selling a project, it is important for Shell to know what they are selling, so that they know which products offer. All projects are implemented by a project team that is based in Waasa (Finland). The service part of Wärtsilä also has a project organization doing upgrades and they work through the local operating units in a similar way to Shell.

A significant part of Shell's customer value proposition (CVP) for Wärtsilä is that Shell is investing in their power plants. This way Wärtsilä has an investor when entering into new market areas. The business idea behind this CVP is that Shell invests a little in the power plant, and at the same time secures the fuel and the lube oil agreement for that power plant and for the end consumer of the energy.

Next to approximately 30 local account managers there are some R&D employees who are regarded as part of the global account team. This is a central group, based in Germany, which will develop new oils and are currently testing new products together with Wärtsilä. It is important to have these kinds of contacts, as they provide a deeper understanding of the customer needs.

Since the start of the program there has been a performance change in the account. Shell seems to have achieved a stronger position in the sharing and negotiating of projects. If a competitor is cheaper, Wärtsilä will offer Shell an opportunity to match the price to secure the deal. The CVP is probably one of the reasons that Wärtsilä gives Shell this option. Shell is not just a strategic supplier to Wärtsilä based on volume, they can also give them something that competitors cannot.

## The Daimler Chrysler Account

Currently the Daimler Chrysler (DC) account has two IKAMs. One is in Europe—a German speaker focuses on Mercedes worldwide and on Hyundai. The other, in North America, focuses on Chrysler, Mitsubishi, Freightliner and Detroit Diesel worldwide, as well as Mercedes and Hyundai in North America. The two IKAMs keep each other informed and work together on issues that cover both accounts, but they otherwise operate as two individual accounts.

Next to the two IKAMS there are seven local account managers working for DC worldwide. The global account organization for automotives in total has seven IKAMs plus around 45 people that are part of the organization and report to the IKAMs. Depending on the requirements of the different countries, the DC account may have a 100 percent dedicated or a shared local account manager.

DC is not very globally coordinated, but it is trying to move in a direction of more globally coordinated buying. The platforms for the vehicles have all been separate, but currently a world engine plant in the US is being built that will start producing engines to fit Hyundai, Mitsubishi and Chrysler vehicles. Because it is moving more and more towards global integration, Shell has decided there should be a single global account manager for DC in the future. However, today that is not the case as DC is still fairly decentralized in its procurement. For example, the purchasing decisions for Mitsubishi Australia are made in Australia and not in Japan (Mitsubishi's HQ). The only current exception is that DC has recently and, for the first time, made a coordinated fuel purchase, but only for certain countries. They say they will start buying factory oil on a global basis—but this will probably not be totally global, and only for the main branches of the company.

Since DC is so fragmented there is no main point of contact for Shell in the organization. Different divisions make different decisions and having a single contact in this situation would not automatically give them preferential treatment as a supplier. Every little piece of business needs to be won separately.

The expectations are that DC will increase its coordinated buying in the future. Its main objective would be price reduction, but Shell is not afraid of lower margins, as the increase in volume and decrease in selling costs will more than make up for this.

## The Unilever Account

The relationship between Unilever and Shell really started becoming global when Shell had the opportunity to assist Unilever in the implementation of Total Productive Maintenance (TPM) in their factories. TPM is a culture-based, production floor approach, which builds an organization that aims to eliminate all losses, consequently realizing a zero-accident, zero-defect, zero-failure objective and improving the overall effectiveness of the production system. One part of TPM is autonomous maintenance, having the responsibility at the line to make sure that maintenance people have their hands free for specialist issues. This is where Shell comes in. Shell knows what is important for TPM and how to provide foolproof maintenance.

After having successfully assisted Unilever in TPM implementation at one of their Dutch factories, it seemed sensible to use this experience in other Unilever factories around the world, as Unilever is rolling out TPM in all parts of the company. Every new site that starts with the TPM implementation and is interested in using Shell will be visited by the IKAM and a local account manager. A presentation on how Shell can help the plant implement TPM will be given, ending with the question: 'Do you want us to be your partner in this?'

Currently, Shell helps Unilever with TPM in 60 plants and this number is continually growing. This would be the time to look at gaining more leverage worldwide from this relationship, and to see if there are opportunities to set up global contracts. However, the Unilever lubricants spend is estimated at only 3–5 percent of the total maintenance budget. This means that buying lubricants on a global basis is not one of Unilever's priorities, and Shell has to win the Unilever business one factory at a time.

The Unilever global account team consists of the IKAM and 40 LKAMs who often have more accounts than just Unilever. The LKAMs report to their local line manager, and have a dotted line to the IKAM. From the IKAM's point of view there is a sales side and a business development side of the account. The IKAM wants to improve the proposition with Unilever and achieve more organic growth. TPM is reaching a mature status and, therefore, Shell must look at all other developments within Unilever and how it can be of service in those. Both Shell and Unilever see this as a partnership where they can find synergy that gives them an edge over competitors.

## The Bosch Account

Bosch and Shell have a long supply history. Good relations exist between the commercial and R&D departments of both companies. R&D is very important, as it provides the best entry to the customer and, therefore, should always be kept in the communications loop. The IKAM has regular meetings with R&D and keeps them in close contact. Bosch is very open, not blocking any information and keen to continue this partnership. In the past Shell focused on the automotive business of Bosch and not the other divisions. The global account organization has changed this and opened Shell's eyes to the business opportunities outside Germany. By coincidence, Shell's 12 key markets happen to be the same as Bosch's key markets. This overlap helps the global relationship. In this situation the Shell global account team for Bosch consists of the IKAM, an R&D focal point, the European sales manager, 25 LKAMs and sometimes other people supporting the account for specific projects.

There is a European supply contract that combines Germany, Switzerland and Austria. Currently Shell and Bosch are working on a global contract. For this situation having an IKAM is a big advantage, as it gives Bosch a single point of contact within Shell. It would be even better if the IKAM had the authority to negotiate on price for other countries. At this time the only way to get authorization is to get the operating units involved, which means involving 25 people to agree on a global contract. The IKAM is also responsible for incoming business. Local projects will go via the local channels, unless they have an international impact or central R&D issues. In these cases local management is not involved unless there are barriers which lead to them being needed.

Shift of production to China and Eastern Europe is a strong trend in the automotive industry. Bosch will also start to invest more in developing regions. It would be hard to grow from the current position without the global account structure. The global approach gives Shell a major competitive edge such as the R&D skills that can be used all over the world and relationships that are already in place.

The performance of the account has gone up since the start of the global relationship. In some cases the IKAM knows more than Bosch itself. This gives him the power of knowledge so he can help Bosch with sharing information and sharing best practices from other countries. This way Shell is involved in projects at an early stage, which creates more global opportunities and a win–win situation for both Bosch and Shell.

# Unilever (as of 2004)

## Introduction to the Company

The Anglo-Dutch company Unilever produces and distributes a vast number of well known brands in the areas of nutrition, hygiene and personal care that are used by consumers all over the world. Unilever employs 234,000 people in approximately 100 countries and is divided into two global divisions: home and personal care and Unilever Bestfoods.

## History of Customer Management

Historically, Unilever has grown to be a very multilocal company. However, while the company used to work with regional supply chains on regional brands, Unilever started to globalize their brands in the early and mid-1990s. This way, they would create stronger global brands for their end consumers. At that time, there was no need to expand globalization for the benefit of the Unilever customers: the retailing companies. The diverging force was language. The operators spoke their local language, and the customer development was very much local for local. Trade term structures were also made on the local level, as this was historically grown. The customer development growth process seemed to be second-class to marketing.

In the second half of the 1990s, a number of customers, led by the French Carrefour, began to organize themselves internationally, first regionally then globally. More and more companies started to set up global buying offices. Unilever was not prepared for that situation, as they were still operating with a local structure: with fiercely independent local companies with a local P&L. Although Unilever had seen the globalization trend, the speed with which the retailers globalized their business took them by surprise. In February 1996 a first meeting of country heads covered the subject of creating a global account management programme for the big customers. The point was raised that Unilever needed to find a product to work on globally with Carrefour, or it would lose out, but there was major resistance against global coordination from the country heads, who had all the autonomy they wanted to work with these customers. However, reality caught up with them quickly, and soon all the relevant Unilever managers saw the necessity for a global coordination programme. Initially, Unilever started to make some ad hoc agreements for the French retailers, with conditions attached as a fig leaf. But as the globalization of the big retailers continued, Unilever soon saw they needed a more structured approach for global account management.

## Objectives and Priorities in Global Selling

Without doubt, the most important objective to start the global account management programme was to keep up with the customer. As the customer is moving to a more globally coordinated operation, they will demand more global deals and service. They have a specific global structure in place and want to work closely with their most important suppliers. Being a supplier the size of Unilever, there is no choice than to cooperate on this. Besides the fact that these are big companies whose business a company like Unilever can't afford to lose, their impact on the markets they operate in goes beyond their market share alone. As these companies often are market leaders, having your products on their shelves is an absolute necessity to be accepted as a leading brand in a specific market. Since the mid-1990s the retail market has seen much consolidation. As it is expected that this trend will continue, working with these ever-growing retailers will help Unilever to gain autonomous growth.

## Designing Global Customer Management

In 1999, Unilever decided there were five customers that they should see as strategic corporate customers, and they appointed one person as vice president to globally coordinate each of them. Two of these customers, Promodes and Carrefour, merged in the same year. One customer, Metro, turned out to be less globally coordinated than expected, and was dropped from the selection, while another customer, Tesco, was added. Initially this was all there was to the global account management organization: five mid-level management people, without any systems or processes. The actions taken per account were completely different. At the end of 1999 a new person was appointed to the position of senior vice president (SVP) global customer development, which later evolved into international customer development. This was the start of the implementation of a more structured organization for global account management.

The SVP worked with a network of managers in different countries who would get together once a year. But as the turnover of people was very high, the SVP role felt like being a general without an army. He reported to the foods director on the Unilever board, at that time Anthony Burgmans, who was very supportive of global account management. This executive support was very important in gaining support from the rest of the company. In 2000 the programme was rolled out for the food, and home and personal divisions. The SVP was responsible for customer development within both divisions but continued to report into food. At this time, the global account management programme is still evolving. Unilever is working toward managing the large international customers like they manage the main international brands. They will have both country P&Ls and a global P&L for the customer. The reporting is still local at this time, but with a global P&L the reporting might shift over time.

There will be a more central organization implemented that will co-appoint the people working on the teams managing the accounts. These teams should be more dedicated than they are at the moment. This central organization needs to be more embedded in the total Unilever organization. An option would be to let the business group Europe take responsibility for the Carrefour account on behalf of all the other business groups, the US business group for the Wal-Mart account, etc. Having one face for the customer is very important.

Unilever is at a turning point in global account management. Up to now they have been very defensive, which meant that Unilever's growth trailed behind that of their customers, so holding them back. Now Unilever has began to work on initiatives to really work together with the global customers and so realize more growth together. Unilever needs to work on developing the perception that they are a global company. Being able to offer global trade terms is a big part of this.

## Customization

Within the current Unilever global account management programme there is a very high level of customization. In the first place this is the case because there is not that much central coordination that forces the account teams to take a rigid approach, but it is also because Unilever has the luxury to customize their approach for each global account, as there are only four of them. These account companies have different areas they focus on in their globalization, and therefore it is good to be able to give them a customized approach.

Wal-Mart is looking to roll out its operating principle around the world. They asked Unilever to do this for them, and to help them open up new territories. At this time they are a predominantly US company, with a few international operations.

Carrefour is focusing on global agreements. This met with a lot of resistance in the beginning, but Unilever now realizes this is the way most global customers are going. At this time, Carrefour is their only truly international customer.

Like Carrefour, Ahold is trying to implement more global agreements, but doesn't seem to have the ability to do so yet. This relationship is still very much at the discussions stage.

Tesco, the last company to be added to the list of Unilever global customers, is still very much a UK company. However, as they have started to expand overseas, they are looking for support from their big suppliers, and could become a very interesting global customer in the future.

## Tools

The main tools that the VPs have to manage their accounts are information systems. Although the basic Unilever metric system is not specifically made to track global data, the majority of the necessary business information is present. Furthermore most account teams work with customer specific intranet pages, where the implementation of international agreements can be checked. No tools are present to use for global reporting. Information and reporting tools would be an important part of the improvements Unilever is trying to make on the global account management programme.

## Company Influences

There is good executive support for global account management. The Unilever chairman meets once a year with the chairmen of top customers. However, due to the current structure of the global account management programme, discussions at the top level cannot have a direct impact on the working of the local parts of the company. With the local companies still having autonomy, it is not possible to just force decisions upon them. This local autonomy is the greatest barrier to doing close global business with the customers. While these customers can be huge in total, they might only have a small percentage market share in a specific country, and therefore the local manager is not always willing to give them better trade terms than their important local customers. The VPs do need to convince the local managers to change this approach, as the total customer represents so much more than business in any one country. It is a tedious and lengthy process to coordinate, for example, getting 50 countries aligned each year to renew the Carrefour deal. Without the formal organization,

P&L responsibility and reliable data in place, the position of VP global account is one requiring much ongoing coordinating and extinguishing of fires.

## Performance

At this time performance is being measured by the standard Unilever systems, but they do not always give satisfactory results. Most of the VP global accounts have set up their own parallel process to collect the necessary information for managing the global account.

There are no real performance improvements that can be contributed to the global account management programme, but the VPs agree that not having global coordination in place will have cost them business in the last few years, and will cost them more in the years to come. Also, global coordination ensures that the global customers get Unilever support in countries where they only have a small market share at this time. The business that Unilever has with the global customers in these countries is not significant to the company today, but a global agreement will ensure this business grows as the customer expands their business there.

## The Future

The Unilever GAM is at a turning point where a decision has to be made on whether it will have only a pedestrian, coordinating function or a more executive function. There are three main requirements that drive the global customers in their pursuit of global suppliers:

1. Operating principles: the customers want to be treated fairly wherever they operate.
2. They want to stop going from deal to deal in each operation, and want more joint business planning. At this time Unilever has fairly sophisticated joint planning systems with all of their global customers.
3. They are looking for suppliers who can match their capabilities, and they want to use suppliers who can help to upgrade their capabilities.

The global relations are currently gravitating to this; they are getting more professional, sophisticated and better informed. Unilever is also undergoing a culture change in their company. It is now more widely recognized that they can't ignore the global aspect. It is expected that consolidation in the retail industry will continue, and therefore Unilever needs to have their global capabilities up to speed, so they can profit from these changes together with their customers.

# Carrefour

Around the mid-1990s, Carrefour had only one word in its vocabulary: global. It wanted global suppliers, global brands, global contracts, etc. After initial resistance from the local companies, Unilever geared up to do global business with Carrefour. Carrefour is the second largest customer for Unilever. Conversely, Unilever is Carrefour's second largest supplier. Therefore, the efforts in global account management are more than justified. At this time, there is a business group in each division. Unilever works with Carrefour in roughly 55 companies, and has 100 managers working dedicatedly on the account worldwide. Between these 55 companies, they respond to eight different business groups. To coordinate the account in a structured way, three business groups are coordinated in Europe, and one each in Asia and Latin America. The five business group coordinators report to their own business groups, but they have a functional role in the Carrefour network that is managed by the vice president for Carrefour. The VP for Carrefour draws upon central resources, or resources that are locally accessible, often because they are in the region where a planned activity takes place. The global Carrefour account network consists of the VP of Carrefour, the five business group coordinators, 100 dedicated key account managers, the account directors and customer development directors in the main Unilever companies.

Between 90 and 95 percent of the business is still being done locally and is managed by the local resources. Most of the international project leaders also work together with the local companies. An important issue at this time is getting the resources to work on the global relationship. So the local companies need to become more willing to share resources to improve the total business with the account.

The biggest barriers to working with Carrefour in a globally coordinated way are linked to the Unilever organization. Because of the high level of local autonomy, there sometimes are very different ways of approaching a business issue in a country or at the regional level. These differences are present in both companies and business groups. It takes a lot of effort to coordinate this. Another barrier is the lack of a good information system specifically designed to work with global companies. The current standard systems measure performance in a way that is only relevant for internal Unilever reporting. Because of this lack, the VP for Carrefour has set up his own process that is customized for the Carrefour business. A Carrefour specific intranet has a scorecard on which the implementation of the international agreements can be tracked.

Better information systems, both for Unilever and Carrefour, and more dedicated functional roles in the Unilever organization would make managing Carrefour as a global account easier and more effective.

## Appendix: Case Studies

## Wal-Mart

The global account management for Wal-Mart really started in 1999. Before that time Unilever did not know how much business they had with Wal-Mart on a global basis. From the moment Wal-Mart was selected as a global customer, the global account organization has evolved from having separate business groups to having a unified approach towards Wal-Mart in 2002. Before that time, Wal-Mart had a global organization, but with the different Unilever companies all handling the account in their own way there were problems. As Wal-Mart represents 8–10 percent of the Unilever business, it was decided to manage them in a more coordinated way.

The vice president for Wal-Mart manages Unilever's global business with Wal-Mart for all the different Unilever business groups. In each country where Unilever and Wal-Mart work together a Wal-Mart account team is set up. Those people are account managers dedicated to a particular part of the business. Typically, there is a team leader who runs the team and who works closely together with the VP. This team leader reports directly to the local business. The VP does not have control of the local P&L or personnel working with Wal-Mart. This structure assures that Unilever is being strategically consistent with Wal-Mart globally, and uses the same operating guideline within the different countries. In total, Unilever has 200 people working with the Wal-Mart account, some of whom are part-time. Five of these people report to the VP for Wal-Mart. They are responsible for different regions, and work with the staff in the local companies.

A set of communication tools enables the VP to manage these people world-wide. In global meetings about 50 people, mainly account personnel, work together with Wal-Mart to set foundation objectives for the following year. Consistent strategies, objectives and operation guidelines are used and sent out to all involved personnel. A global website enables people to get the latest information and statistics. Wal-Mart uses a system called Retail-Link that is the second largest database in the world. Wal-Mart allows Unilever to use Retail-Link for free, which is an enormous source of information. Unilever has a few people who are very skilled in using Retail-Link. There is a specific person responsible for all the number work with Wal-Mart, and this is working very well. This information is valuable for future strategic choices with Wal-Mart, but you need someone to work with the information. If the VP had to do this himself it wouldn't happen due to other more urgent demands on his time.

At the moment the VP for Wal-Mart does not have much influence on who is working on the account. The people in sales in particular countries are responsible for that. They will consult him, but he is not directly responsible. He does not have direct influence on performance rating, but if someone is doing a bad job, he lets the people in the country know.

The main driver to working in this way with Wal-Mart was the demand of the customer. As Wal-Mart wants to work very closely with their top 50 suppliers, the suppliers need to have a structure in place that matches theirs. If a supplier is not focused on the Wal-Mart business globally, they will fall behind other leading suppliers, as Wal-Mart is just too important to everybody's business. Wal-Mart is very focused on relationships. The companies that are able to work closely with them are the ones that will win over time. Wal-Mart is set to continue to grow, and suppliers need to be properly aligned with it to benefit from this growth.

There is sometimes some resistance from the local Unilever companies. Not all activities that take place on a global basis are as interesting to all of the local companies. If the local company doesn't want to cooperate, this can have an impact on the total business with Wal-Mart. However, as the total Wal-Mart business often is bigger than the business in an individual country, it is not so difficult to show the local companies why cooperation is important. Executive support is also an important tool in overcoming resistance. The chairman of Unilever US has ownership of the Wal-Mart account. He supports the global initiative and pays the salaries of the people who are not paid for by any one country's business.

Ideally, the Wal-Mart account should have a senior manager, living close to the customer in Arkansas, who should be responsible for developing the relationship. This person should be responsible for the total Wal-Mart P&L, and would make sure Unilever has the right interface from the supply chain perspective and the right interface with the top level people in Wal-Mart. This way Unilever could develop more leverage from it's size and gain efficiencies.

# Xerox (as of 2004)

## Introduction to the Company

Xerox's core business is document management. The $15.7 billion company provides technology, products and services to businesses to help them find better ways to work with their complete document stream, driving down document costs and streamlining document intensive business processes, hence making organizations more efficient and effective while delivering measurable savings on what is often an unidentified document cost. Their division Xerox Global Services is a global market leader in providing document outsourcing, communication services and business process services. Around the world, Xerox has approximately 60,000 employees. More than half are in the US, where the headquarters are based. The global customer management organization that Xerox has developed is divided over the different major markets. This case study focuses on the European side of the organization which is part of Xerox Global Services Europe.

## History of Customer Management

Xerox has recognized the importance of global customer management for the last few decades. In 1986 a pilot global account management project was started with six customers, which then grew steadily over the subsequent 15 years. During these years the significance of global customer management to the company became embedded in the company culture. However, the global customer management programme manifested itself more as a system of coordination than as an actual organization. The programme was mainly based on the sharing of information between the different employees working with a certain customer.

As Xerox was aware of the new customer requirements that were the result of the increasing globalization, a new global customer management organization was developed, which gave Xerox credibility as a global supplier. The implementation of this new organization started in 2001. The 'Xerox Global Account Operations' programme offered an integrated and coordinated global account strategy through virtual teams across the world.

## Objectives and Importance of Global Selling

The globalization of markets brought a strong demand from customers for a more global approach to account management. Global management and support are becoming a 'mandatory' customer requirement. Xerox realized that global knowledge sharing is a critical success factor and decided to invest a substantial amount of money in people, processes and tools to build the new global customer management organization. For this new organization to succeed they needed to move away from a product approach towards a partnership approach, and manage the relationship and not just the transaction, especially for value-added customers. Customers want a coordinated approach from their key suppliers, including globally compatible systems and global standards. The capability to offer global services gives Xerox a competitive advantage. When Xerox is bidding for national business it will encounter at least 10 other large and small competitors, while in global bids there are very few truly global players. This means the chance of winning the business is much higher in a global situation. A global bid will probably provide lower margins, as the customer tries to use the global volume as leverage, but a global bid also has positive side-effects such as potentially higher volumes, economies of scale and lower selling costs.

## Design of Global Customer Management

The Xerox organization is divided into the North America Solutions Group, the European Solutions Group, Fuji-Xerox (Asia Pacific) and DMO (direct markets, rest of the world). The US and Europe groups each have one person responsible for the global account operations.

In Europe, there is a general manager of global accounts operations (GAO). The companies managed within the global accounts operations are divided into tier 1 and tier 2 accounts. There are four different categories of account managers working with the accounts.

- Global account general manager (GAGM): responsible for one tier 1 account, reports both to GAO and the country manager of the country he or she is operating from and where the tier 1 account is headquartered.

- Global account manager (GAM): responsible for the managing of tier 2 accounts in the headquarters country, plus coordination on a wider basis; is possibly responsible for more than one account; reports to the country manager.

- National Account Manager (NAM): responsible for top national accounts. This person might be part of a global account team (e.g., Siemens a T1 German Global Account in UK will have a NAM in the UK and, Siemens AG has a GAGM in Germany). They are based in the country and manage the largest country opportunities.

- Global Business Manager (GBM): responsible for accounts which are big from a European perspective but where the account is not big enough in any single country to justify having a GAM. Each GBM is responsible for approximately five to ten accounts, which they manage on a European basis. They report to the GAO. They work with the tier 1 GAGM's outside of Europe to ensure Xerox delivers a common account strategy and maximizes the business opportunities in these accounts.

Xerox works with a sender/receiver concept in which the global account general manager (GAGM) works on the sending side, and the global business manager (GBM) works on the receiving side. The GBM manages the business of the sender global account assigned to him or her in the receiving country. The sender country is usually the country of the customer's HQ, where decisions and negotiations are taking place. The tier 1 accounts have a virtual team that is made up of all the people working on the account on a worldwide basis. The GAO is also in control of pricing and contracting in each country. Usually the GAGM (sender) is located as close as possible to the key decision-maker. For example, a German account, Siemens, is very large in many countries. Xerox considers Siemens as a tier 1 customer. The GAGM is based in Germany. He reports to the GAO and the German general manager; he works in all other countries with a virtual team.

Xerox's global capabilities depend on the critical mass in a country. The customer might want the same service in Colombia, a small and remote country, as it has in central London. The business in Colombia will be very small and so the Xerox capabilities will not be the same as in London. The same will usually be true for the customer. Xerox has a pragmatic approach with the countries and has its own version of the 20/80 rule: 'Usually if you concentrate on the top 20 countries you will solve more than 80 per cent of the customer problems'. The tiers depend on what you want to deliver. Tier 1 countries are those in which both the customer and Xerox are strong.

Xerox offers both regional and global agreements. The company operates with a degree of flexibility when implementing global agreements, as it needs to adapt to local reality. The umbrella agreement covers about 80 percent of key needs. Once Xerox has the agreement, it establishes the network of people who will talk to each other to get it implemented in all the relevant countries.

Similar systems to that of Europe are in place in the other Xerox groups. There is a network of organizations that are cooperating to ensure all customers get what they want.

The developing market organization is responsible for Latin America, Eastern Europe, Russia, etc. These are all fully owned except in some minor countries. Fuji–Xerox is a joint venture, but this makes no real difference. Sometimes the equipment is different, but that is because the requirements of the market are also different. So no extra coordination is necessary.

## The Global Accounts

Xerox uses three initial criteria to determine if a company can become a global account:

1. The company has to be truly global: it needs to have operations in more than two regions and a substantial part of the business should be outside of its home market.
2. The size of the account, both in existing and potential business.
3. The customer needs to be organized in a global way, to have global procurement and be willing to collaborate with Xerox in a global manner.

The initiative to set up a global relationship could come from either the customer or Xerox. Some customers actively seek global account management from Xerox and, equally, other companies that have never asked for global account management are asked to join the programme by Xerox, as they see the business opportunities for global account management for the account.

Global account management has to be mutually beneficial for the customer and for Xerox. Not every request for GAM by a customer is granted. Sometimes Xerox does not see the business profitability potential, in which case no effort for GAM with this customer will be made. Furthermore, Xerox will drop accounts from the programme if they no longer comply with the criteria. At the implementation of the global account organization, Xerox has selected a limited number of accounts, which has gone down from 60 to 15 tier 1 global accounts, as they only wanted companies in the global account programme that had a true appetite for global business.

Naturally, there is variation across clients. Size and customer requirements make each account unique. Also the account team and the difference in business opportunities can be very marked. The account teams are fairly customized, yet business driven.

## The GAGM and the Account Team

A good GAGM needs to be capable of internal selling. He or she should be able to put a business case together and understand the company, the culture and industry he or she is working with. The GAGM needs to understand his or her own company's political map, the customer's strategic objectives, his or her company's solutions and how they work towards the customer's strategy. There needs to be a defined period of tenure in the role of GAGM. The position should have a term of least three years and maximum six years. You need a fresh view after this time.

The GAGM is also the facilitator for all account issues, and owns the account strategy. This strategy is outlined in cooperation with the core team members. This means the GAGM will also use the input of national account managers who will actually be implementing the account strategy. This way they ensure adoption on the local level.

Paralleling the business with the global account, a set of dedicated people around the world will be part of the global account team. These people will report locally, but often with a dotted line to the GAGM. The way the GAGM works with these people depends on the requirements of the account.

One of the key challenges of the GAGM is to influence sales activity without direct authority; managing resources and getting target alignment are key areas of focus to maximize success.

## Tools

For virtual networks like the ones that the GAO works with, communication is an important tool. There is a governance process that explains to the GAGMs, GBMs and GAMs what is needed from them in terms of communication. Examples of this process are:

- a monthly management letter setting out the business outlook, digest, key projects, etc;
- a monthly global community conference call;
- a quarterly meeting with about 35 of the global managers in Europe to share best practices;
- global account strategy planning—each GAGM has to make an annual account plan, which is reviewed by the GAO every quarter, and all revenue streams are measured;
- specific management objectives for each GAGM.

The main tool for sharing information on the accounts is a Xerox web-based repository called 'Docushare'. Each GAGM can set up a Docushare group with web pages in their own setup. The pages will include information such as price lists, contract information, who's who, presentations, current projects, success stories and a chat room. The GAGM can give team members' access to the Docushare group in either read only, or read and write status. This is a reference portal for the community and a good way to collect information in a single location. There is also a system that gives global focus information, specifically tailored for executive use.

Besides these repositories for internal use, Xerox is working on developing similar information portals specifically accessible for certain customers. These web-based portals are customized for the account and include information such as the current contracts and which account managers are responsible for the account in each country. Ordering and billing can also be done on this website. A pilot project is currently running with five customer portals.

The 'global account reporting system' helps to get an overview of the global business. This system is set up in all country systems and keeps track of revenue and machine population in more than 5045 countries around the world. An automatic tool, 'Salestracker', shows the selling figures and places in the business pipeline. A central database gives the total outlook. It is a complex system, but gives a good idea about the total global sales to an account as well as the billed revenue.

Xerox also uses a Siebel electronic account planning tool for the global account sales process. This is where all account information relating to active selling cycles is maintained. Every year they will look through all opportunities in the major geographical areas, based on the NAMs annual plans.

## Company Influences

Global business is complicated. Country strategies will collide with global strategies and people tend to do what they are paid for and follow the solid reporting line. Typical barriers that Xerox struggles with are the following:

- Xerox has been organized by geography and product line, and still is today. In many countries there is more of a product view than an account view. GAO has been working to change this. Now each operating company should have a number of account managers to work with top national accounts and global accounts. The critical mass in a country will determine the number of people working on the global accounts and the large national accounts.

- Part of the Xerox business goes through other partners. Most of these partners are national, some of them pan-European. To get a complete view of the market, the cooperation and communication with partners needs to be particularly good. Xerox also tries to find ways to leverage the partnership.

- Country managers can be a barrier when the geographic view is too strong. As the sending country pays for the GAGM, local management tends to push him or her to concentrate on the domestic business. The GAGM is compensated for the worldwide sales to his or her account, but the country manager is not. This barrier is more psychological than the others.

GAO tries to ensure a good balance between the efforts for domestic business and the worldwide business. A good country manager will be supportive of what is good for the company and because it is beneficial to have a GAGM in their country, they are mostly fairly cooperative. GAO also tries to give people enough praise for good work on the global level, and to share the reasons why the global account is important.

Xerox has a focused executive programme working in parallel to the global programme. There is a focus executive (FE) identified for each account on a global basis, and sometimes also on a regional basis. Executive engagement between the two organizations is facilitated. Most country general managers and other senior managers are FEs, but there are also three board members who have an account assigned to them as a FE. Every year the different regions have a contest for FE of the year.

## Performance

The general opinion within Xerox is that the implementation of the global account organization has beneficial effects on the general performance. Xerox has won a number of global deals just because the customers consider the global capabilities to be a competitive advantage. There are not many suppliers who can compete at this level. Besides Xerox, the global players are Hewlett-Packard (strong in value-added products) and Ricoh (strong in cheap commodities). Both their capabilities on GAM are better than average. Ricoh is probably not as strong as Hewlett-Packard or Xerox but it has a good retail network.

Besides having a higher success rate in bidding for global business, the current global accounts seem to have become more rewarding. An example account that was worth $500,000 a year became worth $15 million within three years. At this time, the global accounts in Europe—approximately 100 out of 100,000 customers—make up 15 percent of total business.

Are these accounts more profitable? The current systems do not allow Xerox to measure automatically the true profitability of a given account although they can measure that of a single deal. However, the lower number of competitors combined with the higher level of value-added service sales to these customers lead to the conclusion that the global accounts are more profitable.

The targets for the GAGMs are based on revenue and management objectives. They are split into two levels: the business in the home country and the business in the rest of the world. The local managers in the virtual team are remunerated for their local part of the business.

## The Future

Continuous improvement is important for a dynamic organization. At this time Xerox is trying to achieve a good reporting system with alignment throughout the organization. This system should have a more customer-centric than geographical focus.

Educating customers is another aspect to focus on. Some companies do not know the value of global business and cannot see the bigger picture. Other customers see only the price. An expensive account organization like GAO is wasted on these kinds of account companies. They need to see what the mutual benefits of the global relationship are.

## The Volkswagen Account

Xerox has been in business with Volkswagen (VW) for 35 years—the last four years being in the global account operations programme. The main goals for this account are to win market share, to be their preferred solution provider and bring added value to the account. Xerox wants to support cost reduction with solutions and services, as that fits very well with both the VW and the Xerox visions.

VW is a logistics intensive company with one global quality standard that has zero-fault tolerance. It is sometimes hard for a company like Xerox to understand the needs of such a logistics giant, but that is exactly where the added value of a global relationship can be found.

Xerox needs to know what is going on at VW in order to respond in a way that will add value to the account. At the moment cost reduction is a hot issue at VW as there is a situation of overcapacity in the automotives industry. The culture of VW is that they 'try to protect the jobs of their employees', but they needed more flexibility and so have made the decision to move parts of the company to other countries. A lot of jobs are now moving to Eastern European countries. The GAGM for Xerox needs to know about business plans like these. He will plan how Xerox can help them in this global cost reduction with office equipment, systems and services, translation services and terminology finders, etc.

The global account team for VW consists of a virtual network of account managers in the different countries. The geography of these account managers will mirror the important areas for Xerox business with VW. The GAGM for VW tries to generate understanding for the customer with his virtual team. For global planning the national structure will be used. Within Xerox there are 68 people who work on the VW business and ideally should remain in the same position for at least four years. It is not good for the relationship if the account company sees a different contact person every year. There are also some connections made on a higher level, as executive support for these global accounts is important. The GAGM sees his own role partly as a transporter of information into both organizations. The other important part of his role is coordinating the account activity.

The procurement department within VW has a lot of power. The total VW procurement organization is three times the size of the whole of Xerox Europe. VW's procurement function is not always suitably open to possible opportunities. VW gives its purchases an ABC rating, with 'A' being the mission-critical purchases such as car parts. Xerox is a supplier of 'C' purchases, as its services are not directly related to VW's core business. This means it is hard for Xerox to show VW its true potential.

The GAGM is currently looking for a product opportunity that might be important to VW to give at least one Xerox purchase an 'A' rating, hoping that this status will speed up decisions within the very centralized VW procurement system.

The high level of know-how within VW can prove to be a barrier at times. Too much intelligence blocks progress in the company. VW is a complex organization, and its IT motto seems to be 'never touch a running system'. If it waits too long to implement changes, it might encounter problems in the future. There are always leaders and followers, but sometimes a bit of extra pressure is needed to get things going.

Because of global account coordination there have been significant performance improvements on the VW account. These improvements mainly lie in significant growth of the account due to early involvement in projects, better relationships with contacts in VW, more transparency and good coordination within the virtual global team.

## The HSBC Account

Due to the fact that HSBC has grown by taking over smaller companies and that these companies had different account managers, Xerox's account management for HSBC has traditionally been very fragmented. As HSBC deserved the attention that a global account would get, the company became part of the global account organization. Nowadays there is a single GAGM responsible for the whole of the company, but there still needs to be occasional efforts in integration to include specific people who were initially managing companies that have been acquired by HSBC. The same is true for HSBC, which needs to standardize its working processes throughout the new companies it acquires in different countries. Xerox's services can play a role in this. When HSBC acquires a new company that needs to be integrated into the company, it will call the Xerox GAGM to organize them into a 'look and feel' that fits in with the rest of the company. This would not be possible if Xerox still had a fragmented account management approach towards HSBC.

The GAGM has an account team that consists of national account managers (NAM) in the major areas where Xerox has business with HSBC. As HSBC is very much a UK-centered company, the NAM in the UK is fully dedicated to this account. Other NAMs in other countries will normally be shared with other accounts. The NAM is important for the account as HSBC projects that have run in one country will often be rolled out to different countries, and therefore good communication between the GAGM and the NAMs is vital. The GAGM tries to have the core people in the account team under tight control. Ideally he would like them to be remunerated on a team basis, but at this time that is not the way Xerox works.

Besides the NAMs and other Xerox personnel around the world, there is a more complex layer of distributors. They are a lot more difficult to manage and get information from. For example, HSBC Malta is a large company, but since Xerox does little business in Malta, they are managed by a distributor there. Xerox could not get the distributor to go for the price they wanted with HSBC and therefore they gave the distributor flexible discounting to make sure they could offer HSBC the price they wanted. However, this is a sensitive area and can be very complicated.

HSBC Purchasing has a very advanced communication system. One part of HSBC will be able to tell exactly what Xerox sells to the other parts of HSBC. Having an account with these kinds of global capabilities means Xerox has to make sure its communication is up to date. As the GAGM does not have an administrative assistant in his team, he has to enable and rely on good communication from the team members.

The new integrated way of managing the account is beneficial. The GAGM says that he gets positive feedback from HSBC. The relationship is moving from a 'push' to a 'pull' relationship.

## The Siemens Account

Siemens is Xerox's number one customer in Europe and number eight customer worldwide. In Germany an important 35 percent of the total Xerox revenue comes from Siemens. This makes Siemens a very important customer for Xerox, and therefore it has been in the global account organization from the start.

Siemens's global strategy was one of the reasons why it chose Xerox as a supplier. It needed a supplier that could combine local operations and global management. Xerox is a worldwide player, and will therefore fit in the global purchasing strategy once the buying efforts for this category are fully combined.

Siemens' purchasing is getting stronger. They are already bundling their requirements for commodities, but are not yet coordinated enough to do the same for more complex purchases like the Xerox solutions business. There is a purchasing user council (PuC) that combines the purchasing of standard products and their efforts, which will grow over the next few years, so it is expected that eventually Siemens will want to buy all Xerox products and services on a global basis.

When they started the global relationship, Xerox mapped Siemens' requirements and divided them into two levels. Level 1 countries (Germany, China, US, UK, France) have the highest level of focus. Xerox employees from these countries involved with Siemens are part of a larger account community. The remaining countries are level 2 countries. Within these countries, key individuals with a coordination role hold the Siemens 'linking pin' function. The account network consists in total of about 100 people. Approximately 50 are within the level 1 countries and 50 within the level 2 countries.

There are country specific strategic plans for the five level 1 countries, as the situations for each country are very different. For the level 2 countries, currently a pilot with generic web-based strategic planning is running. This should include a presentation and teleconference.

Siemens runs a very advanced supplier evaluation system in which its purchasing, logistics, quality and technology departments all over the world rate Xerox twice a year. Xerox will be showed the results of this evaluation and based on the results the two companies make an annual business goal agreement. The areas that need to be improved are listed, and together they set up a plan to improve the process, price and quality. They also try to calculate what this procedure will save the companies. There is an itemized action plan set up for a year and signed by management.

In the last four years business with Siemens has doubled, which has contributed to the global programme. Siemens wants a global interface, consistent systems, consistent products, consistent quality, a single level of global escalation and standard logistics. Xerox's global account organization is the perfect partner for that.

## The ABB Account

ABB has 122,000 employees in over 100 countries and an annual revenue of $17 billion. During the last two years ABB has been working on drastic cost reduction. However for purchasing, their focus seems to be on the direct material purchases. As the indirect purchases are only about 5 percent of their total purchases there is less incentive to spend a lot of effort in combining purchases in this category. Therefore the business between Xerox and ABB is focused at the local level. The Xerox GAGM for ABB balances central executive level relationships with frequent visits to local businesses. Twenty key countries together generate 80 percent of the revenue for the ABB account and the GAGM tries to get around those countries as much as possible, every trip being used to visit the local customer. During these trips he focuses on sharing information and will tell the local customer what is happening on the global level. This will create goodwill and leads to receiving more information from their side. In this way the GAGM is a valuable source of information both to Xerox and ABB.

The total (virtual) account team is large. There are 300 people in 54 countries working with the ABB account. All report to their local line manager. All team members are connected through Docushare, in which they can find account planning, account strategy and other useful account documents.

In the UK a national account manager looks after ABB and four other customers. For specific projects a project account manager is appointed in order to obtain subject matter experience and skills. These are often arranged by the country managers, who know their own organization, their people and the skills they have. The NAM will communicate specific aspects of the project within his own local team.

The main ABB contact says he likes the way Xerox handles the ABB account. For him Xerox is personified by the GAGM. He does not know how the account team is organized, but he knows the GAGM and that is all he needs to know. He appreciates the fact that the GAGM has a big network within both ABB and Xerox, and has enough power to make things happen for ABB.

ABB does not expect to start buying all office solutions on a global basis anytime soon. It is very much driven by local factors, such as employment and local costs—e.g., printing in the UK will give a different cost structure from printing in Poland. Some purchases on the hardware side are based on global prices, but on the services side it will take some more work.

# Siemens (as of 2004)

This case study describes the situation of the Siemens Information and Commu-nications Networks (ICN) group in early 2004. In October 2004, the company merged the Information and Communications Networks (ICN) group with the even larger Information and Communications Mobile (ICM) group into a new unit, Siemens Information and Communications. The previous heads of global procurement for ICN were asked to integrate the procurement function of ICM with that of ICN. After the merger, the total purchasing was about € 11 billion. In June 2005, Siemens sold the loss-making mobile devices unit to a Taiwanese company, BenQ. The Information and Communications unit continues to lead the rest of the company in terms of its use of global pro-curement, although other units are expected to increase their level of global integration.

## Introduction to the Company

Originally a German company, Siemens AG employed 430,000 people in more than 190 countries. Siemens provided products, services and solutions divided between the business segments of Automation and Control, Information and Communications, Lighting, Medical, Power, Transportation, and Financing and Real Estate. In these different business segments existed 15 operating groups. In this case study the management of global suppliers within Siemens will be discussed, with a focus on procurement within the Information and Communi-cations Networks group.

## History of Supplier Management

In 2001 the purchasing units at the corporate level bought goods and services from more than 100 material fields (down to 77 by 2006). The global procurement organization started in 2001 when Siemens set the goal to create an innovative and dynamic structure that would be able to meet the new challenges of the globally networked market. Prior to the programme, every production location had its own strategy in purchasing, but the global procurement organization led to an effective pooling of sources. The ICN unit seized the opportunity created by the really terrible industry conditions due to downturn that began in 2001 when nearly every supplier was losing money.

## Objectives and Importance of Global Purchasing

Achieving savings on procurement is an important objective for the Siemens global supplier management organization. However, financial improvements are not the only objective. By consolidating the supplier base, Siemens will be a more important customer for the suppliers that remain as preferred suppliers. Being in the top ten of customers for all the suppliers they work with gives Siemens the guarantee of high level support and service, as most suppliers care most about their biggest customers.

At this time, 50 percent of the total € 3.5 billion purchased by Siemens' group, ICN, was with global suppliers. Group-based procurement optimizes procurement processes and structures within the group and with suppliers. An objective for this is that decisions are based on more than purchase price, but the whole of the value-added chain is taken into account. The cost of ownership is more important than the cost of purchase.

## Design of Global Supplier Management

The central organization of the Siemens global procurement organization is the Global Procurement Board, which has representatives from all the different operating groups, selected regions and the procurement and logistics services. This wide range of representatives will ensure that both the cross-enterprise interests and the specific requirements will be taken into consideration. Also, having the purchasing heads as representatives in the Global Procurement Board ensures that decisions made have practical relevance, as well as making it easier to get decisions implemented in individual areas.

Every operating group, such as Siemens Communications, has a purchasing department which is responsible for the worldwide procurement of raw materials as well as other materials and services for the respective group. The heads of the purchasing groups are represented in the global procurement board and are responsible for the worldwide implementation of decisions that are made, on the corporate level, in their respective groups.

Siemens Global Procurement uses pooling as its purchasing method. Some of the important pooling models are the Lead Buyers, the Purchasing Council, and Procurement Services:

- The lead buyer was the first level of pooling. A lead buyer was based in one group or region, but for specific materials he or she would also handle the purchasing for other groups or regions.

- The purchasing council (PuC) consisted of a representative of the global procurement office, and representatives from different groups or regions. The council has a more strategic role, concluding exclusive master agreements and negotiating terms and conditions. The PuC is a corporate institution and its decisions are binding for the entire company.

- Procurement Services was responsible (until the early 2000s) for procuring the less strategic materials and services. It also covered more operational tasks such as order processing and logistics, while the Lead Buyer and the PuC dealt only with strategic purchasing.

Siemens has operated company-wide supplier relationship and evaluation programmes. A part of those was a corporate level programme for approximately 20 companies: 'Siemens Strategic Suppliers', the so-called $S^3$. An $S^3$ supplier needed to have contact at the corporate level. There was a relationship with a top Siemens executive who would ideally meet the $S^3$ supplier twice a year. The two would discuss strategy, vision, targets and prerequisites. These meetings were not meant for the discussion of operational problems, but it was possible to address requirements at a board level so that the supplier was aware of Siemens' needs and demands. The current version of this programme is even more comprehensive and adds an intranet-based supplier evaluation system.

Every operating group has a number of material group managers (MGM) who are each responsible for the purchases for a particular product group, and the strategy for that group. Furthermore, in general, there is supplier management in the form of the supplier champion, often the MGM with the biggest volume of business with that supplier. The supplier champion will pool the activities for one particular supplier. Among his or her responsibilities are the material strategy, the supplier evaluation, business opportunities, and managing and developing the supplier.

The supplier champion is responsible for the total business with the supplier within the operating group, while the PuC representative is responsible for a particular material. However, it is possible that the supplier champion is seated in the PuC and therefore has both functions. The driver for the PuC is the material; the driver for the supplier champion is the total volume.

Although Siemens purchasing is highly coordinated, there is a decentralized organization with several interfaces to the supplier. There is some pooling, but in a sensible way. There is a structured approach, centred over material segments. Siemens will pool at the corporate level for the things it is possible and sensible to pool, e.g., frame contracts are negotiated at the corporate level. But for many other things, pooling on a high level is not sensible and will only need a lot of specific extra agreements.

## Customization

The selection criteria to become a key supplier are to have a high total volume of businesss and to be a strategic supplier to many divisions. A target agreement and a procurement plan will be made for each supplier. As every MGM works within a strategic material segment, all projects described in these plans should fit within the main strategy of the segment and Siemens as a whole.

For Siemens, to be a key supplier means being globally present, and not that the supplier must have a global strategy or global capabilities. Siemens' global communications are very good, allowing it to take advantage of differing prices in different markets.

There are big differences in material categories. For example, this global way of working works a lot better with technical goods like chips than with power supply. Therefore, if necessary, there is some sense of customization over the different suppliers, but the organizational structure stays the same.

## Tools

One of the most important tools within Siemens' supplier management is the supplier evaluation. This is a cross functional activity that takes place at least once a year. In the supplier evaluation the focus is on cooperation (of which pricing is a key aspect), quality, logistics and technology. Each of those four areas carries an equal weight of 25 percent. From the supplier evaluation comes the supplier rating, with actions to improve and steer the supplier in the right direction. The whole evaluation runs on an intranet-based tool. Next to the supplier evaluation, another tool is the supplier status, which has a more long-term focus. In the supplier status, the supplier gets a classification that will have consequences for its business. Target agreements can be made and controlled, and the supplier comparison factor comes from this.

The supplier comparison factor is used for all suppliers, and can mean a plus or minus based on the classification. This supplier comparison factor is used when comparing quotes. The results of the quote will be multiplied by the supplier comparison factor and, therefore, a more highly approved supplier will have a better chance of landing the contract than one that has a lower supplier comparison factor. The suppliers know that the SCF has a big influence. There are quarterly review meetings and there is an evaluation/controlling loop to optimize the performance of the supplier.

Usually there is a workshop with the supplier where the evaluation feedback is discussed, a target agreement made, areas of improvement identified and an action plan devised. There are also supplier awards in different areas. Although some suppliers do not like to hear the results of this exercise, in general it is seen as a very valuable way to improve the performance and the relationship, as the evaluations force small areas of discontent to surface.

## Company Influences

Some aspects of company organization affect how well global procurement works. For example, the logistics are decentralized and often arranged locally. Hence, from a logistics point of view, there is a slight barrier. Another barrier is that sometimes the strategy used is from a general Siemens point of view, as opposed to an ICN point of view. There is not always a fit between the strategies of the different divisions, technology-wise. Also with the supplier evaluation, the performance over different divisions might not be homogenous. In this case it is hard to come up with corporate action items.

The cross-functional team does not always have similar targets. Sometimes it is easier to work with small flexible companies. Siemens needs a good mix in its supplier base such as some big global companies but also small logistically flexible companies. Sometimes it is necessary to convince the local Siemens people that this mix is necessary, and that the obvious solution for their location is not necessarily the overall best solution.

Siemens overcomes barriers by resolving them in the right place. The Global Procurement Board has been constructed to handle conflicts in an efficient manner. Most strategy conflicts can be resolved within the regular board meetings without many problems. The PuC is material driven over different divisions. They will address complex topics on a relevant level. This helps to overcome the differences between divisions.

## Performance

The Siemens global procurement system for ICN (and then Communications) has been highly successful when measured by the key criterion of cost reduction. For this division (or business area), the system has been able to deliver double digit price reductions year after year, which were necessary to counterbalance price erosion for communication equipment.

## The Future

The current Siemens global procurement programme has been running for only a few years. Expectations are that Siemens will expand the area of global purchasing to more material fields where they see fit.

## Company A as a Supplier

The relationship between Company A and Siemens started in the late 1990s. In the beginning, Siemens found Company A to be typical of many American suppliers in being rather inflexible with regard to their price lists. Siemens is a large company that has high expectations regarding contracts, payment terms, etc., and sometimes the relationship with Company A was a little disappointing. Around 2001, both parties came to an understanding. Company A understood what Siemens needed and wanted and there were new projects running, so as part of the project, Company A accepted the terms. An example was the creation, for the first time, of a Siemens AG worldwide contract with Company A. This contract is negotiated annually.

The most important line of contact between the two companies is between the supplier champion at Siemens and the global account manager at Company A. The role of the supplier champion is covering things that need to be addressed for every material field. When delivery terms are discussed, he will be the one talking to them. It is the same for every material field, so it makes sense to have one person. They use common sense to decide what should be negotiated or discussed on a material or global level within ICN. Whenever there are quarterly business reviews, he will contact all his colleagues to see what topics he needs to discuss. Then he prepares, collects and presents it to Company A and the Siemens management.

For every different group of materials that are being bought from Company A, there is a material group manager (MGM) who is responsible for supplier management, supplier evaluation, and contract and price negotiation. The MGM is responsible for the purchasing of the particular material for all departments. In general, there is one global contract, which the MGM negotiates annually. The local companies buy within this contract. The local units send the forecast to the MGM who then negotiates and sends a pricelist back. They put it in the SAP system and order under those conditions. As the MGM for Telecoms buys approximately 90 percent of the Siemens total at Company A, he is also the supplier champion.

There is a controlling tool called Modias, which produces a monthly update for every location. It shows the volume that was bought, the supplier quantities, and then calculates the average prices from the previous year compared to this year in volume changes, and so on. For some locations this is already working but others it still needs to be implemented.

There is something similar, a volume report, on the measurement level that collects data from SAP. These tools are very important to the MGM. He needs them every month. At the moment this works for existing volumes and is being prepared for future products.

Company A is very important, as a supplier, to both Siemens and ICN. In some products they are a technical leader, but in volume they are also very important. Siemens is also a very important customer for Company A. Siemens has a relatively aggressive growth strategy and Company A wants to aim for increased market share, which is good for Siemens as improved market share produces better prices. About once a year the supplier champion has a meeting with the CEO of Company A who then travels to Germany to meet a representative from the ICN board. He does the same with all the other Siemens business units. A representative of Siemens-wide management on the purchasing level meets with Company A once a year. These high level contacts are very valuable in creating a good working relationship. Although these meetings will not look at every little detail, they can be used to help if there are problems between the companies that cannot be resolved at a local level.

## Company B as a Supplier

Siemens spends about €20 million annually on parts with Company B. Every Siemens group has a materials group manager who is responsible for cost and strategy. Furthermore, there is supplier management in the form of the supplier champion. As this is mostly the MGM with the biggest volume, this is the MGM for products from Company B. The supplier champion for Company B is incentivized on price, terms and conditions, and other factors. However, as with other vendors, the only way for the supplier champion to be a success is to have a good relationship with the supplier as well as internal colleagues. The supplier champion has to cooperate with the cross-functional people and has to think of the wants and needs of the internal customer.

The acceptance of the Siemens way of working with external suppliers is very good. Company B's goal is to have maximum business with Siemens, which can be assured with an annual business of € 20 million. The PuC does the price negotiations for Company B and the supplier management process is done within the division—in this case ICN.

Siemens considers that Company B was a very difficult supplier to start with. For example, early in the relationship, Company B was selling one item in Germany at ten times its price to Siemens in Florida. But this relationship has changed so much that in 2005 Company B received one of Siemens' supplier awards. Company B and Siemens are now strategic partners, but the dependency is not so high that the one cannot exist without the other. There is a good fit between the companies. They are both big global technology-driven companies with a large R&D force. The technological drive for both companies is an important part of the fit. This means the companies understand each other's drives.

# Bibliography

Adams, J. (1976) 'The Structure and Dynamics of Behaviour in Organizational Boundary Roles', in M. D. Dunette (ed.) *Handbook of Industrial and Organizational Psychology*. Chicago: Rand McNally.

Adler, N. and J. Graham (1989) 'Cross-Cultural Interaction: The International Comparison Fallacy?', *Journal of International Business Studies*, October, 13: 515–37.

Akerlof, G. and J. Yellen (1988) 'Fairness and Unemployment', *American Economic Review*, May, 78: 44–52.

Aldrich, H. and D. Herker (1977) 'Boundary Spanning Roles and Organization Structure', *Academy of Management Review*, April, 2: 217–30.

Alexander, J. W. and W. A. Randolph (1985) 'The Fit Between Technology and Structure as a Predictor of Performance in Nursing Subunits', *Academy of Management Journal*, 28(4): 844–59.

Ancona, D. G. and D. F. Caldwell (1997) 'Making Teamwork Work: Boundary Management in Product Development Teams', in M. L. Tushman and P. Anderson (eds.) *Managing Strategic Innovation and Change*. New York: Oxford University Press.

Andal-Ancion, A., under the direction of G. S. Yip (2004*a*) 'Star Alliance (A): A Global Network', European Case Clearing House, No. 305-566-1.

———— ———— (2004*b*) 'Star Alliance (B): A Global Customer', European Case Clearing House, No. 504-128-1.

———— and G. S. Yip (2004) 'Star Alliance (A): A Global Network', in C. A. Bartlett, S. Ghoshal and J. Birkinshaw (eds.), *Transnational Management*, 4th edn. (New York: McGraw-Hill/Irwin), pp. 618–45.

———— ———— (2005) 'Smarter Ways to do Business with the Competition', *European Business Forum*, Spring, 21: 32–6.

Anderson, J. C. and D. W. Gerbing (1988) 'Structural Equation Modeling in Practice: A Review and Recommended Two-Step Approach', *Psychological Bulletin*, 103: 411–23.

Anderson, E. W., C. Fornell and D. R. Lehmann (1994) 'Customer Satisfaction and Market Share, and Profitability', *Journal of Marketing*, July, 56: 53–66.

———— ———— and S. K. Mazvancheryl (2004) 'Customer Satisfaction and Shareholder Value', *Journal of Marketing*, October, 68: 172–86.

Angulo, A., H. Nachtmann and M. A. Waller (2004) 'Supply Chain Information Sharing in a Vendor Managed Inventory Partnership', *Journal of Business Logistics*, 25: 7–27.

Armstrong, M. (2003) *A Handbook of Human Resource Management*. London: Kogan Page.

# Bibliography

Armstrong, M. and A. Baron (1998) *Performance Management: The New Realities*. London: Institute of Personnel and Development.

Arnold, D., J. Birkinshaw and O. Toulan (2001) 'Can Selling Be Globalized? The Pitfalls of Global Account Management', *California Management Review*, 44(2): 8–20.

Arnold, M. P., C. Belz and C. Senn (2001) 'Information and Know-How: The Two Pillars of Knowledge', *Thexis*, 1.

Axelrod, R. (1997) *The Complexity of Cooperation*. Princeton: Princeton University Press.

Bansal, H. S., P. G. Irvin and S. F. Taylor (2004) 'A Three-Component Model of Customer Commitment to Service Providers', *Academy of Marketing Science Journal*, Summer, 14: 234–51.

Barczak, G. and E. F. McDonough III (2003) 'Leading Global Product Development Teams', *Research Technology Management*, November–December, 43: 14–29.

Barney, J. B. (1991) 'Firm, Resources and Sustained Competitive Advantage', *Journal of Management*, 17(1): 99–120.

Barrett, H., J. Balloun and A. Weinstein (2005) 'Success Factors for Organizational Performance: Comparing Business Services, Health Care, and Education', *SAM Advanced Management Journal*, Autumn, 70: 16–28.

Bartlett, C. A. and S. Ghoshal (1989) *Managing Across Borders: The Transnational Solution*. Boston: Harvard Business School Press.

―――― (1990) 'Matrix Management: Not a Structure, a Frame of Mind', *Harvard Business Review*, July–August, pp. 138–45.

―――― (1992) 'What is a Global Manager?', *Harvard Business Review*, September–October, pp. 124–32.

Bartold, K. and L. Haqmann (1992) 'A Key to Effective Teamwork', *Compensation and Benefits Review*, 24: 24–9.

Becherer, R., F. Morgan and R. Lawrence (1982) 'Informal Group Influence Among Situationally/Dispositionally-Oriented Consumers', *Academy of Marketing Science Journal*, Summer, 10: 269–81.

Belz, C. and C. Senn (1999) 'Global Account Management', Special Issue of *Thexis*, 4: 1–64.

Bentler, P. M. (1995) *EQS Structural Equations Program Manual*. Encino, CA: Multivariate Software, Inc.

Benton, W. C. and M. Maloni (2005) 'The Influence of Power Driven Buyer/Seller Relationships on Supply Chain Satisfaction', *Journal of Operations Management*, September, 23: 1–23.

Birkinshaw, J. (2001) 'Why is Knowledge Management so Difficult?', *Business Strategy Review*, Spring, 12(1): 11–18.

―――― and M. Mol (2006) 'How Management Innovation Happens', *MIT Sloan Management Review*, 47(4): 81–8.

―――― O. Toulan and D. Arnold (2001) 'Global Account Management in Multinational Corporations: Theory and Evidence', *Journal of International Business Studies*, 32(2): 231–48.

Black, J. S., H. B. Gregersen, M. E. Mendenhall and L. Stroh (1998) *Globalizing People Through International Assignments*. Reading, MA: Addison Wesley.

Brannen, M. and J. Salk (2004) 'Partnering Across Borders: Negotiating Organisational Culture in a German–Japanese Joint Venture', *Human Relations*, December, 53: 451–87.

Brett, J. and T. Okumura (1998) 'Inter- and Intra-Cultural Negotiations: US and Japanese Negotiators', *Academy of Management Journal*, October, 41: 495–510.

―――― D. Shapiro and A. Lytle (1998) 'Breaking the Bonds of Reciprocity in Negotiations', *Academy of Management Journal*, August, 41: 410–24.

Brouthers, L. E., E. O'Donnell and J. Hadjimarcou (2005) 'Generic Product Strategies for Emerging Market Exports into Triad Nation Markets: A Mimetic Isomorphism Approach', *Journal of Management Studies*, January, 42: 225–46.

Brown, W. B. and R. C. Schwab (1984) 'Boundary-Spanning Activities in Electronic Firms', *IEEE Transactions of Engineering Management*, April, 31: 105–12.

Bollen, K. and R. Lennox (1991) 'Conventional Wisdom and Measurement: A Structural Equation Perspective', *Psychological Bulletin*, 110(2): 305–14.

Bourgeois, L. J., III (1985) 'Strategic Goals, Perceived Uncertainty, and Economic Performance in Volatile Environments', *Academy of Management Journal*, 28(3): 548–73.

Burt, R. (1992) *Structural Holes: The Social Structure of Competition*. Cambridge, MA: Harvard University Press.

―――― (1997) 'The Contingent Value of Social Capital', *Administrative Science Quarterly*, March, 42: 339–65.

―――― (2001) 'Attachment, Decay, and Social Network', *Journal of Organizational Behaviour*, December, 22: 619–43.

―――― (2004) 'Structural Holes and Good Ideas', *American Journal of Sociology*, March, 110: 349–99.

Buzzell, R. D. (1984) 'Citibank: Marketing to Multinational Customers', Harvard Business School case No. 9-584-016, revised 1/85, Harvard Case Services, Boston, MA.

Cannon, J. P. and C. Homburg (2001) 'Buyer–Seller Relationships and Customer Firm Costs', *Journal of Marketing*, January, 65: 29–43.

Capon, N. (2001) *Key Account Planning and Management*. New York: The Free Press.

Cavusgil, S., P. Ghauri and M. Agarwal (2002) *Doing Business in Emerging Markets: Entry and Negotiation Strategies*. Thousand Oaks: Sage.

Cheverton, P. (2003) *Key Account Management—The Route to Profitable Key Supplier Status*. London: Kogan Page.

Cohen, M. A., M. Fisher and R. Jaikumar (1989) 'International Manufacturing and Distribution Networks: A Normative Model Framework', in K. Ferdows (ed.) *Managing International Manufacturing*. Amsterdam: North-Holland, pp. 67–93.

Conner, K. and C. K. Prahalad (1996) 'A Resource-Based View of the Firm: Knowledge Versus Opportunism', *Organization Science*, October, 7: 477–501.

Copacino, W. C. and D. B. Rosenfield (1987) 'Methods of Logistics Systems Analysis', *International Journal of Physical Distribution and Materials Management*, 17(6): 38–59.

# Bibliography

Cox, A., C. Lonsdale, J. Sanderson and G. Watson (2004) *Business Relationships for Competitive Advantage*. London: Palgrave.

Daniel, D. R. (1961) 'Management Information Crisis', *Harvard Business Review*, September–October, 39: 325–31.

Davis, G. (1993) 'Agents Without Principles? The Spread of the Poison Pill through the Intercorporate Network', *Administrative Science Quarterly*, August, 38: 583–613.

Deephouse, D. (1996) 'Does Isomorphism Legitimate?', *Academy of Management Journal*, August, 39: 1024–38.

de Jong, R. (2001) *Global Teams*. Pale Alto, CA: Davies-Black Publishing.

de la Torre, J., Y. Doz and T. Devinney (2001) *Managing the Global Corporation: Cases in Strategy and Management*. New York: McGraw-Hill.

DeSanto, B. and D. Moss (2004) 'Rediscovering What PR Managers Do: Rethinking the Measurement of Managerial Behaviour in the Public Relations Context', *Journal of Communication Management*, March, 9: 179–95.

Deshpandé, R., J. U. Farley and F. E. Webster, Jr. (1993) 'Corporate Culture, Customer Orientation, and Innovativeness in Japanese Firms: A Quadrad Analysis', *Journal of Marketing*, January, 57: 23–7.

de Waal, A. (2001) *Power of Performance Management: How Leading Companies Create Sustained Value*. Chichester: John Wiley & Sons.

_____ (2002) 'The Power of World-Class Performance Management: Use It!', *Measuring Business Excellence*, August, 6: 9–22.

DiMaggio, P. and W. Powell (1983) 'The Iron Cage Revisited: Institutional Isomorphism and Collective Rationality in Organizational Fields', *American Sociological Review*, January, 48: 147–60.

DiStefano, J. and M. Maznevski (2000) 'Creating Value with Diverse Teams in Global Management', *Organizational Dynamics*, January, 29: 45–63.

_____ and A.-V. Ohlsson (2000) 'Schneider Electric Global Account Management', case study IMD-3-0940, Lausanne, Switzerland.

Dunning, J. (1993) *The Globalisation of Strategy*. London: Routledge.

Earl, M. J. and D. Feeny (1996) 'Information Systems in Global Business', in M. J. Earl (ed.) *Information Management: The Organizational Dimension*. Oxford: Oxford University Press.

Egelhoff, W. G. (1992) 'Information Processing Theory and the Multinational Enterprise', *Journal of International Business Studies*, 23(3): 341–68.

Erez, M. and C. Earley (1993) *Culture, Self-Identity and Work*. New York: Oxford University Press.

Ezzamel, M. and H. Willmott (1998) 'Accounting, Remuneration and Employee Motivation in the New Organisation', *Accounting & Business Research*, Spring, 28: 97–110.

*Financial Times* (2005) 'Smarter Links in the Modern Supply Chain', 8 November, p. 13.

Fleming, S. (1999) 'Global Procurement—A Universal Trend and How Canon Succeeds', *Thexis*, 4: 42–3.

Fornell, C., M. D. Johnson, E. W. Anderson, J. Cha and B. Bryant (1996) 'The American Customer Satisfaction Index: Description, Findings, and Implications', *Journal of Marketing*, October, 60: 7–18.

Foss, N. J. (1996) 'Knowledge-Base Approaches to the Theory of the Firm: Some Critical Comments', *Organization Science*, October, 7: 470–6.

Friedman, R.A. and J. Podolny (1992) 'Differentiation of Boundary Spanning Roles: Labour Negotiations and Implications for Role', *Administrative Science Quarterly*, January, 37: 28–41.

Fritschi, A. (1999) 'Global Key Account Management bei ABB: Erfolg Kennt Keine (Länder-) Grenzen', *Thexis*, 4: 26–9.

Fullerton, G. (1999) 'The Three Types of Customer Commitment', *American Marketing Association Conference Proceedings*, 10: 138–9.

Furst, S., M. Reeves, B. Rosen and R. Blackburn (2004) 'Managing the Life Cycle of Virtual Teams', *Academy of Management Executive*, May, 18: 6–20.

Gabel, M. and H. Bruner (2003) *Global Inc*. New York: New Press.

Gefen, D. and A. Ragowsky (2005) 'A Multi-Level Approach to Measuring the Benefits of an ERP System in Manufacturing Firms', *Information Systems Management*, Winter, 22: 18–32.

Ghoshal, S. (1987) 'Global Strategy: An Organizing Framework', *Strategic Management Journal*, January, 21: 425–40.

Goldberger, A. S. (1964) *Econometric Theory*. New York: Wiley.

Goodbody, J. (2005) 'Critical Success Factors for Global Virtual Teams', *Strategic Communication Management*, February–March, 9: 18–24.

Gooderham, G. and B. Maskell (1998) 'Information Systems that Support Performance Management', *Journal of Strategic Performance Measurement*, February/March, 12: 23–35.

Govindarajan, V. and A. Gupta (2001) 'Building an Effective Global Business Team', *MIT Sloan Management Review*, Summer, 42: 63–71.

Graham, J., A. Mintu and W. Rodgers (1994) 'Explorations of Negotiation Behaviours in Ten Foreign Cultures using a Model Developed in the United States', *Management Science*, January, 40: 72–95.

Grant, R.M. (1996) 'Towards a Knowledge-Based View of the Firm', *Strategic Management Journal*, Winter Special Issue, 17: 109–22.

Grossman, T. and J. Walsh (2004) 'Avoiding the Pitfalls of ERP System Implementation', *Information Systems Management*, Spring, 21: 38–42.

Grundy, J. and J. Ginger (1998) 'Global Teams for the Millennium', *Management Decision*, January, 36: 31–5.

Grönroos, C. (1997) 'Value-Driven Relational Marketing: From Products to Resources and Competencies', *Journal of Marketing Management*, 13(5): 407–20.

Gulati, Ranjay (1995) 'Social Structure and Alliance Formation Patterns: A Longitudinal Analysis', June, 40: 619–52.

———— (1998) 'Alliances and Networks', *Strategic Management Journal*, March, 19: 293–317.

# Bibliography

Gulati, Ranjay (1999) 'Network Location and Learning: The Influence of Network Resources and Firm Capabilities on Alliance Formation', *Strategic Management Journal*, March, 20: 397–420.

———— and M. Gargulio (1999) 'Where Do Interorganizational Networks Come From?', *American Journal of Sociology*, October, 104: 1439–93.

———— and N. Nohria (2000) 'Strategic Networks', *Strategic Management Journal*, March, 21: 381–404.

Hamel, G. and C. K. Prahalad (1985) 'Do You Really Have a Global Strategy?' *Harvard Business Review*, July-August, pp. 139–48.

Hannan, M. and J. Freeman (1977) 'The Population Ecology of Organizations', *American Journal of Sociology'*, September, 82: 929–64.

Hargie, O. and D. Tourish (1999) 'Internal Communications and the Management of Change', in R. Baker, H. Hearnshaw and N. Robertson (eds.) *Implementing Change With Clinical Audit*. (New York: Wiley.

———— D. Dickson and D. Tourish (1999) *Communication in Management*. Gower: Aldershot.

Harvey, M. and M. Novicevic (2002) 'The Co-ordination of Strategic Initiatives Within Global Organizations: The Role of Global Teams', *International Journal of Human Resource Management*, June, 13: 660–76.

Hennessey, H. D. and J.-P. Jeannet (2003) *Global Account Management: Creating Value*. New York: Wiley.

Hickins, M. (1998) 'Creating a Global Team', *Management Review*, September, 87: 6–7.

Ho, L. and G. Lin (2004) 'Critical Success Factor Framework for the Implementation of Integrated-Enterprise Systems in the Manufacturing Environment', *International Journal of Production Research*, October, 42: 3731–42.

Hofstede, G. (1980) *Culture's Consequences*. Beverly Hills, CA: Sage.

———— (1991) *Culture and Organisations*. London: McGraw-Hill.

———— and W. Luo (1996) 'A Framework for Studying Computer Support of Organizational Infrastructure', *Information and Management*, January, 31: 13–24.

Holsapple, C. and A. Whinston (1996) *Decision Support Systems—A Knowledge-Based Approach*. St. Paul, MN: West Publishing Company.

Houlihan, J. B. (1986) 'International Supply Chain Management', *International Journal of Physical Distribution and Materials Management*, 15(1): 22–38.

Huang, Z. and A. Gangopadhyay (2004) 'A Simulation Study of Supply Chain Management to Measure the Impact of Information Sharing', *Information Resources Management Journal*, July–September, 17: 540–56.

Huang, S., Y. Hung, H. Chen and C. Ku (2004) 'Transplanting the Best Practice for Implementation of an ERP System: A Structured Inductive Study of an International Company', *Journal of Computer Information Systems*, Summer, 44: 101–10.

Hult, G. T. M., D. J. Ketchen, Jr. and S. F. Slater (2004) 'Information Processing, Knowledge Development, and Strategic Supply Chain Performance', *Academy of Management Journal*, 47: 241–53.

Jackson, B. B. (1985) *Winning and Keeping Industrial Customers*. New York: Lexington Books.

Jaeger, A. (1986) 'Organizational Development and National Culture: Where's the Fit?', *Academy of Management Review*, January, 11: 178–90.

Jarvis, C. B., S. B. MacKenzie and P. M. Podsakoff (2003) 'A Critical Review of Construct Indicators and Measurement Model Misspecification in Marketing and Consumer Research', *Journal of Consumer Research*, September, 30: 199–218.

Johansson, J. K. (1997) *Global Marketing*. New York: Irwin.

——— and G. S. Yip (1994) 'Exploiting Globalization Potential: U.S. and Japanese Strategies', *Strategic Management Journal*, 15: 579–601.

Johlke, M. C. and D. F. Duhan (2001) 'Supervisor Communication Practices and Boundary Spanner Role Ambiguity', *Journal of Managerial Issues*, January, 13: 87–101.

Kale, S. and J. Barnes (1992) 'Understanding the Domain of Cross-National Buyer–Seller Interactions', *Journal of International Business Studies*, January, 23: 101–32.

Kalwani, U. M. and N. Narayandas (1995) 'Long-Term Manufacturer–Supplier Relationships: Do They Pay Off for Supplier Firms?' *Journal of Marketing*, 59: 1–16.

Karimi, J. and B. R. Konsynski (1991) 'Globalization and Informationa Management Strategies', *Journal of Information Management Systems*, Spring, 7(4): 7–26.

Kauffeld, S. (2006) 'Self-Directed Work Groups and Team Competence', *Journal of Occupational and Organizational Psychology*, March, 79: 1–21.

Keller, R. T. and W. F. Holland (1975) 'Boundary Spanning Roles in a Research and Development Organization: An Empirical Investigation', *Academy of Management Journal*, April, 18: 388–93.

Kelley, E. (2001) 'Keys to Effective Virtual Global Teams', *The Academy of Management Executive*, May, 15: 132–5.

Kim, K. (2001) 'On the Effects of Customer Conditions on Distributor Commitment and Supplier Commitment in Industrial Channels of Distribution', *Journal of Business Research*, February, 51: 87–9.

Kim, W. C. and R. Mauborgne (1995) 'A Procedural Justice Model of Strategic Decision Making', *Organization Science*, 6(1): 44–61.

Kirkman, B., B. Rosen, P. Tesluk and C. Gibson (2004) 'The Impact of Team Empowerment on Virtual Team Performance: The Moderating Role of Face-to-Face Interaction', *Academy of Management Journal*, April, 47: 175–92.

Kogut, B. (1985) 'Designing Global Strategies: Profiting from Operational Flexibility', *Sloan Management Review*, Fall, pp. 27–38.

——— (1985) 'A Note on Global Strategies', *Strategic Management Journal*, April, 10: 383–9.

——— 'What Firms Do? Coordination, Identity, and Learning', *Organization Science*, October, 7: 502–18.

Kotabe, M. and G. S. Omura (1989) 'Sourcing Strategies of European and Japanese Multinationals: A Comparison', *Journal of International Business Studies*, Spring, 20(1): 113–30.

# Bibliography

Kraljic, P. (1983) 'Purchasing Must Become Supply Management', *Harvard Business Review*, September–October, 61: 109–17.

Kumar, N. (2004) *Marketing as Strategy*. Boston: Harvard Business School Press.

Lawler, E. (1981) *Pay and Organisation Development*. Reading, MA: Addison-Wesley.

Lawrence, P. R. and J. W. Lorsch (1967) *Organization and Environment*. Boston: Graduate School of Business Administration, Harvard University.

Lee, H. L., K. C. So and C. S. Tang (2000) 'The Value of Information Sharing in a Two-Level Supply Chain', *Management Science*, May, 46: 626–44.

Levitt, T. (1983) 'The Globalization of Markets', *Harvard Business Review*, May–June, pp. 92–102.

Levy, M. (1990) 'Sun Microsystems Automates Financial Reporting', *Management Accounting*, January, 71: 24–8.

Lovelock, C. H. and G. S. Yip (1996) 'Developing Global Strategies for Service Businesses', *California Management Review*, Winter, 37(3): 64–86.

MacKenzie, S. B. (2003) 'The Dangers of Poor Construct Conceptualization', *Journal of the Academy of Marketing Science*, 31(3): 323–6.

Madapusi, A. and D. D'Souza (2005) 'Aligning ERP Systems with International Strategies', *Information Systems Management*, Winter, 22: 7–17.

Malnight, T. W. (1995) 'Globalization of an Ethnocentric Firm: An Evolutionary Perspective', *Strategic Management Journal*, 16(2): 119–42.

Malone, T. and K. Crowston (1994) 'The Interdisciplinary Study of Coordination', *ACM Computing Surveys*, January, 26: 87–119.

Marshall, C., L. Prusak and D. Shpilberg (1996) 'Financial Risk and the Need for Superior Knowledge Management', *California Management Review*, March, 38.

Mendoza, L., M. Pérez and A. Grimán (2006) 'Critical Success Factors For Managing Systems Integration', *Information Systems Management*, Spring, 23: 56–75.

Meyer, J. and B. Rowan (1977) 'Institutionalised Organisations: Formal Structure as Myth and Ceremony', *American Journal of Sociology*, September, 82: 340–63.

McCall, Jr., M. W. and G. P. Hollenbeck (2002) *Developing Global Executives*. Boston: Harvard Business School Press.

McClelland, M. K. (1992). 'Using Simulation to Facilitate Analysis of Manufacturing Strategy', *Journal of Business Logistics*, 13(1): 215–37.

McDonough III, E. F. and D. Cedrone (2000) 'Meeting the Challenge of Global Team Management', *Research Technology Management*, July–August, 43: 12–19.

McKinsey & Company (1999) *Managing International Retailers*. London: McKinsey & Company.

Newell, S. C. Tansley and J. Huang (2004) 'Social Capital and Knowledge Integration in an ERP Project Team: The Importance of Bridging and Bonding', March, 15: 43–57.

Newton McClurg, L. (2001) 'Team Rewards: How Far Have We Come?', *Human Resource Management*, Spring, 40: 73–92.

Mentzer, J. T., D. J. Flint, and G. T. M. Hult (2001) 'Logistics Service Quality as a Segment-Customized Process', *Journal of Marketing*, October, 65: 82–104.

Miles, R., C. C. Snow and J. Pfeffer (1974) 'Organization-Environment: Concepts and Issues', *Industrial Relations*, 13: 244–64.

Millman, T. (1996) 'Global Key Account Management and Systems Selling', *International Business Review*, 5(6): 631–45.

Mirhan, G. (1993) 'Advantage: Hewlett-Packard', *Global Executive*, March/April: 10–13.

Mollenkopf, D., D. J. Closs, D. Twede, S. Lee and G. Burgess (2005) 'Assessing the Viability of Reusable Packaging: A Relative Cost Approach', *Journal of Business Logistics*, 26(1): 169–98.

Momani, F. and T. Richter (1999) 'Standardisation versus Differentiation in European Key Account Management: The Case of the Adidas-Salomon AG', *Thexis*, 4: 44–7.

Montgomery, D. B. and G. S. Yip (2000) 'The Challenge of Global Customer Management', *Marketing Management*, 9(4): 22–9.

—— —— and B. Villalonga (1999) 'Demand For and Use of Global Account Management', Report No. 99–115, Marketing Science Institute, Cambridge, MA.

Moore, K. and J. M. Birkinshaw (1998) 'Managing Knowledge in Global Service Firms: Centres of Excellence', *Academy of Management Executives*, December.

Morgan, R. M. and S. D. Hunt (1994) 'The Commitment–Trust Theory of Relationship Marketing', *Journal of Marketing*, 58(3): 20–38.

Moriarty, R. T. and J. E.G. Bateson (1982) 'Exploring Complex Decision Making Units: A New Approach', *Journal of Marketing Research*, May, 19: 182–91.

Moschis, G. (1976) 'Social Comparison and Informal Group Influence', *Journal of Marketing Research*, August, 13: 235–42.

Nahapiet, J. (1994) 'Servicing the Global Client: Towards Global Account Management?', Paper presented at the 14th Annual Conference of the Strategic Management Society, Groupe HEC, Jouy-en-Josas, France.

Narayandas, D., J. Quelch and G. Swartz (2000) 'Prepare our Company for Global Pricing', *MIT Sloan Management Review*, Fall, 42(1): 61–70.

Nicholson-Crotty, S., N. A. Theobald and J. Nicholson-Crotty (2006) 'Disparate Measures: Public Managers and Performance-Measurement Strategies', *Public Administration Review*, January–February, 66: 101–14.

Nickerson, J. A. and B. S. Silverman (2003) 'Why Firms Want to Organize Efficiently and What Keeps Them From Doing So: Inappropriate Governance, Performance, and Adaptation in a Deregulated Industry', *Administrative Science Quarterly*, September, 48: 433–66.

Nohria, N. and C. Garcia-Pont (1991) 'Global Strategic Linkages and Industry Structure', *Strategic Management Journal*, January, 12: 105–24.

Nohria, N. and R. G. Eccles (1992) *Networks and Organizations: Structure, Form, and Action*. Boston, MA: Harvard Business School Press.

Nohria, N. and C. Garcia-Pont (1992) 'Local versus Global Mimetism: The Dynamics of Alliance Formation in the Automobile Industry', *Strategic Management Journal*, February, 23: 307–21.

# Bibliography

Nonaka, I. (1991) 'The Knowledge Creating Company', *Harvard Business Review*, November–December.

Ohlsson, A.-V. and J. DiStefano (2000), 'Schneider Electric Global Account Management', case study IMD-3-0949, Lausanne, Switzerland.

Ohmae, K. (1989) 'Managing in a Borderless World', *Harvard Business Review*, May–June, 67: 2–9.

O'Neill, G. (1995) 'Framework for Developing A Total Reward Strategy', *Asia Pacific Journal of Human Resources*, Spring, 33: 103–17.

Palmer, D., D. Jennings and X. Zhou (1993) 'Late Adoption of the Multidivisional Form by Large U.S. Corporations: Institutional, Political, and Economic Activity', *Administrative Science Quarterly*, January, 38: 100–31.

Parvatiyar, A. and T. Gruen (2001) 'Global Account Management Effectiveness: A Contingency Model', working paper, Goizueta School of Business, Emory University, Atlanta, GA, 25 May.

Peebles, D. M. (1989) 'Don't Write Off Global Advertising: A Commentary', *International Marketing Review*, 6(1): 73–8.

Porter, M. E. (1980) *Competitive Strategy*. New York: Free Press.

—— (1986) 'Changing Patterns of International Competition', *California Management Review*, 28(2): 9–40.

Powell, W. and P. DiMaggio (1991) *The New Institutionalism in Organizational Analysis*. Chicago: University of Chicago Press.

Prahalad, C. K. and Y. L. Doz (1987) *The Multinational Mission: Balancing Local Demands and Global Vision*. New York: The Free Press.

Provan, K. G. and J. B. Gassenheimer (1994) 'Supplier Commitment in Relational Contract Exchanges with Buyers: A Study of Interorganizational Dependence and Exercised Power', *The Journal of Management Studies*, January, 31: 55–69.

Quinn, J. (1992) *The Intelligent Enterprise*. New York: Free Press.

Rau, P. A. and J. F. Preble (1987) 'Standardization of Marketing Strategy by Multinationals', *International Marketing Review*, Autumn: 18–28.

Reynolds, C. 'Global Compensation and Benefits in Transition', *Compensation & Benefits Review*, January–February, 32: 28–41.

Rockart, J. (1979) 'Chief Executives Define their Own Data Needs', *Harvard Business Review*, March–April, 57: 81–93.

—— (1986) 'A Primer on Critical Success Factors', in J. Rockart and C. Bullen (eds.) *The Rise of Managerial Computing: The Best of the Center for Information Systems Research*. Homewood, IL: Dow Jones-Irwin.

Roos, J., G. von Krogh and G. S. Yip (1994) 'An Epistemology of Globalizing Firms', *International Business Review*, Special Issue on Organizations' Knowledge, Knowledge Transfer and Cooperative Strategies, November/December, 3(4): 395–409.

Rucci, A., S. Kim and R. Quinn (1998) 'The Employee–Customer–Profit Chain at Sears', *Harvard Business Review*, January/February, pp. 34–56.

Rust, R. T. and A. J. Zahorik (1993) 'Customer Satisfaction, Customer Retention, and Market Share', *Journal of Retailing*, Summer, 69: 145–56.

Sackman, S. (1992) 'Cultures and Sub-Cultures: An Analysis of Organizational Knowledge', *Administrative Science Quarterly*, January, 37: 140–61.

Schary, P. B. and T. Skjott-Larsen (2001) *Managing the Global Supply Chain*, 2nd edn. Copenhagen: Copenhagen Business School Press.

Schneider, S. (1983) 'National vs. Corporate Culture: Implications for Human Resource Management', *Human Resource Management*, March, 27: 231–46.

Scott, R. (1987) *Organizations: Rational, Natural, and Open Systems*. Englewood Cliffs, NJ: Prentice-Hall.

Scott, W. R. (1998) *Organizations: Rational, Natural and Open Systems*. Englewood Cliffs, NJ: Prentice-Hall.

Shapiro, B. P. (1989) 'Close Encounters of the Four Kinds: Managing Customers in a Rapidly Changing Environment', Note No. 9-589-015, Harvard Business School, Boston, MA.

—— and R. T. Moriarty (1980) 'National Account Management: Emerging Insights', Report No. 80-104, Marketing Science Institute, Cambridge, MA.

Simons, R. (2000) *Performance Measurement and Control Systems for Implementing Strategy*. Englewood Cliffs, NJ: Prentice-Hall.

Singh, J. and G. K. Rhoads (1991) 'Boundary Role Ambiguity in Marketing-Oriented Positions: A Multidimensional, Multifaceted Operationalisation', *Journal of Marketing Research*, April, 28: 328–38.

Sloan, P. (1993) 'Why Reebok Fired Chiat, Once and For All', *Advertising Age*, 30 September, 13–158.

Smith, J. (1992) 'Reward Management and HRM', in P. Blyton and E. Turnbull (eds.) *Reassessing Human Resource Management*. London: Sage.

Speare N. and S. J. Reese (2002) *Successful Global Account Management: Key Strategies and Tools for Managing Global Customers*. London: Miller Heiman.

Spender, J. (1996) 'Making Knowledge the Basis of a Dynamic Theory of the Firm', *Strategic Management Journal*, Winter Special Issue, 17.

Starbuck, W. H. (1976) 'Organizations and Their Environments', in M. D. Dunette (ed.) *Handbook of Industrial and Organizational Psychology*. Chicago: Rand McNally.

Starbuck, W. (1992) 'Learning by Knowledge-Intensive Firms', *Journal of Management Studies*, November, 29: 713–40.

Stevens, C. (2003) 'Enterprise Resource Planning: A Trio of Resources', *Information Systems Management*, Summer, 20: 61–70.

Stredwick, J. (2000) 'Aligning Rewards to Organisation Goals—A Multinational's Experience', *European Business Review*, January, 12: 9–21.

Swan, J. (2003) 'Knowledge Management in Action', in C. Holsapple (ed.) *Handbook on Knowledge Management*. Berlin: Springer, pp. 286–9.

Teece, D. (2000) *Managing Intellectual Capital*. New York: Oxford University Press.

Tourish, D. and O. Hargie (2004) *Key Issues in Organisational Communication*. London: Routledge.

—— (2005) 'Critical Upward Communication: Ten Commandments for Improving Strategy and Decision Making', *Long Range Planning*, May, 38: 485–503.

# Bibliography

Triandis, H. (1994) *Culture and Social Behaviour*. New York: McGraw-Hill.

Tung, R. (1984) 'How to Negotiate with the Japanese', *California Management Review*, April, 26: 62–77.

_____ (1991) 'Handshakes Across the Sea: Cross-Cultural Negotiating for Business Success', *Organizational Dynamics*, October, 19: 30–40.

Tyler, K. and E. Stanley (2001) 'Corporate Banking: The Strategic Impact of Boundary Spanner Effectiveness', *International Journal of Bank Marketing*, June, 19: 246–60.

van Weele, A. J. (1997) *Inkoop in strategisch perspectief*. Samson: Alphen aan de Rijn.

Venkatraman, V. (1989) 'The Concept of Fit in Strategy Research: Toward Verbal and Statistical Correspondence', *Academy of Management Review*, 14(3): 423–44.

Venkatraman, N. and V. Ramanujam (1986) 'Measurement of Business Performance in Strategy Research: A Comparison of Approaches', *Academy of Management Review*, 11(4): 801–14.

Wakeford, N. (2003) 'The Embedding of Local Culture in Global Communication', *New Media and Society*, August, 5: 379–99.

Walters, P. G. P. (1986) 'International Marketing Policy: A Discussion of the Standardization Construct and its Relevance for Corporate Policy', *Journal of International Business Studies*, Summer, pp. 55–69.

Weber, Y., O. Shenkar and A. Raveh (1996) 'National and Corporate Cultural Fit in Mergers/Acquisitions: An Exploratory Study', *Management Science*, October, 42: 1215–27.

Weiss, S. (1993) 'Analysis of Complex Negotiations in International Business', *Organization Science*, April, 4: 269–300.

_____ (1994) 'Negotiating with Romans', *Sloan Management Review*, October, 35: 859–74.

Wentz, L. (1993) 'Shops Flourish in '90s: Decade of Alignment', *Advertising Age*, 30: September, 11–110.

Wernerfelt, B. (1989) 'From Critical Resources to Corporate Strategy', *Journal of General Management*, 14(3): 4–12.

Verbeke, A. (2003) 'The Evolutionary View of the MNE and the Future of Internalization Theory', Journal of International Business Studies, November, 34(6): 498–504.

Verra, G. J. (2003) *Global Account Management*. London: Routledge.

Westney, D. E. and S. Zaheer (2001) 'The Multinational Enterprise as an Organization', in Alan M. Rugman and Thomas L. Brewer (eds.) *The Oxford Handbook of International Business*. Oxford: Oxford University Press, ch. 13, pp. 349–79.

Williamson, O. E. (1975) *Markets and Hierarchies: Analysis and Antitrust Implications*. New York: The Free Press.

Wilson, K. J. (1999) 'Developing Global Account Management Programmes: Observations from a GAM Panel Presentation', *Thexis*, 4: 30–5.

Wilson, K., S. Croom, T. Millman, and D. C. Weilbaker (2000) 'The Global Account Management Study Research Report', sponsored by Strategic Account Management Association (SAMA) and the Sales Research Trust.

Yip, G. S. (1989) 'Global Strategy ... In a World of Nations?', *Sloan Management Review*, 31(1): 29–41.

―――― (1992) *Total Global Strategy*. Upper Saddle River, NJ: Prentice-Hall.

―――― (1997) 'Hewlett-Packard (A): The Global Sales Problem' and 'Hewlett-Packard (B): The Global Account Solution', in J. K. Johansson (ed.) *Global Marketing*. New York: Irwin, pp. 684–91.

―――― (2003) *Total Global Strategy II*. Upper Saddle River, NJ: Prentice-Hall.

―――― and T. L. Madsen (1996) 'Global Account Management: The New Frontier in Relationship Marketing', *International Marketing Review*, 13(3): 24–42.

―――― ―――― (2001) 'Hewlett-Packard (A)' in J. de la Torre, Y. Doz and T. Devinney (eds.) *Managing the Global Corporation: Cases in Strategy and Management*, New York: McGraw-Hill, pp. 364–74.

―――― G., T. M. Hult and A. Bink (2007) 'Static Triangular Simulation as a Methodology for Strategic Management Research', in *Research Methodology in Strategy and Management*, Vol. 4, David J. Ketchen and Donald D. Bergh (eds.) Oxford: Elsevier JAI.

# Index

# Index

# Index

# Index

# Index

# Index

# Index

# Index